T0329977

Economics and Evolution

Economics and Evolution

Edited by
Jan Reijnders
Department of Social Economics
Utrecht University, The Netherlands

Belgian–Dutch Association for Post-Keynesian Studies

Edward Elgar
Cheltenham, UK • Lyme, US

Published by
Edward Elgar Publishing Limited
8 Lansdown Place
Cheltenham
Glos GL50 2HU
UK

Edward Elgar Publishing, Inc.
1 Pinnacle Hill Road
Lyme
NH 03768
US

A catalogue record for this book
is available from the British Library

ISBN 978 1 85898 555 8

Printed and bound by CPI Group (UK) Ltd, Croydon, CR0 4YY

Contents

Figures

Tables

Contributors

Esben Sloth Andersen
Senior Lecturer Descriptive Economics, Department of Business Studies, Aalborg University, Denmark.

Ron Boschma
Lecturer of European Studies and Economic Geography, Department of Public Administration and Public Policy, University of Twente, Enschede, The Netherlands.

Nicolai J. Foss
Associate Professor of Strategic Management and the Theory of Economic Organisations, Copenhagen Business School, Denmark.

Geoffrey M. Hodgson
University Lecturer, Judge Institute for Management Studies at Cambridge University, England.

Bert van der Knaap
Professor of Economic and Social Geography, Department of Applied Economics, Erasmus University, Rotterdam, The Netherlands.

Jan P.G. Reijnders
Associate Professor of Economics, Department of Social Economics, Utrecht University, The Netherlands.

Gerald Silverberg
Program coordinator at Maastricht Economic Research Institute on Innovation and Technology (MERIT), University of Maastricht, The Netherlands, and International Institute for Applied Systems Analysis (IIASA), Laxenburg, Austria.

Bart Verspagen
Fellow of the Royal Netherlands Academy of Arts and Sciences at Maastricht Economic Research Institute on Innovation and Technology (MERIT), University of Maastricht, The Netherlands.

Jack J. Vromen

Assistant Professor in Philosophy of Economics, Department of Philosophy of Erasmus University Rotterdam and the Department of Economics and Econometrics of the University of Amsterdam, The Netherlands.

Acknowledgements

The editor of this volume, also organizer of the Conference on Economics and Evolution of the Belgian–Dutch Association of Post-Keynesian Studies gratefully acknowledges the financial and logistical support of the Department of Social Economics of Utrecht University, the Reaal Groep N.V. Utrecht, the Royal Netherlands Academy of Sciences (KNAW) and the Netherlands School for Social and Economic Policy Research (AWSB) Utrecht.

Many thanks to the contributors to this volume for complying with the editor's requests and meeting deadlines so efficiently.

A special message of thanks goes to Maiumi Sadler for being a mainstay in the editing process and for turning the typescript into camera-ready copy.

1. Variety in the Garden of Heterodox Economics: An Introduction

Jan P.G. Reijnders

If one had to picture a panorama of economic theory in general, one would probably end up with an image of the lower reaches of a river delta. Somewhere in the middle one would envision the orthodox 'mainstream' meandering through the economic landscape. It hardly changes its course, it merely meanders, that is, slowly adapts to the historical changes that its object of investigation undergoes. Outside this mainstream one would picture several types of heterodox currents. Sometimes these are mere branches of the mainstream itself that are bound to join it again further downstream. Sometimes these are true diversions that endeavour to find their own way to the sea. In spite of its possible beauty, this picture would be unsatisfactory because it can only give a static, two-dimensional view of the situation. Static because it does not mirror economic change, the transformation of the object of observation that is the ultimate cause of changes of direction, of 'revolutions' in economic theory. Static because it does not show the dynamic interrelations that exist between the orthodox 'mainstream' and various heterodox currents. The last mentioned do play important roles in the development of the discipline. Because they venture beyond the boundaries of orthodox theory, they fertilize the mainstream and provide it with new ideas and because they remain critical towards its basic propositions, point out its shortcomings and inconsistencies, they safeguard it against complacency.

It so happens that the expression used to illustrate the inadequacy of the earlier mentioned image of economic theory is also the principal catchword that heterodox economists use to voice the uneasy feelings they harbour against orthodox theory. Heterodox economists have complained for a long time that the equilibrium orientation of mainstream neoclassical economics makes it an essentially static theory. It regards a deterministic world in which everything is fixed from the outset. There is little room for endogenous economic change, and as far as change is incorporated in the neoclassical model its analysis is merely cast in comparative static terms. This denies the cumulative and irreversible nature of economic change and ignores the existence of historical time. Neither is there room for uncertainty, chance, spontaneity and human agency. Rather than accepting them an 'error term' is inserted as a kind of stochastic apology for the unknown forces that have not been included in the model (Mirowski, 1989). Such complaints are common among several groups of heterodox economists. They appear to apply especially to the branch of heterodoxy that is designated 'evolutionary economics'.

Evolutionary economics as such can be traced back to the synergy between biology and economics in the days of the very emergence of these modern sciences in the eighteenth and nineteenth centuries (Hodgson, 1993, p. 55). This is exemplified by the work of Charles Darwin, whose ideas were strongly influenced by the work of Classical economists such as Smith and Malthus. In turn, his ideas had an impact on contemporary economists such as, for instance, Marx and later Veblen and Marshall. On the brink of the twentieth century Veblen proclaimed that the time was ripe for a fundamental reorientation of the discipline and urged economists to develop an up-to-date evolutionary approach. This idea was endorsed by Alfred Marshall who thought that the Mecca of economists would lie in 'economic biology'. Unfortunately these hopes did not materialize. Instead evolutionary economics submerged into a 'dark age' (Sanderson, 1990, p. 2) where Schumpeter had to concede that the evolutionary idea in economics had been discredited and where evolutionism came to be considered as 'supremely intelligent after-dinner talk' (Lord Robbins, according to Elster, 1983, p. 112). There was a revival of evolutionary economics after the Second World War but it led a rather secluded life until its final re-emergence in the early eighties. Evolutionary economics has been gaining momentum ever since. Its revitalization can be traced to the impact of Nelson and Winter's classic *An Evolutionary Theory of Economic Change* published in 1982. Since then there has been a burgeoning literature on this subject of which one can say that it produced sufficient variety to fulfil the very first requirement for starting an evolutionary process of its own. These 'thousand flowers blooming' in the garden of heterodox economics did not fail to attract the attention of the Belgian–Dutch Association of Post-Keynesian Studies, which has a keen interest in the whereabouts and activities of its fellow travellers. The Association therefore decided to select 'Economics and Evolution' as the subject for its sixteenth annual conference to be held at Utrecht University, in Utrecht, The Netherlands in November 1995. The objective was to present the members of the Association with an overview of the principal characteristics of the modern evolutionary approach, to acquaint them with the ideas of some of its important representatives and to give them an impression of its fields of application. This volume offers a collection of papers presented at this conference.

In his contribution, Geoffrey Hodgson presents a concise history of evolutionary economics and introduces the variety of approaches within the subject. Earlier, in his *Economics and Evolution: Bringing Life Back into Economics* (1993), he presented a taxonomy of evolutionary economics that revolved around the distinction between ontogenetic and phylogenetic concepts of change. In his contribution to the present volume he tries a new taxonomy that concentrates on the ontological and methodological foundations of the theories in question. He distinguishes four criteria for his classification of evolutionary theories: an *ontological* one that concentrates on the generation of novelty, a *methodological* one that centres around reductionism, a *temporal* one that pertains to gradualism and a *metaphorical* one associated with the use of biological analogies. This leads to an ideal type that he then designates as NEAR (Novelty Embracing, Anti-Reductionist) evolutionary economics, the 'institutional' wing of the evolutionary approach.

It appears that only a very small number of authors fit within the confines of this approach. The intriguing thing about Hodgson's list is that it excludes authors (notably Schumpeter) who, as we will subsequently see, are regarded by others as the forerunners *par excellence* of all modern evolutionary economics. Instead, Hodgson draws up a list of ancestors of the NEAR approach, that, apart from the 'old' institutionalists like Veblen, Commons and Mitchell, consists of Hobson and Keynes.

In contrast to Hodgson who effectively limits the number of scholars who are allowed to sail under the banner of evolutionary economics, Jack Vromen specifically aims at enlarging this number again. He counteracts the view that evolutionary economics by its very nature is alien to neoclassical economics and everything for which such theories are supposed to stand. He argues that this view is misguided, first because he thinks that evolutionary theory can be invoked to give a radical reinterpretation of standard neoclassical analysis and second because he thinks that evolutionary theorizing can yield neoclassical results (see Vromen, 1995, p. 108 ff.). He subsequently concentrates on the 'orthodox' group of evolutionary theorists. It goes without saying that his list of precursors of the 'orthodox' group of evolutionary theorists considerably differs from the group of precursors of Hodgson's NEAR-evolutionists. Vromen considers the contributions of the '(neo)Austrians', the 'sociobiologists' and the 'Chicago economists'. From these only the (neo)Austrians want to replace the neoclassical analytical apparatus by explicit analyses of processes of economic evolution. Characteristic of all proponents of evolutionary economics is that they take Darwin's idea of biological evolution through natural selection as their point of departure. This notion is incorporated by modern evolutionary economists by introducing rules or routines as the economic counterpart of genes. At first sight, rule-governed behaviour seems to contradict neoclassical assumptions. In Vromen's view, however, this is not necessarily true because rules do not fix the standard operating behaviour of economic agents once and for all. The rules may include higher-order rules that guide changes in standard behaviour. In this sense evolutionary economics does not exclude neoclassical economics. It may even be considered to complement it because it endogenizes the changes in variables and parameters that neoclassical economics treats as exogenous shocks.

Also Nicolai Foss considers the relationship between evolutionary and neoclassical economics. He concentrates on their respective theories of the firm and tries to answer the question whether they are competitive or complementary. Historically the theory of the firm was closely connected with evolutionary economics. Marshall's analysis of industry and the controversy over profit maximization are cases in point. Although modern evolutionary economics and the modern (contractual) theory of the firm emerged at almost the same time, they made relatively little contact. The contractual theory kept strong leanings toward neoclassical economics and the evolutionary theory of the firm did not quite develop, probably because of the dominant population perspective in evolutionary theory. In fact there is no evolutionary theory of the firm, in the sense of a theory that addresses the existence, the boundaries and the internal organization of the firm. To remedy this, Foss opts for the development of an ontogenetic evolutionary perspective on the firm. He expects from this a theory that explains the structure and the behaviour of firms as emergent results of two sets of interactions: one between agents within the firm and one between the firm and its environment. Such a theory would have the same objects of explanation as the neoclassical theory of the firm. In this sense there is a strong case for regarding the two types of theories as competitors. On the other hand there is scope for the expectation that the two types of theories are complementary in a certain way. Therefore, an effort to combine propositions from the two approaches seems a promising avenue of research (see also: Foss, 1994a,b).

Esben Sloth Andersen takes up the gauntlet that Hodgson flung down when he removed Schumpeter from the list of precursors of evolutionary economics. He takes Hodgson's challenge as an opportunity to rethink the relationship between Schumpeter's developmental work and the modern model-building evolutionary economists, who have a self-declared affiliation with Schumpeter. According to Andersen, there are two reasons why Schumpeter did not embrace the idea of an evolutionary economics. First, he was reluctant to associate himself with an idea that was discredited in his time. Second, he had a 'tool problem', that is, he did not have at his disposal the sophisticated analytical apparatus required to intellectually master the intricacies involved in evolutionary reasoning. By posing the proper questions, however, Schumpeter provided his present day followers with a rich problem area.

The prototypical solution to part of Schumpeter's tool problem is incorporated in the standard variant of Nelson and Winter's model of Schumpeterian competition. (Andersen, 1994, p. 104 ff.) Despite its merits as a means for clarifying Schumpeterian competition, however, this variant of the Nelson and Winter model provides only a partial solution. In the eyes of Andersen, much can be gained by extending the model with elements of a complementary approach. Especially Marshall's theory of economic evolution seems to have promising features in this respect. Andersen subsequently delineates the contours of such a modified version of the Nelson and Winter model that incorporates Schumpeterian (discrete innovations) as well as Marshallian (incremental technical progress) elements.

In their earlier work Gerald Silverberg and Bart Verspagen (1994; 1995) clearly manifested themselves as representatives of, what Andersen calls, 'modern model building evolutionary economics'. In their contribution to the present volume, they develop an evolutionary model that describes the relation between endogenous technological change and economic growth. Technological change is considered the principal propelling force of the evolutionary process. In line with the tradition in evolutionary model building, the economy is disaggregated into distinct individual behavioural subunits which are connected by dynamic interaction patterns. Selection takes place on the basis of a mechanism that is driven by market competition based on differential profit rates. Economic agents use boundedly rational procedures for selecting their investment and R&D strategies and learning is modelled by allowing for mutation and imitation rules on the agent's strategy parameters.

The authors try to identify what they call an 'evolutionary attractor', a stable configuration of R&D strategies to which the economy will converge from particular classes of initial conditions. To this end they present density plots of the results of multiple simulation experiments indicating the existence of such phenomena. Silverberg and Verspagen's model demonstrates that economic competition leads to an approximately steady-state growth path with a positive rate of technical change and R&D investment. The mere existence of such a steady-state growth path does, however, not mean that history does not matter. On the contrary. The authors establish experimentally that an 'artificial' society starting with no or very low rates of R&D will pass through several stages and will ultimately 'bootstrap' itself to higher rates of R&D and technical change.

It is obvious that the key issues of evolutionary economics do not limit themselves to the domain of economics alone. They trickle down into other fields of the social sciences where they establish themselves as regular fields of investigation. Economic geographers, for instance, take a keen interest in the emergence of novelty and the nature of technological change because these are important determinants of the way in which spatial economic systems evolve over time. In their contribution, Ron Boschma and Bert van der Knaap relate to these issues by their analysis of the way in which innovations, that give rise to new industries, are distributed over space. To this end they apply a concept called 'windows of locational opportunity' (Boschma, 1994). Conventional theory predicts that the spatial distribution of new industries is mainly determined by the regional distribution of beneficial locational factors, that constitute the 'selection environment'. Contrary to this, Boschma and van der Knaap argue that the outcome strongly depends upon the type of innovation that forms the basis of the new industry. If innovations are discontinuous and form a violent break with the past, they have such strong internal dynamics that the attraction of the selection environment is overwhelmed. The 'windows of locational opportunity' open up and spatial patterns become unpredictable. If innovations are gradual, the selection environment becomes dominant which stabilizes the development of the spatial system.

REFERENCES

Andersen, E.S. (1994), *Evolutionary Economics: Post-Schumpeterian Contributions*, London: Pinter.

Boschma, R.A. (1994), *Looking through a window of locational opportunity. A long term spatial analysis of techno-industrial upheavals in Great Britain and Belgium*, Tinbergen Institute Research Series no. 75, Amsterdam: Thesis Publishers.

Elster, J. (1983), *Explaining Technical Change: A Case Study in the Philosophy of Science*, Cambridge: Cambridge University Press.

Foss, N.J. (1994a), 'Realism and Evolutionary Economics', *Journal of Social and Evolutionary Systems*, **17**, 21–40.

Foss, Nicolai J. (1994b), 'Why Transaction Cost Economics Needs Evolutionary Economics', *Revue d'Economie Industrielle*, **64**, 7–26.

Hodgson, G.M. (1993), *Economics and Evolution: Bringing Life Back into Economics*, Cambridge: Polity Press.

Mirowski, P. (1989), 'The Probabilistic Counter Revolution, or How Stochastic Concepts Came to Neoclassical Economic Theory', *Oxford Economic Papers*, **42**(2), 217–35.

Nelson, R. and S.G. Winter (1982), *An Evolutionary Theory of Economic Change*, Cambridge: Bellknap Press of Harvard University Press.

Sanderson, Stephen K. (1990), *Social Evolutionism: A Critical History*, Oxford: Blackwell.

Silverberg, G. and B. Verspagen (1994), 'Learning, Innovation and Economic Growth: A Long-Run Model of Industrial Dynamics', *Industrial and Corporate Change*, **3**, 199–223.

Silverberg, G. and B. Verspagen (1995), 'An Evolutionary Model of Long Term Cyclical Variations of Catching Up and Falling Behind', *Journal of Evolutionary Economics*, **5**, 209–27.

Vromen, J.J. (1995), *Economic Evolution: An Enquiry into the Foundations of New Institutional Economics*, London: Routledge.

2. Economics and Evolution and the Evolution of Economics

Geoffrey M. Hodgson[1]

INTRODUCTION

The term 'evolutionary economics' is currently applied to a confusingly wide variety of approaches within the subject. At least six main groupings using the phrase can be identified:

- A century ago Thorstein Veblen (1898a) argued for an 'evolutionary' and 'post-Darwinian' economics. Institutionalists in the tradition of Veblen and John Commons frequently describe their approach as 'evolutionary economics', often using the terms 'institutional' and 'evolutionary' as virtual synonyms, as exemplified in the title of the Association for Evolutionary Economics – the USA-based association of institutional economists.
- Joseph Schumpeter (1942, p. 82) famously described capitalist development as an 'evolutionary process'. Work influenced by Schumpeter is also described as 'evolutionary economics' as evidenced by the title of the *Journal of Evolutionary Economics*, published by the International Joseph Schumpeter Association.
- The approach of the Austrian School of economists is often described as 'evolutionary', as portrayed in Carl Menger's theory of the evolution of money and other institutions, and by the extensive use of an evolutionary metaphor from biology in the later works of Friedrich Hayek, especially in relation to the concept of spontaneous order.

---

[1]. This essay makes use of material from Hodgson (1993, 1995b, forthcoming a). Thanks are due to participants at the eleventh meeting of the Belgian–Dutch Association for Post-Keynesian Economics, especially Esben Sloth Andersen and Uskali Mäki, for helpful criticisms of an earlier draft.

- In addition, the economics of assorted writers such as Adam Smith, Karl Marx, Alfred Marshall and others is also sometimes described as 'evolutionary' in character.
- Evolutionary game theory is a prominent recent development in mathematical economics and has been inspired by related mathematical work in theoretical biology.
- The word 'evolutionary' is sometimes attached to work in what is also described as 'complexity theory', typically that associated with the Santa Fe Institute in the United States, involving applications of chaos theory and various other types of computer simulation. In this and allied simulation work the use of replicator dynamics, genetic algorithms, genetic programming, and so on, can be found.

With such a wide variety of uses, it is unlikely that there is a single, underlying and coherent message. Indeed, the use of the word 'evolutionary' in economics seems very much to be a matter of fashion. It is arguable that the increasing use of the term 'evolutionary economics' today can be largely traced to the impact of Richard Nelson and Sidney Winter's classic (1982) work *An Evolutionary Theory of Economic Change*, although other developments in both orthodox and heterodox economics are also important. Apart from the institutionalist and Schumpeterian fringes, the use of the word 'evolutionary' did not become widespread in economics until after 1982.

Following the 'golden age' of the late nineteenth century, the period up to the Second World War has been described by Stephen Sanderson (1990, p. 2) as the 'dark age' for evolutionism in social science: 'During this time evolutionism was severely criticized and came to be regarded as an outmoded approach that self-respecting scholars should no longer take seriously ... even the word "evolution" came to be uttered at serious risk to one's intellectual reputation' (Sanderson, 1990, p. 2).

Even Schumpeter (1934, p. 57) accepted in 1912 that 'the evolutionary idea is now discredited in our field'. The re-emergence of the word 'evolution' in economics was even later than in other social sciences, particularly anthropology, where the use of it became quite common in the 1960s. The number of relevant works in economics encountered by the present author in the years from 1914 to 1980 inclusive with 'evolution' in their title or subtitle is 17.[2] If the years 1914 to 1969 inclusive are

---

[2]. The few discovered in those 67 years include Alchian (1950), Boulding (1978), Edgell (1975), Haavelmo (1954), Harris (1934), Hayek (1967a), Hunt (1975), von Mises (1957), Nelson and Winter (1973, 1974), Robbins (1970), Sowell (1967) and Tang et al. (1976).

considered then the overall number is just seven, or about one every eight years. In contrast, the number since 1980 is already well into three figures.

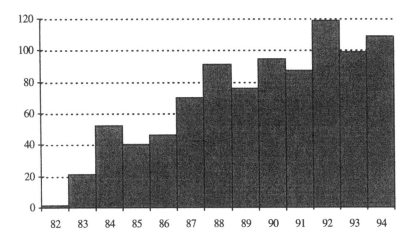

Figure 2.1   Citations to Nelson and Winter's Evolutionary Theory of Economic Change

Figure 2.1 gives some indication, using Social Science Citations Index data, of the growing impact of Nelson and Winter's (1982) work.[3]

Three of these have clear Veblenian origins and two are by prominent Austrian economists. The remainder have varied intellectual pedigrees. The author would be interested to hear of any others that have been omitted. In contrast, a relatively large number appeared prior to 1920 and there has been a veritable explosion since 1982. It should be noted, however, that the 'evolution'-in-the-title criterion is relatively rough and loose, particularly as it allows Georgescu-Roegen (1971) to pass through the net. Nevertheless, a severe scarcity of biological metaphors is indicated. Reasons why this may be so are discussed in Hodgson (forthcoming b).

[3]. However, Alexander Rosehberg (1994, p. 402) wrote of the Nelson and Winter (1982) volume: 'The capstone of two distinguished careers, few books can have had a more disappointing reception in current economics ... it has fallen stillborn from the presses'. Yet a growth of annual citation rates to a level of 119 just ten years after publication is no small achievement. Consider the fate of another heterodox classic, Sraffa's *Production of Commodities by Means of Commodities* (1960). Ten years after its publication its annual citation rate was just 15, and its all-time highest level was only 49, achieved in 1982. If there is a grain of truth in Rosenberg's contention it is the following. Casual inspection of the citations to *An Evolutionary Theory of Economic Change* in the Social Science Citations Index suggests that this work is cited much more frequently in management and business publications, rather than in the core theoretical journals of mainstream economics.

By the late 1980s, work in 'evolutionary economics' had been broadened and accelerated by the growth in both America and Europe of various institutional, Austrian and Schumpeterian approaches to economics.[4] There have been notable and fruitful applications of these ideas, particularly in the sphere of technological change.[5] Evolutionary economics has already established an impressive research programme and has had a major impact on economic policy, particularly in the areas of technology policy, corporate strategy and national systems of innovation. A substantial body of work is now clearly visible, and worthy of reflective evaluation.

Nevertheless, there is still no established consensus on what 'evolutionary economics' should mean. Many economists use the term whilst wrongly taking it for granted that a common and obvious meaning is implied. As the biologist Jacques Monod is reported to have said in a lecture on biological evolution: 'Another curious aspect of the theory of evolution is that everybody thinks that he understands it!' Likewise, a curious aspect of 'evolutionary economics' is that many people use the term as if it required little further explanation and that everyone knows what it means.

Furthermore, 'evolutionary economists' are typically muddled about their own intellectual history. Leading exponents such as Nelson and Winter (1982) ignored the Veblenian precedent, although to some extent they have now rectified that sin. Even attempts at a 'history' of evolutionary economics can go back as far as Adam Smith but downplay Thomas Robert Malthus and entirely ignore the elusive Veblen (Langlois and Everett, 1994).

Arguably the impact to date of the book on mainstream economic theory has been detectable but no more than marginal.

[4]. The European Association for Evolutionary Political Economy and the International Joseph Schumpeter Association were both formed in the late 1980s. Relevant books appearing since 1980 include Andersen (1994), Basalla (1989), Blaas and Foster (1992), Boulding (1981), Clark and Juma (1987), Day and Chen (1993), Delorme and Dopfer (1994), Dosi et al. (1988), England (1994), Faber and Proops (1990), Foster (1987), Goodwin (1990), Gordon and Adams (1989), Hamilton (1991), Hannan and Freeman (1989), Hanusch, (1988), Hayek (1988), Heertje and Perlman (1990), Hodgson (1988, 1993, 1995a, 1995b), Hodgson and Screpanti (1991), Hodgson et al. (1994), Kay (1982), Langlois (1986), Loasby (1991), Magnusson (1994), McKelvey (1982), Metcalfe (1994), Mirowski (1994), Mokyr (1990), Van Parijs (1981), Pantzar (1991), Rutherford (1994), Saviotti and Metcalfe (1991), Verspagen (1993), Vromen (1994) and Witt (1987, 1992, 1993a, 1993b). The *Journal of Evolutionary Economics* commenced publication in 1991 and articles on 'evolutionary economics' have also appeared in the *Journal of Economic Issues* (published by the US-based Association for Evolutionary Economics), the *Journal of Economic Behavior and Organization* and other journals.

[5]. Note in particular the contributions in Dosi et al. (1988) and Freeman (1990).

Nothing is more guaranteed to generate confusion and to stultify intellectual progress than to raise a muddled term to the centrepiece of economic research, whilst simultaneously suggesting that a clear and well-defined approach to scientific enquiry is implied. It is important both to sort out the different meanings of the term and to consider carefully its conceptual history.

Elsewhere (Hodgson, 1993, chapter 3), a taxonomy of relevant meanings of 'evolutionary economics' has been attempted. There the principal focus is on the important difference between 'ontogenetic' and 'phylogentic' conceptions of change. This distinction is useful because it exposes the more limited character of the former type of 'evolution'.

In biology, ontogeny involves the development of a particular organism from a set of given and unchanging genes. Its environment will also affect its development, but nevertheless the growth of the organism is the result of genetic instructions. Hence the genes represent a given set of (environmentally-dependent) developmental possibilities. In contrast, phylogeny is the complete and ongoing evolution of a population, including changes in its composition and that of the genepool. It involves changes in the genetic potentialities of the population, as well as their individual phenotypic development.

By analogy, in economic evolution ontogeny traces institutional and other developments in the context of an environment but with fixed 'genetic material'. If we reject the argument that socio-economic evolution can be explained in terms of the human biotic inheritance[6] then an alternative and analogous supposition is to assume inert individuals with given purposes or preference functions. For example, for the purposes of theoretical explanation, given individuals are assumed in Menger's ([1871] 1981) account of the evolution of money and Hayek's (1982, 1988) discussion of the 'evolution' of spontaneous order. By contrast, Veblen (1899, 1919) gives more emphasis to changing purposes, preferences, habits and beliefs in his accounts of economic evolution.

However, as in biology, phylogenesis subsumes ontogenesis. The phylogenetic development of a population includes the ontogenetic development of the individuals within it. Hence the objection here to Menger's account of the evolution of money or Hayek's description of the evolution of spontaneous order is not so much as they are wrong, but they are only part of the story. Indeed, in some other passages in his later works, Hayek (1982, 1988) goes some way to broaden the evolutionary picture,

---

[6]. Such a view was indeed popular in the latter part of the nineteenth century, and popularized by Herbert Spencer, William Graham Sumner and others (Degler, 1991).

considering changes in cultures and individual habits. In fact it is an emerging view that the differences between Hayekian and Veblenian economics may not be as wide as formerly supposed (Boettke, 1989; Leathers, 1990; Rutherford, 1989, 1994; Samuels, 1989; Wynarczyk, 1992).

Accordingly, the distinction between ontogenetic and phylogentic conceptions of evolution does not involve mutually exclusive categories. These two concepts are useful to distinguish the broader from the narrower notions of 'economic evolution' but they are of only limited use in polarizing and patterning the kaleidoscope of methodological approaches and ontological possibilities.

For this reason an alternative and perhaps more fundamental classification is attempted here. This pays particular attention to the varied ontological and methodological foundations of the theories involved.

VARIETIES OF 'EVOLUTIONARY ECONOMICS': ANOTHER TAXONOMY

Approaches to 'evolutionary economics' are here classified with regard to the following four criteria.

1. The ontological criterion – novelty: Whether or not substantial emphasis is given to the assumption that 'evolutionary' processes in economics involve ongoing or periodic novelty and creativity, thus generating and maintaining a variety of institutions, rules, commodities and technologies.

Conceptions of 'economic evolution' that stress novelty typically highlight indeterminacy and the possibility of cumulative divergence, in contrast with convergence and equilibria (Andersen, 1994; Foss, 1994; Hodgson, 1993; Witt, 1987). Notably, the Austrian School of economists give pronounced stress both to the indeterminacy and the potential novelty of human imagination, action and choice (Lachmann, 1977; Loasby, 1976; Shackle, 1955). Kenneth Boulding (1991, p. 13) wrote: 'One very fundamental principle in evolutionary processes is their profound indeterminacy.' Outside economics, Karl Popper's stress on indeterminacy, novelty, and emergent properties can be mentioned (Popper, 1982). However, novelty does not necessarily involve indeterminacy. For instance, chaos theory highlights potential novelty and divergence, and does this using unpredictable but essentially deterministic systems (Gleick, 1988).

2. The methodological criterion – reductionism: Whether explanations in 'evolutionary economics' are reductionist or non-reductionist. Reductionism sometimes involves the notion that wholes must be explained entirely in terms of their elemental, constituent parts. More generally, reductionism can be defined as the idea that all aspects of a complex phenomenon must be explained in terms of one level, or type of unit. According to this view there are no autonomous levels of analysis other than this elemental foundation, and no such thing as emergent properties upon which different levels of analysis can be based.

In social science in the 1870–1920 period, reductionism was prominent and typically took a biological form. Accordingly, attempts were made to explain the behaviour of individuals and groups in terms of their alleged biological characteristics. Reductionism is still conspicuous in social science today and typically appears as methodological individualism. This is defined as 'the doctrine that all social phenomena (their structure and their change) are in principle explicable only in terms of individuals – their properties, goals, and beliefs' (Elster, 1982, p. 453). It is thus alleged that explanations of socio-economic phenomena must be reduced to properties of constituent individuals and relations between them.[7] Allied to this is the sustained attempt since the 1960s to found macroeconomics on 'sound microfoundations'. There are other versions of reductionism, however, including versions of 'holism' that suggest that parts should be explained in terms of wholes. Reductionism is countered by the notion that complex systems display emergent properties at different levels that cannot be completely reduced to or explained wholly in terms of another level. By contrast, anti-reductionism generally emphasizes emergent properties at higher levels of analysis that cannot be reduced to constituent elements. Accordingly, notions such as group selection in biology and group knowledge in the social sciences can be sustained (Bhaskar, 1975, 1979; Hodgson, 1988, 1993; Mayr, 1985; Murphy, 1994).

3. The temporal criterion – gradualism: Whether the alleged gradualism of economic 'evolution' is stressed or, by contrast, the possibility of intervening periods of rapid change and disruption.

---

[7]. Note that this popular term is sometimes used in additional, ambiguous and contradictory ways. Confusingly, Winter (1988) defends 'methodological individualism' whilst repeatedly invoking concepts such as organisational knowledge and group learning (Winter, 1982). However, what Winter seems to have in mind here by 'methodological individualism' is a rejection of the idea that intentions and interests can be attributed to groups and organizations, rather than individuals. Contrary to Winter, the emphasis here is rightfully on the issue of explanation, not on the attribution or non-attribution of qualities to individuals or groups. The idea that intentions and interests should not be attributed, at least in an unqualified manner, to groups and organizations equally as well as to individuals, is compatible with a rejection of methodological individualism. It is arguable that in the proper, methodological (that is, explanatory) sense Winter is not a methodological individualist.

A notable appearance of this dichotomy is in the controversy between gradualistic and punctuated – or saltationist – theories of technological evolution in particular (Basalla, 1989; Mokyr, 1990, 1991) and economic evolution in general (Loasby, 1991; Marshall, 1890; Schumpeter, 1942).

4. The metaphorical criterion – biology: Whether extensive use is made of metaphors from biology or not. A motivation for the use of biological metaphors is to replace the mechanistic paradigm which dominates mainstream economics.[8]

It has been frequently argued that economies are closer in their constitution to biotic than to mechanical systems, and that a biological metaphor is thus more appropriate in economics (Georgescu-Roegen, 1971; Hodgson, 1993; Marshall, 1890; Nelson and Winter, 1982). Others have distanced themselves in varying degrees from biological metaphors (Schumpeter, 1954; Witt, 1992).

These four binary criteria give 16 possible classifications, portrayed in Figure 2.2. The shaded area in this diagram represents four out of the 16 possibilities and is referred to as 'NEAR' (Novelty-Embracing, Anti-Reductionist) Evolutionary Economics.

Of course, the ordering of the four criteria is largely arbitrary. Nevertheless, it has been suggested that the ontological criterion is the most fundamental (Hodgson, 1993; Foss, 1994). Further than this, space does not permit a detailed justification of the classification system. Notably, some of the variants evade precise classification because of ambiguities in the works of the authors involved. An important example here is Hayek, who is placed in two boxes because of the ambiguity of his attachment to reductionism and methodological individualism. Despite claiming allegiance to this methodological imperative, especially in his later works, he has championed group selection and a departure from strict reductionism and methodological individualism has thus been identified (Böhm, 1989; Vanberg, 1986).

Taxonomic classifications of authors' theoretical systems are generally problematic and the individual classifications here cannot be fully justified. As in many taxonomies, the precise application of the criteria is difficult and in some cases it must be tentative, for example with the criterion of 'extensive use' of the biological metaphor. For this reason this – arguably important – criterion is given the lowest implicit ranking of the four in Figure 2.2.

---

[8].   For discussions of the nature of this paradigm see Georgescu-Roegen (1971), Sebba (1953) and Thoben (1982).

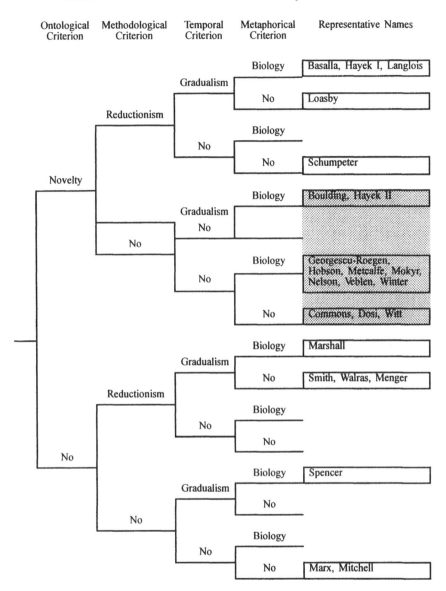

Ontological Criterion	Methodological Criterion	Temporal Criterion	Metaphorical Criterion	Representative Names
		Gradualism	Biology	Basalla, Hayek I, Langlois
			No	Loasby
	Reductionism	No	Biology	
			No	Schumpeter
Novelty		Gradualism No	Biology	Boulding, Hayek II
	No			
		No	Biology	Georgescu-Roegen, Hobson, Metcalfe, Mokyr, Nelson, Veblen, Winter
			No	Commons, Dosi, Witt
		Gradualism	Biology	Marshall
	Reductionism		No	Smith, Walras, Menger
		No	Biology	
No			No	
		Gradualism	Biology	Spencer
	No		No	
		No	Biology	
			No	Marx, Mitchell

Key: ▒▒ = 'NEAR' (Novelty-Embracing, Anti-Reductionist) Evolutionary Economics

Figure 2.2   *'Evolutionary Economics' – another possible taxonomy*

As well as a judgement as to what is and is not 'extensive', there is a further judgement required on the nature and degree of the 'use' of the metaphor. Is it explicit or implicit, for instance? For example, although allusions to the biological metaphor are found in the work of John Commons and Wesley Mitchell, unlike Veblen the use of it is not here deemed to be extensive. Accordingly, there is an important difference on this question within the 'old' institutionalist tradition. Commons is thus put with Ulrich Witt (1992, p. 7), who has criticized the use of the biological metaphor, and with Giovanni Dosi, who like Commons has made no such criticism but does not in practice apply the metaphor explicitly and extensively.

In part the problem here is that the use of metaphor is not admitted, or is even opposed, by those who are using it. The metaphorical criterion is the lowest ranked for taxonomic purposes primarily because the use of constitutive metaphors is often inadvertent or covert. Elsewhere, it is argued that in economics metaphor plays a deeper role, and is often used less consciously than Philip Mirowski's (1989) engaging treatise on mechanistic metaphors in economics would suggest (Hodgson, 1996). More widely, a number of other authors argue that metaphor has a deeply constitutive and subterranean presence in science (Black, 1962; Hesse, 1966, 1980; Klamer and Leonard, 1994; Maasen, 1995).

The criterion of gradualism also raises some difficulties, particularly where authors have not made their position clear. Fortunately, however, others have stressed either gradualism or 'punctuated' approaches in their writings.

Further problems of taxonomic classification arise with Smith, Marx, Menger, Marshall and Walras. They all recognized invention and innovation in economic processes, but their stress on determinism or unilinear development (Smith), or on a teleological view of history as a progression towards a given end (Marx), or on equilibrium outcomes (Menger, Marshall, Walras), means that they pay less attention than others to novelty and creativity.

A further difference within the 'old' institutionalism arises when we consider Mitchell. He is put with Marx because he put much less emphasis than Commons on the role of human will and purposeful behaviour.

In addition to the evident lack of unanimity in the 'old' institutionalist camp, there may be several surprises in this classificatory schema. The biggest and most significant one might be Schumpeter. However, the classification can be defended. First, it was Schumpeter himself who coined the term 'methodological individualism' and repeatedly tried to emulate and develop reductionist approaches in economics, particularly Walras's attempt to base explanations of systemic economic phenomena on the 'microfoundations' of individual actors. Second, Schumpeter expressed an uneasiness with the extensive use of metaphors from the natural and physical sciences. He defined the word 'evolution' in broad developmental terms, making no reference to biology (for example, Schumpeter, 1954, p. 964). In particular he proclaimed that in general in economics: 'no appeal to biology would be of the slightest use' (ibid., p. 789).

The NEAR zone of Evolutionary Economics includes works of Boulding, Commons, Dosi, Foster, Georgescu-Roegen, Hayek, Hobson, Metcalfe, Mokyr, Nelson, Veblen, Winter and Witt. Again there are some surprises here, particularly the placing of the later Hayek and some 'old' institutionalists in this same zone. The remainder of this essay is devoted to outlining the NEAR approach and arguing for the recognition of its earlier legacy in the writings of Veblen, Commons and Hobson.

EMBRACING NOVELTY

Ulrich Witt (1992, p. 3) writes: 'for a proper notion of socioeconomic evolution, an appreciation of the crucial role of novelty, its emergence, and its dissemination, is indispensable.' Accordingly, Nicolai Foss (1994) argues forcefully for an ontological characterization of the divergence between evolutionary and neoclassical thinking in economics. He argues that evolutionary economics of the type developed by Dosi, Nelson, Winter, Witt and others is concerned with 'the transformation of already existing structures and the emergence and possible spread of novelties' (p. 21). Indeed, whereas evolutionary economics theorizes on the basis of a universe that is open, in the sense that the emergence of novelties is allowed, neoclassical economics addresses closed systems and suppresses novelty. In short, evolutionary and neoclassical economics start from very different ontological assumptions about the social world.

One major source of novelty is individual creativity and choice. Arguably, genuine creativity, real choices and willed changes of purpose mean that human action must contain an element of indeterminacy in the sense of an uncaused cause.[9] To choose or to create means that our choice or our creation is undetermined: we could have acted otherwise. Accordingly, it has been argued (for example, Loasby, 1976, p. 9) that the neoclassical idea of behaviour programmed by fixed preference functions

---

[9]. Note that this concept is quite different from stochastic 'indeterminacy', where the probability of an event is determined by a probability function. It is thus more accurate to speak of 'stochastic determination' rather than indeterminacy in this case.

does not admit genuine choice. However, the idea of an 'uncaused cause' does not have a widespread appeal, most physical and social scientists assuming that every event must have a prior cause. Even within the Austrian School of economists the notion of an 'uncaused cause' is not ubiquitous and clear statements in its favour are not common. These are confined to a handful of economists.

Notably, Frank Knight (1921, p. 221) argued: 'If there is real indeterminateness ... there is in a sense an opening of the door to a conception of freedom in conduct.' More recently, George Shackle (1972, p. 122) writes: 'if the world is determinist, then it seems idle to speak of choice'. Shackle (1989, p. 51) further asserts that 'economics is about choice as a *first cause*, that is the coming into being of decisive thoughts not in all respects to be explained by antecedents.' Ludwig Lachmann (1969, p. 93) comes from the same intellectual tradition, arguing that individual plans cannot be a response 'to anything pre-existent' and thus they are wholly spontaneous and undetermined. Their common anti-determinism is based on a conception of the essential indeterminacy of human decision-making: of individual decision and action as a first or uncaused cause.[10]

The development of non-linear dynamics and chaos theory raise additional questions about indeterminacy and the meaning of novelty. Chaos theory suggests that even if the world is deterministic we would have to treat it as if it were indeterministic and unpredictable. Even if novelty is caused, it may appear as entirely spontaneous and free. Thus the very distinction between determinacy and indeterminacy is undermined. We can never know for sure if any event is caused or uncaused, but chaos theory suggests that we have to treat non-linear systems as if they were indeterministic. A number of key and well known features emerge. First, the chaos literature blurs the boundary between randomness and determinism. Second, precise predictability is confounded by the high degree of sensitivity to initial parameter values. Third, this sensitivity means that there is path dependency and history matters (Arthur, 1989). Fourth, bifurcations and 'butterfly effects' also suggest and reinforce a notion of irreversibility. Fifth, the amplification of small fluctuations can provide endless novelty. Sixth, chaotic systems can exhibit emergent, higher-order properties. Seventh, chaos

---

[10]. See the discussion and references in Hodgson (1993, pp. 155, 214–33). A notable philosophical defence is in Thorp (1980).

theory challenges a reductionist view that a system can be understood by breaking it down and studying each of its component parts.[11]

Consider the question of endogeneity and exogeneity in the light of this discussion of novelty. In his studies of economic development, Schumpeter repeatedly emphasized the sources of change from within. Likewise, Witt defines evolution as 'the transformation of a system over time through endogenously generated change' (Witt, 1991, p. 87, emphasis removed). Similarly, Esben Sloth Andersen (1994, p. 1) regards an 'evolving' as a 'self-transforming' economic system. We may note in passing that, apart from mere Schumpeterian precedent, it is difficult to find a justification for this stance. In biology, neither individuals or species of even ecosystems are entirely 'self-transforming'. Evolution takes place within open systems involving both exogenous and endogenous change.

Further, there is a problem reconciling the emphasis on endogenous change with the notions of novelty and creativity. If the possibility of an uncaused cause is admitted then the concepts of exogeneity and endogeneity require refinement. The distinction between them is typically based on the source of determination. The demarcating criterion is as follows: is the variable causing change inside or outside the system? But if some events are uncaused then is the absence of such a prior cause defined as exogeneity or endogeneity? Clearly the question is absurd in this case.

Taking recourse to chaos theory does not solve this particular problem. Even if chaos theory makes indeterminacy deterministic, it does so by undermining the possibility of a reductionist or full causal explanation and by instating the concept of emergence. If emergent properties are possible, and not capable of full, reductive explanation by a set of other elements, then the same problem of demarcation arises. Emergent properties could be rightly described as endogenous but they are not subject to a complete explanation in terms of endogenous factors.

Given the above problems, and the past association of the concepts of exogeneity and endogeneity with the unqualified notion of causal determination it would be better if the exclusive emphasis on endogeneity was abandoned. The idea of an 'open system' is much more relevant. The distinction between an open and a closed system was first made by Ludwig von Bertalanffy in 1950. The term has been taken up and emphasized by

---

[11]. See, for example, Crutchfield et al. (1986), Gleick (1988), Mirowski (1990), and the related work of Prigogine and Stengers (1984). However, Khalil (1993) argues that it is not possible to derive an adequate concept of purposeful behaviour from such nonlinear systems alone. Nevertheless, such developments involve a catastrophic slippage in the deterministic world view and show that even with deterministic premises we must treat the world as if it was indeterministic.

institutional economists such as K. William Kapp (1976) and the realist
philosopher Roy Bhaskar (1975, 1979). In particular, Bhaskar discusses the
intrinsic and extrinsic conditions of closure. He argues that extrinsic closure
is absent in socio-economic systems because such systems interact with their
environment. National economic systems export and import, and even the
world economic system extrudes waste and is dependent on energy flows
from the sun. Intrinsic closure concerns human agents: even if the system
was otherwise closed then outcomes would not be determinate because of
the potential novelty of human agency. If human beings are more than
automata they are not merely programmed responders to external stimuli;
their actions cannot always be predicted. For these two crucial reasons
socio-economic systems should not be regarded as closed.[12]

For Andersen (1994), Metcalfe (1988), Nelson (1991, 1994), Witt (1987)
and others, novelty and creativity are a major source of variety within
evolving socio-economic systems. Accordingly, a population of entities
cannot be represented by a few distinct characteristics which represent their
essence. Such 'typological essentialism' is rejected in favour of 'population
thinking'. In population thinking, species are described in terms of a
distribution of characteristics. Whereas in typological thinking novelty and
variation are classificatory nuisances, in population thinking they are of
paramount interest because it is precisely the variety of the system that fuels
the evolutionary process (Foss, 1994; Hodgson, 1993; Mayr, 1985).

It should be noted that much work describing itself as 'evolutionary
economics' makes extensive use of mathematics. Some contributors are
enthusiastic about such mathematical developments, seeing this as a way of
making evolutionary economics part of the mainstream (Heertje, 1994, p.
275). However, as Witt (1992, pp. 9–10) points out: 'Regardless of which
mathematical concept seems the most promising, none of them have yet
found or, perhaps, even considered an answer to the question of how the
emergence of novelty may be adequately represented in a formal treatment
of the evolutionary process'.

Arguably, mathematical modelling taken to its limits in economics would
greatly constrain novelty. Even if chaotic systems can seemingly generate
novelty they are limited by their own formal assumptions. In such models
the system needs to be defined by formal assumptions in finite dimensions
that limit the possible results. Even a stochastic process constrains the
variance and defines a given parametric space.

---

[12]. Bhaskar's argument has been applied extensively to economics by Lawson (1989a, 1989b, 1994).

By its nature, novelty defies the boundaries of formalism. To endogenize the novelty-creating process within a formal framework is always to limit greatly the set of possible novel outcomes (Bonaccorsi et al., 1995). Thus, it would appear that modelling within evolutionary economics founders when it reaches the emergence of novelty.

THE LIMITS OF REDUCTIONISM

It is a courageous soul that challenges reductionism in economics. Jon Elster (1983, pp. 20–4) expresses a common view when he writes:

> The basic building block in the social sciences, the elementary unit of explanation, is the individual action guided by some intention. ... Generally speaking, the scientific practice is to seek an explanation at a lower level than the explandum. ... The *search for micro-foundations*, to use a fashionable term from recent controversies in economics, is in reality a pervasive and omnipresent feature of science. (Emphasis in the original)

The project to attempt to place macroeconomics on 'sound microfoundations' gathered pace in the 1970s. The idea of explaining wholes in terms of individual parts is now seen as the *sine qua non* of science. Accordingly, theories based on supposed aggregate behaviour are regarded as scientifically unsound and *ad hoc*. Confidence in the necessity of reductionism in science has reached the point that the Nobel Laureate James Tobin (1986, p. 350) wrote that:

> This [microfoundations] counter-revolution has swept the profession until now. It is scarcely an exaggeration to say that no paper that does not employ the 'microfoundations' methodology can get published in a major professional journal, that no research proposal that is suspect of violating its precepts can survive peer review, that no newly minted Ph.D. who can't show that his hypothesized behavioral relations are properly derived can get a good academic job.

However, several years ago the microfoundations project reached insurmountable difficulties and it has essentially collapsed due to the weight of its internal difficulties. This truth is not widely broadcast but it accounts for the rise in interest in the alternative paradigm of game theory in the 1980s. The fact remains that Hugo Sonnenschein (1972, 1973a, 1973b), Mantel (1974) and Debreu (1974) showed that, starting from the assumption of individual utility maximization, the excess demand functions in an exchange economy can take almost any form. There is thus no basis for the assumption that they are downward sloping. This problem is essentially one of aggregation when individual demand functions are combined. The consequences for neoclassical general equilibrium theory are devastating (Kirman, 1989). As Rizvi (1994, p. 363) puts it, the work of Sonnenschein, Mantel and Debreu is quite general and is not restricted to counterexamples:

> Its chief implication ... is that the hypothesis of individual rationality, and other assumptions made at the micro level, gives no guidance to an analysis of macrolevel phenomena: the assumption of rationality or utility maximisation is not enough to talk about social regularities. This is a significant conclusion and brings the microfoundations project in [general equilibrium theory] to an end.

Further, recent research into the problems of the uniqueness and stability of general equilibria have shown that they may be indeterminate and unstable unless very strong assumptions are made, such as the supposition that society as a whole behaves as if it were a single individual. Again, this demolishes the entire microfoundations project (Lavoie, 1992, pp. 36–41; Screpanti and Zamagni, 1993, pp. 344–53). Facing such profound problems, Alan Kirman (1992, p. 118) writes: 'there is no plausible formal justification for the assumption that the aggregate of individuals, even maximizers, acts itself like an individual maximizer'. He concludes: 'If we are to progress further we may well be forced to theorize in terms of groups who have collectively coherent behaviour. ... The idea that we should start at the level of the isolated individual is one which we may well have to abandon' (Kirman 1989, p. 138).

Methodological individualism carries similar problems of intractability. Indeed it has never been fully carried out in practice. Lars Udéhn (1987) has argued convincingly that not only is methodological individualism flawed but because of the problems of analytical intractability involved it is inoperable as a methodological approach. The reductionist explanation of all complex socioeconomic phenomena in terms of individuals is over-ambitious, and has never succeeded. Aggregation and simplification are always necessary.

Both the microfoundations project and methodological individualism wave reductionist banners but involve partial reductionism only. As David Sloan Wilson and Elliott Sober (1989) argue, to settle on the individual as the unit of selection involves an inconsistency. Adequate reasons why explanations should be reduced simply to the level of the individual, and stop there, have not been provided. The same arguments concerning explanatory reduction from the macro to the micro, from groups to individuals' apply equally to explanatory reduction from individual to gene, gene to molecule, and so on.

If we can reduce explanations to individual terms why not further reduce them to the terms of genes? Or molecules? To avoid this 'double standard' one must either accept multiple levels of analysis, each with their own partial autonomy, or reduce everything to the lowest possible level as the biological reductionists attempted in the nineteenth century.

The version of reductionism that suggests that wholes must be explained in terms of parts must take the parts as given. To take a contrary view suggests an infinite regress, in which each part has to be explained in terms of its relations with other parts, and so on, without end. This reductionist injunction assumes that which must eventually reach the basic, unperturbable and irreducible parts or individuals where the analysis can come to a stop (Hodgson, 1988, 1993). A preferable stance is to argue that parts and wholes, individuals and institutions, mutually constitute and condition each other, and none has analytical priority (Giddens, 1984; Lawson, 1985; Nozick, 1977).

It should be pointed out at the outset that the general idea of a reduction to parts is not being overturned here. Some degree of reduction to elemental units is inevitable. Even measurement is an act of reduction. Science cannot proceed without some dissection and some analysis of parts.

However, although some reduction is inevitable and desirable, complete reductionism is both impossible and a philosophically dogmatic diversion. What is important to stress is that the process of analysis cannot be extended to the most elementary subatomic particles presently known to science, or even to individuals in economics or genes in biology. Complete reductionism would be hopeless and interminable. As Karl Popper has declared: 'I do not think that there are any examples of a successful reduction' to elemental units in science (Popper and Eccles, 1977, p. 18). Reduction is necessary to some extent, but it can never be complete.

Notably, the adoption of an organicist ontology implies that the reductionist and methodological individualist project to explain all social and economic phenomena in terms of given individuals and the relations between them is confounded. The adoption of an organicist ontology means precisely that the individual is not given (Winslow, 1989). Organicism obstructs the treatment of individuals as elemental or immutable building blocks of analysis. Exponents of organicism argue further that both the explanatory reduction of wholes to parts and parts to wholes should be rejected. Just as society cannot exist without individuals, the individual does not exist prior to the social reality. Individuals both constitute, and are constituted by, society. Unidirectional modes of explanation, such as from parts to wholes – and vice versa – or from one level to another are thus thwarted. There is both 'upward' and 'downward' causation.

Philosophers Roy Bhaskar, Arthur Koestler, Alfred Whitehead and others propose that reality consists of multi-levelled hierarchies. The existence of emergent properties at each level means that explanations at that tier cannot be reduced entirely to phenomena at lower levels. As the biologist Ernst Mayr (1985, p. 58) puts it:

> Systems at each hierarchical level have two characteristics. They act as wholes (as if they were a homogeneous entity), and their characteristics cannot (not even in theory) be deduced from the most complete knowledge of the components, taken separately or in other partial combinations. In other words, when such systems are assembled from their components, new characteristics of the new whole emerge that could not have been predicted from a knowledge of the components. ... Perhaps the two most interesting characteristics of new wholes are that they can in turn become parts of still higher-level systems, and that they can affect properties of components at lower levels (downward causation) ... Recognition of the importance of emergence demonstrates, of course, the invalidity of extreme reductionism. By the time we have dissected an organism down to atoms and elementary particles we have lost everything that is characteristic of a living system.

James Murphy (1994, p. 555) develops a similar argument:

> The theory of emergence ... is a nonreductionist account of complex phenomena. ... The notion that from complexity emerges new phenomena that cannot be reduced to simpler parts is at the center of modern biology ... Complex systems very often have a hierarchical structure, and the hierarchical structure of living systems shares some important features with our hierarchy, one being that higher levels can affect properties of components at lower levels.

This again implies 'downward causation' (Sperry, 1969; Campbell, 1974). The fact that structures or elements on one level can profoundly affect those at another level confounds reductionism. Although reductionism is still prominent, both in biology and in the social sciences, in biology strong and influential voices can be found against it.

ANCESTORS OF NEAR EVOLUTIONARY ECONOMICS

Our search for precedents for the NEAR stance will be confined to economists who have made their major contribution in this genre prior to 1930. The boundaries of NEAR exclude many. Consider four. Menger and Schumpeter are ruled out because of their adherence to methodological individualism. Marshall embraced reductionism and gave little attention to the question of novelty. Although Knight (1921) gave great emphasis to the reality of indeterminacy and novelty in economic systems, his extreme individualism masked any anti-reductionist feelings.

Three prominent candidates remain: John A. Hobson (1848–1940), Thorstein B. Veblen (1857–1929) and John R. Commons (1862–1945). Veblen and Commons are well known as founders of American institutionalism and Hobson is the British economist with the foremost claim to the 'institutionalist' label. Apart from a belated and extensive recognition by John Maynard Keynes (1936, pp. 19, 364–71) of Hobson's importance, he has since been largely ignored by economists.

Veblen

In the sense that Veblen (1898a, 1899) was the first economist to apply extensively the Darwinian ideas of variety, heredity and selection to economic evolution, he is rightly described as the first evolutionary economist. However, his commitment to NEAR principles is not so forthright. A reason for this is that he was hampered by a prevailing conception of science in which ideas such as an uncaused cause would be an anathema. It took the rise of quantum physics in the first three decades of the twentieth century to break the hold of strict determinism in science. Writing earlier, Veblen was thus at a disadvantage.

It is sometimes alleged that Veblen 'teeters between free will and determinism' (Seckler, 1975, p. 56), and entertained a conception of science from which purpose and intentionality were excluded (Commons, 1934, p. 654). However, in one of his first articles Veblen (1884) addressed the problem of human freedom and indeterminacy. Furthermore, his subsequent emphasis on human purposefulness is repeated and significant: 'Economic action is teleological, in the sense that men always and everywhere seek to do something' (Veblen, 1898a, 1919, p. 75). Human beings are 'endowed with a proclivity for purposeful action' (Veblen, 1898b, 1934, p. 80).

Nevertheless, the nature and definition of what is meant by 'purposeful action' is not always clear, and this is perhaps one source of controversy over Veblen's line of thought (Seckler, 1975; Langlois, 1989). However, Veblen's (1914) emphasis on 'idle curiosity', for instance, as well as many of his own explicit statements, would seem to retain a crucial role for human agency in his theory. In his *Instinct of Workmanship* Veblen also wrote: 'Neither the manner of life imposed by the machine process, nor the manner of thought inculcated by habituation to its logic, will fall in with the free movement of the human spirit' (Veblen, 1914, p. 334).

Notably, and in contrast to many of his contemporaries, Veblen's approach was interactionist and anti-reductionist. It was interactionist in the sense that actor and structure interact and mutually condition each other to the degree that explanations based on either actor or structure alone are unwarranted: 'both the agent and his environment being at any point the outcome of the last process' (Veblen, 1898a, p. 391). It was also interactionist in the sense that socio-economic systems interact with their biotic foundation to the degree that explanations based on biology alone are unsuitable and that full explanations of some socio-economic phenomena may involve biological factors. Although Veblen (1909, p. 300) acknowledged the biotic foundations of social life, he resisted the view that human behaviour could be explained purely and simply in terms of genetic inheritance.

Commons

Commons (1934, p. 55) was aware of the quantum revolution in physics and lived to see the growing arguments for indeterminacy in the human sphere. However, while consistently emphasizing the importance of purposeful action, his position on this question is ambiguous. In one passage Commons (1924, p. 82) saw the argument between determinacy and indeterminacy as irrelevant 'for economic purposes'. Despite this, he consistently held to the view that the exercise of human will drastically limit the role of prediction in economics. Nevertheless, the emphasis on purposeful behaviour remains central. Commons (1950, p. 36) went so far as to argue that the 'science of the human will' acting in both 'individuals and all collective organizations' is the 'twentieth century foundation' of economic science.

Despite a degree of vagueness in the specification of his terms, Neil Chamberlain (1963, p. 93) has argued that this recognition of the role of individual 'human will' and of the place of 'collective action' comprise Commons's two great achievements. Commons's concepts of 'collective action' and 'collective will' are complex and controversial but they are in part sustained by a belief in units and levels of analysis apart from the atomistic individual.[13] His writings suggest an organicist conception of the human agent, in which people both mould and are moulded by their circumstances.

---

[13]. Despite Langlois (1986, 4n.), Commons did not take these terms to mean that an organization or collective has a distinct will of its own (Biddle, 1990; Ramstad, 1990; Rutherford, 1983; Vanberg, 1989).

Hobson

In a work published in the same year as Veblen's *Instinct of Workmanship*, Hobson (1914, pp. 240–1, 336) saw the role of human error and playful inventiveness as decisive in creating mutations in behavioural patterns, and thereby a source of continuous evolutionary innovation. Interestingly, he gave more stress to the function of the 'freedom of the human will' than Veblen in this context. However, Hobson did not go so far as Veblen to incorporate this idea into an evolutionary theory of the Darwinian and phylogenetic type. There is not a theory of evolutionary change in Hobson's writings that comes close to this.[14]

Hobson drew strong methodological and anti-reductionist conclusions from his own version of organicism, writing: 'An organized unity, or whole, cannot be explained adequately by an analysis of its constituent parts: its wholeness is a new product, with attributes not ascertainable in its parts, though in a sense derived from them' (Hobson, 1929, p. 32). Hobson thus expressed the idea of emergent properties and higher, irreducible levels of analysis.

In his book on *Veblen*, Hobson (1936, p. 216) approvingly notes an important shift of thinking in the early decades of the twentieth century:

> Emergent evolution brings unpredictable novelties into the processes of history, and disorder, hazard, chance, are brought into the play of energetic action. Intuition is invoked as an independent source of information regarding the higher values, and ... this line of thought ... does distinctly contravene the doctrines of mechanical causation in their moulding of modern thought and sentiment. Its emphasis upon novelty in evolutionary processes, and upon elements of chance constitutes a direct challenge to the logic of ordinary thought as well as to the determinist philosophy.

Accordingly, Hobson forcefully rejected mechanical metaphors, seeing them as 'squeezing out humanity' and denying human novelty and creativity (Freeden, 1988, pp. 89, 173). Although Hobson was older than Veblen and Commons, he provided the clearest expression of the essentials of the NEAR paradigm.

---

[14]. This is my excuse for not having a chapter on Hobson in my *Economics and Evolution* (1993) book. In retrospect, the omission is probably an error of judgement.

Enter Mitchell... and Keynes

Wesley Mitchell (1874–1948) was the third in the founding generation of American institutionalists, and, additionally, one of the fathers of modern macroeconomics. Mitchell's work is notable not for its stress on novelty and creativity but for its anti-reductionist thrust and its consequent contribution to the development of Keynesian macroeconomics. It is for this reason, and for his links with NEAR 'old' institutionalists Veblen and Commons, that he is considered here.

Mitchell (1937, p. 26) argued that economists need not begin with a theory of individual behaviour but with the statistical observation of 'mass phenomena'. Mitchell and his colleagues in the National Bureau of Economic Research in the 1920s and 1930s played a vital role in the development of national income accounting, suggesting that aggregate, macroeconomic phenomena have an ontological and empirical legitimacy.

This was an important incursion against reductionism in economics. It created space for the construction of Keynesianism but the counter-attack from reductionism has been persistent up to the present day. Notably, in defending Mitchell's approach against the reductionist criticisms of Tjalling Koopmans (1947), Rutledge Vining (1949, p. 79) argued that phenomena such as 'trade fluctuations' were not merely aggregates 'of the economizing units of traditional theoretical economics'. Further, 'we need not take for granted that the behaviour and functioning of this entity can be exhaustively explained in terms of the motivated behaviour of individuals who are particles within the whole'. This is a classic rejection of reductionism, in terms of the existence of emergent properties that cannot be completely explained in terms of the constituent parts.

For Keynesianism, Mitchell's anti-reductionist thrust was crucial. Being traditionally linked with organicist or holistic views, institutionalism developed and sanctioned the conceptualization and measurement of economic aggregates. Through the development of national income accounting the work of Mitchell and his colleagues influenced and inspired the macroeconomics of Keynes (Mirowski, 1989, p. 307). It was with institutionalism as a midwife that Keynesian macroeconomics was born.

Keynes's own views have been a persistent source of controversy. However, insofar as Keynes is influenced by ideas of the indeterminacy of the human will, of 'animal spirits' and the capacity for creativity and novelty, he fulfils one criterion of the NEAR paradigm. Clearly, in developing an economic theory based on aggregates he was breaking from reductionism. The second criterion is thus also satisfied. It is thus perhaps no accident that Keynes was so full of praise for Hobson, and even wrote personally to Commons in the following terms: 'Judging from limited evidence and at great distance, there seems to be no other economist with whose general way of thinking I find myself in such genuine accord.'[15]

CONCLUSION

The challenge provided by evolutionary economics is not only theoretical but ontological, epistemological and methodological. The stress on ontology coincides with a general movement in philosophy back towards matters of ontological grounding that were dismissed as 'metaphysical' in the era of logical positivism.

Arguably, 'evolutionary economics' has now reached a crossroads in its own development, and faces the possibility of both degenerative and regenerative outcomes. Despite the difficulties involved, at least we are now in a position to identify some of the most pressing problems and the philosophical roots of an approach which differs radically from mainstream economics.

The NEAR or 'institutional' wing of evolutionary economics legitimates a number of allied endeavours: less in formal modelling and more in economic philosophy, the history of economic thought, economic history, the study of technical and institutional change, empirical enquiry, and the development of economic, industrial and environmental policies.

Clearly, evolutionary economics is at a crucial stage in its history. A dozen years after *An Evolutionary Theory of Economic Change* there is much mutation and variety within this species of economics. It will be very interesting to observe the evolution of the different strains as we approach and pass the centenary of Veblen's famous 1898 essay.

REFERENCES

Alchian, A.A. (1950), 'Uncertainty, Evolution and Economic Theory', *Journal of Political Economy*, **58**, June, 211–22.

Andersen, E.S. (1994), *Evolutionary Economics: Post-Schumpeterian Contributions*, London: Pinter.

Arthur, W.B. (1989), 'Competing Technologies, Increasing Returns, and Lock-in by Historical Events', *Economic Journal*, **99**(1), 116–31. Reprinted in Freeman (1990).

---

[15]. Keynes to Commons, dated 26 April 1927 (John R. Commons Papers, State Historical Society of Wisconsin, 1982).

Basalla, G. (1989), *The Evolution of Technology*, Cambridge: Cambridge University Press.

Bertalanffy, L. von (1950), 'The Theory of Open Systems in Physics and Biology', *Science*, No. 111, 23–9.

Bhaskar, R. (1975), *A Realist Theory of Science*, Leeds: Leeds Books. 2nd edn (1978), Brighton: Harvester.

Bhaskar, R. (1979), *The Possibility of Naturalism: A Philosophic Critique of the Contemporary Human Sciences*, Brighton: Harvester.

Biddle, J.E. (1990), 'Purpose and Evolution in Commons's Institutionalism', *History of Political Economy*, **22**(1), 19–47.

Blaas, W. and J. Foster (eds) (1992), *Mixed Economies in Europe: An Evolutionary Perspective on their Emergence, Transition and Regulation*, Aldershot: Edward Elgar.

Black, M. (1962), *Models and Metaphors: Studies in Language and Philosophy*, Ithaca: Cornell University Press.

Boettke, P.J. (1989), 'Evolution and Economics: Austrians as Institutionalists', *Research in the History of Economic Thought and Methodology*, **6**, 73–89.

Böhm, S. (1989), 'Hayek on Knowledge, Equilibrium and Prices: Context and Impact', *Wirtschaftspolitische Blatter*, **36**(2), 201–13.

Bonaccorsi, A., F. Pammolli and S. Tani (1995), 'On R&D and the Nature of the Firm', University of Pisa, mimeo.

Boulding, K.E. (1978), *Ecodynamics: A New Theory of Societal Evolution*, Beverly Hills: Sage.

Boulding, K.E. (1981), *Evolutionary Economics*, Beverly Hills, CA: Sage Publications.

Boulding, K.E. (1991), 'What is Evolutionary Economics?', *Journal of Evolutionary Economics*, **1**(1), 9–17.

Campbell, D.T. (1974), '"Downward Causation" in Hierarchically Organized Biological Systems', in F.J. Ayala and T. Dobzhansky (eds) (1974), *Studies in the Philosophy of Biology*, Berkeley and Los Angeles: University of California Press, pp. 179–86.

Chamberlain, N.W. (1963), 'The Institutional Economics of John R. Commons', in J. Dorfman, C.W. Ayres, N.W. Chamberlain, S. Kuznets and R.A. Gordon (1963), *Institutional Economics: Veblen, Commons, and Mitchell Reconsidered*, Berkeley, CA: University of California Press, pp. 63–94.

Clark, N.G. and C. Juma (1987), *Long-Run Economics: An Evolutionary Approach to Economic Growth*, London: Pinter.

Commons, J.R. (1924), *The Legal Foundations of Capitalism*, New York: Macmillan. Reprinted 1968, Madison: University of Wisconsin Press and 1974, New York: Augustus Kelley.

Commons, J.R. (1934), *Institutional Economics – Its Place in Political Economy*, New York: Macmillan. Reprinted 1990 with a new introduction by M. Rutherford, New Brunswick: Transaction.

Commons, J.R. (1950), *The Economics of Collective Action*, edited by K.H. Parsons, New York: Macmillan.

Crutchfield, J.P., J.D. Farmer, N.H. Packard and R.S. Shaw (1986), 'Chaos', *Scientific American*, **255**(6), 38–49.

Day, R.H. and P. Chen (eds) (1993), *Nonlinear Dynamics and Evolutionary Economics*, New York: Oxford University Press.

Debreu, G. (1974), 'Excess Demand Functions', *Journal of Mathematical Economics*, **1**(1).

Degler, C.N. (1991), *In Search of Human Nature: The Decline and Revival of Darwinism in American Social Thought*, Oxford and New York: Oxford University Press.

Delorme, R. and K. Dopfer (eds) (1994), *The Political Economy of Diversity: Evolutionary Perspectives on Economic Order and Disorder*, Aldershot: Edward Elgar.

Depew, D.J. and B.H. Weber (eds) (1985), *Evolution at a Crossroads: The New Biology and the New Philosophy of Science*, Cambridge, MA: MIT Press.

Dosi, G., C. Freeman, R. Nelson, G. Silverberg and L. Soete (eds) (1988), *Technical Change and Economic Theory*, London: Pinter.

Edgell, S. (1975), 'Thorstein Veblen's Theory of Evolutionary Change', *American Journal of Economics and Sociology*, **34**, July, 267–80.

Elster, J. (1982), 'Marxism, Functionalism and Game Theory', *Theory and Society*, **11**(4), 453–82.

Elster, J. (1983), *Explaining Technical Change*, Cambridge: Cambridge University Press.

England, R.W. (ed.) (1994), *Evolutionary Concepts in Contemporary Economics*, Ann Arbor: University of Michigan Press.

Faber, M. and J.L.R. Proops (1990), *Evolution, Time, Production and the Environment*, Berlin: Springer.

Foss, N.J. (1994), 'Realism and Evolutionary Economics', *Journal of Social and Evolutionary Systems*, **17**(1), 21–40.

Foster, J. (1987), *Evolutionary Macroeconomics*, London: George Allen and Unwin.

Freeden, M. (ed.) (1988), *J.A. Hobson: A Reader*, London and Boston: Unwin Hyman.

Freeman, C. (ed.) (1990), *The Economics of Innovation*, Aldershot: Edward Elgar.

Georgescu-Roegen, N. (1971), *The Entropy Law and the Economic Process*, Cambridge, MA: Harvard University Press.

Giddens, A. (1984), *The Constitution of Society: Outline of the Theory of Structuration*, Cambridge: Polity Press.

Gleick, J. (1988), *Chaos: Making a New Science*, London: Heinemann.

Goodwin, R.M. (1990), *Chaotic Economic Dynamics*, Oxford: Oxford University Press.

Gordon, W. and J. Adams (1989), *Economics as a Social Science: An Evolutionary Approach*, Riverdale, MD: Riverdale.

Haavelmo, T. (1954), *A Study in the Theory of Economic Evolution*, Amsterdam: North-Holland.

Hamilton, D.B. (1991), *Evolutionary Economics: A Study in Change in Economic Thought*, 3rd edn, New Brunswick, NJ: Transaction.

Hannan, M.T. and J. Freeman (1989), *Organizational Ecology*, Cambridge, MA: Harvard University Press.

Hanusch, H. (ed.) (1988), *Evolutionary Economics: Applications of Schumpeter's Ideas*, Cambridge: Cambridge University Press.

Harris, A.L. (1934), 'Economic Evolution: Dialectical and Darwinian', *Journal of Political Economy*, 42(1), 34–79.

Hayek, F.A. (1967a), 'Notes on the Evolution of Systems of Rules of Conduct', from Hayek (1967b), pp. 66–81. Reprinted in Witt (1993b).

Hayek, F.A. (1967b), *Studies in Philosophy, Politics and Economics*, London: Routledge and Kegan Paul.

Hayek, F.A. (1982), *Law, Legislation and Liberty*, 3-volume combined edn, London: Routledge and Kegan Paul.

Hayek, F.A. (1988), *The Fatal Conceit: The Errors of Socialism, the Collected Works of Friedrich August Hayek*, vol. I, ed. W.W. Bartley III, London: Routledge.

Heertje, A. (1994), 'Neo-Schumpeterians and Economic Theory', in Magnusson (1994), pp. 265–76.

Heertje, A. and M. Perlman (eds) (1990), *Evolving Technology and Market Structure: Studies in Schumpeterian Economics*, Ann Arbor, MI: University of Michigan Press.

Hesse, M.B. (1966), *Models and Analogies in Science*, Notre Dame: University of Notre Dame Press.

Hesse, M.B. (1980), *Revolutions and Reconstructions in the Philosophy of Science*, Brighton: Harvester Press.

Hobson, J.A. (1914), *Work and Wealth: A Human Valuation*, London: Macmillan.

Hobson, J.A. (1929), *Wealth and Life: A Study in Values*, London: Macmillan.

Hobson, J.A. (1936), *Veblen*, London: Chapman and Hall. Reprinted 1991 by Augustus Kelley.

Hodgson, G.M. (1988), *Economics and Institutions: A Manifesto for a Modern Institutional Economics*, Cambridge and Philadelphia: Polity Press and University of Pennsylvania Press.

Hodgson, G.M. (1993), *Economics and Evolution: Bringing Life Back Into Economics*, Cambridge, UK and Ann Arbor, MI: Polity Press and University of Michigan Press.

Hodgson, G.M. (ed.) (1995a), *Economics and Biology*, Aldershot: Edward Elgar.

Hodgson, G.M. (1995b), 'The Evolution of Evolutionary Economics', *Scottish Journal of Political Economy*, 42(4), November, 469–88.

Hodgson, G.M. (1996) 'Metaphor and Pluralism in Economics: Mechanics and Biology', in A. Salanti and E. Screpanti (eds) (1996), *Pluralism in Economics: New Perspectives in History and Methodology*, Aldershot: Edward Elgar.

Hodgson, G.M. (forthcoming a), 'Evolutionary Economics', in J.B. Davis, D.W. Hands and U. Mäki (eds), *Handbook of Economic Methodology*, Aldershot: Edward Elgar, forthcoming.

Hodgson, G.M. (forthcoming b), 'Decomposition and Growth: Biological Metaphors in Economics from the 1880s to the 1980s', in K. Dopfer (ed.) (forthcoming), *Evolutionary Principles of Economics*, Boston: Kluwer.

Hodgson, G.M. and E. Screpanti (eds) (1991), *Rethinking Economics: Markets, Technology and Economic Evolution*, Aldershot: Edward Elgar.

Hodgson, G.M., W.J. Samuels and M.R. Tool (eds) (1994), *The Elgar Companion to Institutional and Evolutionary Economics*, Aldershot: Edward Elgar.

Hunt, E.K. (1975), *Property and Prophets: The Evolution of Economic Institutions*, New York.

Kapp, K.W. (1976), 'The Nature and Significance of Institutional Economics', *Kyklos*, **29**, Fasc. 2, 209–32. Reprinted in W.J. Samuels (ed.) (1988), *Institutional Economics*, Aldershot: Edward Elgar, vol. 1.

Kay, N.M. (1982), *The Evolving Firm: Strategy and Structure in Industrial Organisation*, London: Macmillan.

Keynes, J.M. (1936), *The General Theory of Employment, Interest and Money*, London: Macmillan.

Khalil, E.L. (1993), 'Is Poincaréan Nonlinear Dynamics the Alternative to the Selection Theory of Evolution?', *Journal of Social and Evolutionary Systems*, **16**(4), 489–500.

Kirman, A.P. (1989), 'The Intrinsic Limits of Modern Economic Theory: The Emperor Has No Clothes', *Economic Journal (Conference Papers)*, **99**, 126–39.

Kirman, A.P. (1992), 'Whom or What Does the Representative Individual Represent?', *Journal of Economic Perspectives*, **6**(2), 117–36.

Klamer, A. and T.C. Leonard (1994), 'So What's an Economic Metaphor?', in Mirowski (1994), pp. 20–51.

Knight, F.H. (1921), *Risk, Uncertainty and Profit*, New York: Houghton Mifflin.

Koopmans, T.C. (1947), 'Measurement Without Theory', *Review of Economics and Statistics*, **29**, August, 161–72.

Lachmann, L.M. (1969), 'Methodological Individualism and the Market Economy', in E.W. Streissler (ed.) (1969), *Roads to Freedom: Essays in Honour of Friedrich A. von Hayek*, London: Routledge and Kegan Paul, pp. 89–103. Reprinted in L.M. Lachmann (1977), *Capital, Expectations and the Market Process*, edited with an introduction by W.E. Grinder, Kansas City: Sheed Andrews and McMeel.

Lachmann, L.M. (1977), *Capital, Expectations and the Market Process*, edited with an introduction by W.E. Grinder, Kansas City: Sheed Andrews and McMeel.

Langlois, R.N. (ed.) (1986), *Economics as a Process: Essays in the New Institutional Economics*, Cambridge: Cambridge University Press.

Langlois, R.N. (1989), 'What Was Wrong With the Old Institutional Economics (and What is Still Wrong With the New)?', *Review of Political Economy*, **1**(3), 270–98.

Langlois, R.N. and M.J. Everett (1994), 'What is Evolutionary Economics?' in Magnusson (1994), pp. 11–47.

Lavoie, M. (1992), *Foundations of Post-Keynesian Economic Analysis*, Aldershot: Edward Elgar.

Lawson, T. (1985), 'Uncertainty and Economic Analysis', *Economic Journal*, **95**(4), 909–27.

Lawson, T. (1989a), 'Abstraction, Tendencies and Stylised Facts: A Realist Approach to Economic Analysis', *Cambridge Journal of Economics*, **13**(1), 59–78. Reprinted in A. Lawson, J.G. Palma and J. Sender (eds) (1989), *Kaldor's Political Economy*, London: Academic Press.

Lawson, T. (1989b), 'Realism and Instrumentalism in the Development of Econometrics', *Oxford Economic Papers*, **41**(1), 236–58. Reprinted in N. de Marchi and C. Gilbert (eds) (1990), *The History and Methodology of Econometrics*, Oxford: Oxford University Press.

Lawson, T. (1994), 'Realism, Philosophical', in G.M. Hodgson, W.J. Samuels and M.R. Tool (eds) (1994), *The Elgar Companion to Institutional and Evolutionary Economics*, vol. 2, Aldershot: Edward Elgar, pp. 219–25.

Leathers, C.G. (1990), 'Veblen and Hayek on Instincts and Evolution', *Journal of the History of Economic Thought*, **12**(2), 162–78.

Loasby, B.J. (1976), *Choice, Complexity and Ignorance: An Enquiry into Economic Theory and the Practice of Decision Making*, Cambridge: Cambridge University Press.

Loasby, B.J. (1991), *Equilibrium and Evolution: An Exploration of Connecting Principles in Economics*, Manchester: Manchester University Press.

Maasen, S. (1995), 'Who is Afraid of Metaphors?' in Maasen et al. (1995), pp. 11–35.

Maasen, S., E. Mendelsohn and P. Weingart (eds) (1995), *Biology as Society, Society as Biology: Metaphors*, Sociology of the Sciences Yearbook, **18**, 1994, Boston: Kluwer.

Magnusson, L. (ed.) (1994), *Evolutionary and Neo-Schumpeterian Approaches to Economics*, Boston: Kluwer.

Mantel, R. (1974), 'On the Characterization of Aggregate Excess Demand', *Journal of Economic Theory*, **12**(2).

Marshall, A. (1890), *Principles of Economics: An Introductory Volume*, 1st edn, London: Macmillan.

Mayr, E. (1985), 'How Biology Differs from the Physical Sciences', in Depew and Weber (1985), pp. 43–63.

McKelvey, W. (1982), *Organizational Systematics: Taxonomy, Evolution, Classification*, Berkeley, CA: University of California Press.

Menger, C. (1981), *Principles of Economics*, edited by J. Dingwall and translated by B.F. Hoselitz from the German edition of 1871, New York: New York University Press.

Metcalfe, J.S. (1988), 'Evolution and Economic Change', in A. Silberston (ed.) (1988), *Technology and Economic Progress*, Basingstoke: Macmillan, pp. 54–85. Reprinted in Witt (1993b).

Metcalfe, J.S. (1994), 'Evolutionary Economics and Technology Policy', *Economic Journal*, **104**(4), 931–44.

Mirowski, P. (1989), *More Heat Than Light: Economics as Social Physics, Physics as Nature's Economics*, Cambridge: Cambridge University Press.

Mirowski, P. (1990), 'From Mandelbrot to Chaos in Economic Theory', *Southern Economic Journal*, **57**(2), 289–307.

Mirowski, P. (ed.) (1994), *Natural Images in Economic Thought: Markets Read in Tooth and Claw*, Cambridge: Cambridge University Press.

Mises, L. von (1957), *Theory and History: An Interpretation of Social and Economic Evolution*, New Haven: Yale University Press.

Mitchell, W.C. (1937), *The Backward Art of Spending Money and Other Essays*, New York: McGraw-Hill.

Mokyr, J. (1990), *The Lever of Riches: Technological Creativity and Economic Progress*, Oxford: Oxford University Press.

Mokyr, J. (1991), 'Evolutionary Biology, Technical Change and Economic History', *Bulletin of Economic Research*, **43**(2), 127–49. Reprinted in Hodgson (1995a).

Murphy, J.B. (1994), 'The Kinds of Order in Society', in Mirowski (1994), pp. 536–82.

Nelson, R.R. (1991), 'Why Do Firms Differ, and How Does it Matter?', *Strategic Management Journal*, **12**, Special Issue, Winter, 61–74.

Nelson, R.R. (1994), 'The Role of Firm Difference in an Evolutionary Theory of Technical Advance', in Magnusson (1994), pp. 231–42.

Nelson, R.R. and S.G. Winter (1973), 'Towards an Evolutionary Theory of Economic Capabilities', *American Economic Review (Papers and Proceedings)*, **63**(2), 440–9.

Nelson, R.R. and S.G. Winter (1974), 'Neoclassical vs. Evolutionary Theories of Economic Growth: Critique and Prospectus', *Economic Journal*, **84**(4), 886–905. Reprinted in Freeman (1990).

Nelson, R.R. and S.G. Winter (1982), *An Evolutionary Theory of Economic Change*, Cambridge: Bellknap Press of Harvard University Press.

Nozick, R. (1977), 'On Austrian Methodology', *Synthese*, **36**, 353–92.

Pantzar, M. (1991), *A Replicative Perspective on Evolutionary Dynamics*, Helsinki: Labour Institute for Economic Research, Research Report 37.

Popper, Sir K.R. (1982), *The Open Universe: An Argument for Indeterminism*, from the *Postscript to the Logic of Scientific Discovery*, edited by W.W. Bartley, III, London: Hutchinson.

Popper, Sir K.R. and J.C. Eccles (1977), *The Self and Its Brain*, Berlin: Springer International.

Prigogine, I. and I. Stengers (1984), *Order Out of Chaos: Man's New Dialogue With Nature*, London: Heinemann.

Ramstad, Y. (1990), 'The Institutionalism of J.R. Commons: Theoretical Foundations of a Volitional Economics', *Research in the History of Economic Thought and Methodology*, **8**, 53–104.

Rizvi, S. Abu Turab (1994), 'The Microfoundations Project in General Equilibrium Theory', *Cambridge Journal of Economics*, **18**(4), 357–77.

Robbins, L. (1970), *Evolution of Modern Economic Theory*, London: Macmillan.

Rosenberg, A. (1994), 'Does Evolutionary Theory Give Comfort or Inspiration to Economics?', in Mirowski (1994), pp. 384–407.

Rutherford, M. (1983), 'J.R. Commons's Institutional Economics', *Journal of Economic Issues*, **17**(3), 721–44. Reprinted in W.J. Samuels (ed.) (1988), *Institutional Economics*, Aldershot: Edward Elgar, vol. 1.

Rutherford, M.C. (1989), 'Some Issues in the Comparison of Austrian and Institutional Economics', *Research in the History of Economic Thought and Methodology*, vol. 6, 159–71.

Rutherford, M.C. (1994), *Institutions in Economics: The Old and the New Institutionalism*, Cambridge: Cambridge University Press.

Samuels, W.J. (1989), 'Austrian and Institutional Economics: Some Common Elements', *Research in the History of Economic Thought and Methodology*, vol. 6, 53–71.

Sanderson, S.K. (1990), *Social Evolutionism: A Critical History*, Oxford: Blackwell.

Saviotti, P.P. and J.S. Metcalfe (eds) (1991), *Evolutionary Theories of Economic and Technological Change: Present Status and Future Prospects*, Reading: Harwood.

Schumpeter, J.A. (1934), *The Theory of Economic Development*, translated by R. Opie from the German edition of 1912, Cambridge, MA: Harvard University Press.

Schumpeter, J.A. (1942), *Capitalism, Socialism and Democracy*, 1st edn, London: George Allen and Unwin.

Schumpeter, J.A. (1954), *History of Economic Analysis*, New York: Oxford University Press.

Screpanti, E. and S. Zamagni (1993), *An Outline of the History of Economic Thought*, Oxford: Clarendon Press.

Sebba, G. (1953), 'The Development of the Concepts of Mechanism and Model in Physical Science and Economic Thought', *American Economic Review (Papers and Proceedings)*, **43**(2), 259–68. Reprinted in Hodgson (1995a).

Seckler, D. (1975), *Thorstein Veblen and the Institutionalists: A Study in the Social Philosophy of Economics*, London: Macmillan.

Shackle, G.L.S. (1955), *Uncertainty in Economics*, Cambridge: Cambridge University Press.

Shackle, G.L.S. (1972), *Epistemics and Economics: A Critique of Economic Doctrines*, Cambridge: Cambridge University Press.

Shackle, G.L.S. (1989), 'What Did the "General Theory" Do?', in J. Pheby (ed.) (1989), *New Directions in Post Keynesian Economics*, Aldershot: Edward Elgar, pp. 48–58.

Sonnenschein, H. (1972), 'Market Excess Demand Functions', *Econometrica*, **40**(3).

Sonnenschein, H. (1973a), 'Do Walras's Identity and Continuity Characterize the Class of Community Excess Demand Functions?', *Journal of Economic Theory*, **6**(4).

Sonnenschein, H. (1973b), 'The Utility Hypothesis and Market Demand Theory', *Western Economic Journal*, **11**(4).

Sowell, T. (1967), 'The "Evolutionary" Economics of Thorstein Veblen', *Oxford Economic Papers*, **19**(2), 177–98. Reprinted in M. Blaug (ed.) (1992), *Thorstein Veblen (1857–1929)*, Aldershot: Edward Elgar.

Sperry, R.W, (1969), 'A Modified Concept of Consciousness', *Psychological Review*, **76**, 532–36.

Sraffa, P. (1960), *Production of Commodities by Means of Commodities: Prelude to a Critique of Economic Theory*, Cambridge: Cambridge University Press.

Tang, A. et al. (eds) (1976), *Evolution, Welfare and Time in Economics: Essays in Honor of Nicholas Georgescu-Roegen*, Lexington, MA: Lexington Books.

Thoben, H. (1982), 'Mechanistic and Organistic Analogies in Economics Reconsidered', *Kyklos*, **35**, Fasc. 2, 292–306. Reprinted in Hodgson (1995a).

Thorp, J. (1980), *Free Will: A Defence Against Neurophysiological Determinism*, London: Routledge and Kegan Paul.

Tobin, J. (1986), 'The Future of Keynesian Economics', *Eastern Economic Journal*, **13**(4).

Udéhn, L. (1987), *Methodological Individualism: A Critical Appraisal*, Uppsala: Uppsala University Reprographics Centre.

Van Parijs, P. (1981), *Evolutionary Explanations in the Social Sciences: An Emerging Paradigm*, London: Tavistock.

Vanberg, V.J. (1986), 'Spontaneous Market Order and Social Rules: A Critique of F.A. Hayek's Theory of Cultural Evolution', *Economics and Philosophy*, **2**(1), 75–100. Reprinted in Witt (1993b).

Vanberg, V.J. (1989), 'Carl Menger's Evolutionary and John R. Commons' Collective Action Approach to Institutions: A Comparison', *Review of Political Economy*, **1**(3), 334–60. Reprinted in V.J. Vanberg (1994), *Rules and Choice in Economics*, London: Routledge.

Veblen, T.B. (1884), 'Kant's Critique of Judgement', *Journal of Speculative Philosophy*, **43**, 260–74. Reprinted in Veblen (1934).

Veblen, T.B. (1898a), 'Why is Economics Not an Evolutionary Science?', *Quarterly Journal of Economics*, **12**(3), 373–97. Reprinted in Veblen (1919).

Veblen, T.B. (1898b), 'The Instinct of Workmanship and the Irksomeness of Labor', *American Journal of Sociology*, **4**, September, 187–201. Reprinted in Veblen (1934).

Veblen, T.B. (1899), *The Theory of the Leisure Class: An Economic Study of Institutions*, New York: Macmillan.

Veblen, T.B. (1909), 'Fisher's Rate of Interest', *Political Science Quarterly*, **24**, June, 296–303. Reprinted in Veblen (1934).

Veblen, T.B. (1914), *The Instinct of Workmanship, and the State of the Industrial Arts*, New York: Augustus Kelley. Reprinted 1990 with a new introduction by M.G. Murphey and a 1964 introductory note by J. Dorfman, New Brunswick: Transaction Books.

Veblen, T.B. (1919), *The Place of Science in Modern Civilisation and Other Essays*, New York: Huebsch. Reprinted 1990 with a new introduction by W.J. Samuels, New Brunswick: Transaction.

Veblen, T.B. (1934), *Essays on Our Changing Order*, ed. Leon Ardzrooni, New York: The Viking Press.

Verspagen, B. (1993), *Uneven Growth Between Interdependent Economies: An Evolutionary View on Technology Gaps, Trade and Growth*, Aldershot: Avebury.

Vining, R. (1949), 'Methodological Issues in Quantitative Economics', *Review of Economics and Statistics*, **31**, May, 77–86.

Vromen, J.J. (1994), *Evolution and Efficiency: An Inquiry into the Foundations of the 'New Institutional Economics'*, Delft: Eburon.

Wilson, D.S. and E. Sober (1989), 'Reviving the Superorganism', *Journal of Theoretical Biology*, **136**, 337–56.

Winslow, E.A. (1989), 'Organic Interdependence, Uncertainty and Economic Analysis', *Economic Journal*, **99**(4), 1173–82.

Winter, S.G. (1982), 'An Essay on the Theory of Production', in S.H. Hymans (ed.) (1982), *Economics and the World Around It*, Ann Arbor, Michigan: University of Michigan Press, pp. 55–91.

Winter, S.G. (1988), 'On Coase, Competence, and the Corporation', *Journal of Law, Economics, and Organization*, **4**(1), 163–80. Reprinted in Williamson and Winter (eds) (1991), *The Nature of the Firm: Origins, Evolution, and Development*, Oxford: Oxford University Press.

Witt, U. (1987), *Individualistiche Grundlagen der evolutorischen Ökonomie*, Tübingen: Mohr.

Witt, U. (1991), 'Reflections on the Present State of Evolutionary Economic Theory', in Hodgson and Screpanti (1991), pp. 83–102.

Witt, U. (ed.) (1992), *Explaining Process and Change: Approaches to Evolutionary Economics*, Ann Arbor, MI: University of Michigan Press.

Witt, U. (ed.) (1993a), *Evolution in Markets and Institutions*, Heidelberg: Physica-Verlag.

Witt, U. (ed.) (1993b), *Evolutionary Economics*, Aldershot: Edward Elgar.

Wynarczyk, P. (1992), 'Comparing Alleged Incommensurables: Institutional and Austrian Economics as Rivals and Possible Complements?', *Review of Political Economy*, **4**(1), 18–36.

3. Evolutionary Economics: Precursors, Paradigmatic Propositions, Puzzles and Prospects

Jack J. Vromen

1 INTRODUCTION

What approaches and theories sail under the banner of 'evolutionary economics'? One way of tackling this question is to give an overview of the writings that have been labelled 'evolutionary economics' either by their authors or by commentators. But unless some organizing principles have been chosen, such an overview easily deteriorates into a lengthy and dreary compilation of summaries that does not really contribute to our understanding of what is at stake. To avoid this I have clustered my overview around four vantage points. The first vantage point I have called 'precursors': which economists laid the seeds for the present-day attempts at evolutionary theorizing in economics (and for the current interest in them)? 'Paradigmatic propositions', the second vantage point from which I look on evolutionary economics, deals with both assumptions and hypotheses (or claims) that typically distinguish evolutionary from non-evolutionary theorizing in economics. The third vantage point, 'puzzles', concerns intricate and as yet unresolved problems in economic evolutionary theorizing. Finally, the fourth vantage point, 'prospects', relates to future lines of research in evolutionary economics that we may extrapolate from current theoretical developments.

The four vantage points chosen are by themselves neutral to the subject matter. That is to say, they do not prejudge the question what writings are and what writings are not discussed. Yet the restricted space I have been given makes selection mandatory. My selection is partly based on the fact that certain branches within evolutionary economics are given due attention in other papers in this volume. To be more precise, the so-called second generation of post-Nelson and Winter type of evolutionary analyses (see, for example, Dosi et al., 1988; Saviotti and Metcalfe, 1991) is discussed and exemplified in Silverberg and Verspagen's paper. And the types of

41

evolutionary theorizing in economics associated with Schumpeter and – among others – with Veblen and Georgescu-Roegen are dealt with in the papers of Andersen and Hodgson respectively. In an attempt to complement their discussions I will concentrate on branches within evolutionary economics that get less attention in their papers. In particular, I focus on lines of evolutionary theorizing that are much less discontinuous with mainstream neoclassical economics than the lines just mentioned.

I also want to make clear right from the outset, however, that my emphasis on non-dissident examples of evolutionary theorizing in economics is not only prompted by my wish to complement their discussions. It is also instigated by my desire to counteract the view that by its very nature evolutionary thinking is alien to neoclassical analysis, with its emphasis on rational individual behaviour and equilibria. Many people seem to think that embracing evolutionary thinking by definition implies a break with everything such theories are supposed to stand for. I shall argue that this view is misguided for several reasons. For one thing, evolutionary thinking can be invoked, and has been invoked, to give a radical reinterpretation of standard neoclassical analysis. For another, evolutionary theorizing can, and sometimes does, yield neoclassical results. Examining the precise relation between evolutionary theorizing and neoclassical analysis and neoclassical results will be one of the central concerns of this paper.

2   PRECURSORS

There is now ample historical evidence that in his laborious search for a general principle that could unite his empirical findings Darwin was helped a lot by getting acquainted to ideas that were developed by economists. In the Preface of *The Origins of Species*, Darwin explicitly expresses his debt to Thomas Malthus's *Essay on the Principle of Population*. In fact, it seems that Darwin's indebtedness to economists goes back to Adam Smith and other representatives of the Scottish moral philosophers (see Schweber, 1968). Later on there have also been major contributions of economists to evolutionary biology. R.A. Fisher's *The Evolution of Sex* (1930) is a case in point. And so are von Neumann and Morgenstern's *Theory of Games and Economic Behaviour* (1944), Luce and Raiffa's *Games and Decisions* (1957) and other contributions of economists to game theory that paved the way for the development of evolutionary game theory in population genetics (see Maynard Smith, 1982).

I do not want to dwell here on the influence economics and economists had on evolutionary biology, however. I rather want to focus on economists that anticipated and stimulated the current interest of economists in evolutionary theorizing. In particular, I discuss writings of economists upon which later attempts at evolutionary theorizing have been built or that otherwise have been a source of inspiration.

These writings can be distinguished by and large into two groups: an 'orthodox' and a 'heterodox' group. The 'heterodox' group consists of writings in which a replacement of orthodox economic theory (most of the time (neo)classical theory) by an altogether different evolutionary economic theory is pleaded for. The leading idea behind these writings is that what is needed is an economic theory that is capable of dealing with dynamic processes of economic change. Orthodox economic theory is by its very nature taken to be non-evolutionary or pre-evolutionary, capable of dealing only with static phenomena, and therefore to be discarded. A typical example is Thorstein Veblen's *Why is Economics not an Evolutionary Science?* (1898).[1] Veblen argues that it is high time to abandon static (neo)classical analysis, with its emphasis on an alleged unalterable 'human nature', for a truly evolutionary analysis centred around the notion of cumulative causation. 'Cumulative causation' is meant to bring out clearly that evolutionary processes form one long causal chain over time: the results of past evolutionary processes provide the starting point of present evolutionary processes which in turn produce effects that future evolutionary processes build upon, and so on *ad infinitum*. In Veblen's ideas, there is no presumption that such processes will ever come to an end. Veblen seemed to be convinced that in an evolutionary economic science the notion of equilibrium would be robbed from the central role it plays in (neo)classical analysis.

The 'orthodox' group of writings anticipating our current interest in evolutionary theorizing in economics is much less antithetical (hostile) to orthodox economic theory. These writings do not go as far as to claim that orthodox economic theory is an evolutionary theory. But they do maintain in one sense or another that orthodox economic theory and evolutionary theorizing do not stand in opposition to each other. Some of these writings are led by the idea that evolutionary theories in economics are likely to produce results that are similar, if not identical, to the results that are taken to be typical of orthodox economic theory. In others it is held that orthodox economic theory and evolutionary theory supplement or complement each other or that they can learn from each other. In yet other writings it is even argued that appearances notwithstanding orthodox economic theory is about

---

[1]. The work of K.E. Boulding (1981) can also be mentioned in this respect. See, for an overview, Khalil (1992).

(the outcomes of) evolutionary economic processes. Let us consider each of these subgroups within the orthodox group in more detail.

The first (sub)category within this orthodox group that I want to distinguish here consists of (neo)Austrian economists who draw on the pioneering work of Carl Menger and Friedrich Hayek. Carl Menger is famous for his path-breaking insight that prevailing institutions need not have originated as the intended outcome of the concerted actions of a group of individuals (see Menger, 1985). The institution of money, for example, can be said to be an 'organic institution'. It emerged as an unintended consequence of the actions of a multitude of individuals. This insight has been taken up and elaborated upon by Hayek. For a substantial part of his long life, Hayek argued that social order can, and to a large extent in fact does, evolve spontaneously (see, for example, Hayek, 1964 and 1978). We should suppress our intellectual habit of assuming that, when we encounter (and marvel at) some instance of order (in nature or in society), it must be consciously designed. As the notion of an unintended consequence already suggests, both Menger and Hayek draw inspiration from Adam Smith and other members of the Scottish Enlightenment. Hayek urges economists to return to these Darwinians *avant la lettre*. According to Hayek, the Darwinians-before-Darwin developed a notion of spontaneous cultural evolution in which mechanisms of adaptive learning and imitation anticipated mechanisms of natural selection and genetic inheritance in Darwinist biology.

Menger and Hayek shared the belief that the institutions that make for the social order that emerge out of processes of organic spontaneous cultural evolution are mutually beneficial for the individuals involved. Indeed, they go as far as to claim that processes of spontaneous evolution result in outcomes that are optimal for the group or society in question. Subsequent attempts to make Menger's and Hayek's ideas more precise by using game theory (see, for example, Schotter, 1981; Sugden, 1986) focus on the issue whether the processes of spontaneous evolution that Menger and Hayek had in mind result in institutions that sustain optimal Nash equilibria. Thus it seems that despite Menger's and Hayek's uneasiness with mainstream neoclassical thought, some notion of equilibrium is retained in their own view. The notion of equilibrium does not function as some sort of a natural state society (or the economy) is in, but as an outcome that evolutionary processes can converge on. It is for this reason that the type of (neo)Austrian economics that Menger and Hayek fostered can be said to be closer to neoclassical economics than Veblen and his (neo)institutional followers.

A second subcategory within the orthodox group has an even greater affinity with neoclassical thought. This subcategory comprises economists like Becker, Tullock, Hirshleifer and Frank who hold that insights of sociobiologists can supplement and complement (rather than supplant) neoclassical analysis.[2] Becker's *Altruism, egoism and genetic fitness: economics and sociobiology* (1976) stands out as one of the first attempts to combine economic and sociobiological analysis. By economic analysis Becker means standard indifference curve analysis (under the standard neoclassical assumption that individuals maximize some utility function under budget constraints). From sociobiology Becker takes over the assumption that only the fitter behavioural dispositions survive. That is, those behavioural dispositions evolve under the pressure of natural selection that yield the best material results for the organisms having the dispositions. Becker points out not only that altruistic dispositions can evolve, but also that altruistic persons can entice egoistic·persons to behave as if they too were altruistic (that is, to behave nonselfishly).[3]

In contrast to the (neo)Austrians, Becker and his associates hold that Darwinian biological evolution is of interest to economics. They argue that economic agents are biological organisms in a very real and literal sense: economic agents pass on their genes to their offspring (if they have any) and are subject (or at least have been subject) to the pressure of natural selection. What Becker shares with Hirshleifer and Frank is the 'programmatic contention' that preference patterns have survived because they have proven to be adapted to environmental circumstances.[4] In other words, they have the presumption in common that (socio)biology can cast an interesting new light on the problem of preference formation. (Socio)biology holds out the promise that prevailing preference patterns that neoclassical economists tend to treat as given, exogenous data can once be fully understood. In this sense, Becker *cum suis* believe that standard neoclassical analysis can be supplemented or complemented by a more profound understanding of evolutionary processes.

Alongside Alchian and Friedman, Becker features prominently also in the third (sub)category within the orthodox group. Alchian (1950), Friedman

---

[2]. It can perhaps be said that more than any one else, Hirshleifer has urged economists to pay more attention to evolutionary biological thought. See, for example, Hirshleifer (1977, 1978 and 1982).

[3]. To avoid possible confusions concerning the notion of altruism (does it refer to a disposition/preference or to self-sacrificing behaviour?), Hirshleifer proposes to stop talking of altruism altogether and to investigate instead: under what conditions can competition be expected to lead to cooperation?

[4]. See Becker (1976, p. 826), Hirshleifer (1977, p. 18) and Frank (1988, p. 37). See also Coase (1978) and Demsetz (1988) for expressions of similar views.

(1953) and Becker (1962) all argue that processes of economic evolution lead to standard neoclassical results. Friedman even states that the standard assumption of profit-maximizing firms in neoclassical analysis should be understood as summarizing the conditions for survival. Only those firms survive processes of market selection that manage to make maximum profits. Appearances notwithstanding, Friedman argues, the assumption of profit maximization does not entail any claim concerning the processes of deliberation (if any) that businessmen go through before arriving at their decisions. The assumption only claims that businessmen behave as if they are maximizing profits: the overt behaviour that businessmen actually display is the behaviour that businessmen would display if they really were to carry out the calculations that are ascribed to them in neoclassical theory.[5] According to Friedman, it does not matter what actually determines the behaviour of businessmen. *Ex post* market 'natural selection' will see to it that only those firms remain in business who happen to make maximum profits.

Friedman's claim that the assumption of profit maximization summarizes the conditions for survival for firms has been proven to be unwarranted. Or to say the least, it has been shown to be subject to many qualifications (see, for example, Winter, 1964; Hansen and Samuelson, 1988; Schaffer, 1989). Making maximum profits may be a sufficient condition for firms to survive, it is by no means a necessary condition. It is perfectly possible that firms that make less than maximum profits survive processes of market selection. But it can be argued that for Friedman this was just an intermediate claim (see Langlois, 1986). The ultimate claim that Friedman and Alchian and Becker are arguing for is that market selection processes lead to standard neoclassical results. In their opinion standard neoclassical results pertain not to the behaviour of individual firms but to tendencies at the industry (or market) level. A paradigmatic example is the claim that market demand for some factor of production tends to go down if prices go up. Such instances of 'rational market behaviour', as Becker calls them, need not be the result of rational firm behaviour. Market selection will produce rational market behaviour even if firms display irrational behaviour.

The idea that 'natural selection' mimics rational decision making is by no means alien to evolutionary biology. Friedman's 'as if' understanding of the behavioural assumptions of neoclassical theory is mirrored in the use that the biologist Dawkins makes of teleological statements (see Dawkins, 1976, 1986). Dawkins describes the behaviour of biological organisms in

---

[5].   Latsis (1976) and Simon (1976 and 1978) also argue that neoclassical economics does not say anything on decision-making processes.

terms of the goals that this behaviour serves. But he hastens to add that, of course, there is no presumption in evolutionary theory that the organisms are really pursuing goals consciously. Their behaviour is rather taken to be instructed or programmed by their genes. But under pressure of natural selection genes will be selected that let organisms behave as if they were maximizing their fitness. As Maynard Smith (1982) and other founders of evolutionary game theory point out, natural selection may drive a population of organisms in the direction of a so-called evolutionarily stable strategy (ESS). If an ESS is established, then no mutant strategy can get a foothold because no mutant strategy can exceed ESS in fitness. The intriguing thing about 'ESS' is that it bears some resemblance to marginalist principles in neoclassical theory. For example, some evolutionary games, such as the prototypical Hawk–Dove game, have no pure strategies. They only have mixed ESSs. Mixed ESSs can be found by calculating at which frequency (proportion) of (pure) strategies the gains in fitness of the (pure) strategies are equalized. Gains in fitness can then be said to be equal at the margin. This is similar to the typical neoclassical idea that equilibria can be found by calculating at what ratio marginal magnitudes are equalized. For example, a rise in the price of a factor of production will *ceteris paribus* change (relative) marginal costs and will hence lead to a new equilibrium ratio in the use of factors of production.

What the selection arguments of Alchian, Friedman and Becker suggest, to repeat, is that the shift to the new equilibrium ratio is not brought about by instantaneously responding and rationally deliberating entrepreneurs, but by a force that is akin to natural selection in biology: market selection. It thus invites a reinterpretation of marginal analysis: marginal analysis does not represent the deliberations of perfectly rational agents. What it does represent are the results of selection processes at the industry (or market) level. In the eyes of these Chicago economists, marginal analysis is not to be replaced by evolutionary theorizing, but is believed to be reconfirmed by evolutionary thought. In this respect, they differ from the (neo)Austrians who also hold that evolutionary theorizing is likely to produce similar results as neoclassical analysis, but who nevertheless argue that neoclassical analysis has to make room for evolutionary theorizing.

To sum up, what we have seen in this section is that the notion of economic evolution has been taken up not only by precursors who believed that it would undermine the whole edifice of neoclassical economists. These 'heterodox' precursors held that with the replacement of the analytical apparatus of neoclassical economics by evolutionary theorizing, the standard results of neoclassical economics would be refuted also. There have also been more 'orthodox' ancestors of the present interest in evolutionary theorizing, however, who argued that evolutionary theorizing leaves neoclassical results untouched. In particular, this latter group maintained that processes of economic evolution are likely to lead to the type of equilibria that neoclassical theory predicts. The second and third (sub)categories that I distinguished within this group, the 'sociobiologists' and the 'Chicago economists', also want to retain the analytical apparatus of neoclassical theory. Only the first (sub)category, the (neo)Austrians, want to replace the neoclassical analytical apparatus by explicit analyses of processes of economic evolution.

3 PARADIGMATIC PROPOSITIONS

When discussing the paradigmatic propositions of evolutionary economics, we can distinguish between characteristic presumptions and assumptions of evolutionary economics on the one hand and its typical theoretical results on the other. What is modelled and theorized and what are the outcomes of the models and theories? I shall argue that what distinguishes evolutionary economics from other schools and traditions in economic thought, notably neoclassical analysis among them, is not so much its theoretical results as the forces and mechanisms that are modelled explicitly in it. This is not to say that the theoretical results of evolutionary economists coincide with those of neoclassical economists. Sometimes the results coincide, sometimes they do not. The only reliable way to tell evolutionary from neoclassical economics is by looking at the forces and mechanisms that are modelled in either case.

Thus far we have been talking of 'evolutionary' and 'evolution' as if they were clear and unproblematic notions. Unfortunately, this is not the case. The notions have been understood in quite different ways. For a start we can observe that 'evolution' is often taken to imply development or change. And, indeed, we can say that proponents of evolutionary theorizing in economics plead for a focus on processes of change rather than on stationary states. Evolutionary economists urge economists to develop truly dynamic analyses rather than to refine and indulge in comparative static analysis. Yet another connotation that often goes with the notion of evolution, progress or growth, is not taken into the bargain by many evolutionary economists. That is to say, evolutionary economists do not seem to have *a priori* convictions that processes of evolutionary economic change entail either progress and growth or regress and decay. In general, they seem to endorse the view that it all depends on prevailing conditions and circumstances whether or not such processes are progressive.

Sometimes, 'evolution' and 'evolutionary' are contrasted with 'revolution' and 'revolutionary'. Although some of the proponents of evolutionary theorizing in economics do hold that economic processes display gradual changes (as opposed to sudden major revolutionary changes), this does not seem to be central to their evolutionary project. What does seem to be central is that they take processes of economic change to be governed by forces and mechanisms that are identical, or at least similar, to the forces and mechanisms that govern biological evolution. All proponents of evolutionary theorizing seem to take 'Darwin's dangerous idea' of biological evolution produced by natural selection as a point of reference in developing their own ideas about the nuts and bolts of economic evolution.

What precisely is entailed in the notion of natural selection? Darwin himself specified three conditions for natural selection to produce evolution. First there must be variation. If all organisms in some population were identical (with respect to the relevant features), then natural selection would have no bite. It would not produce any change then. The second condition is heredity. If the features that are selected on are not inheritable (if they are not passed on to descendants), then no selection effects obtain. Finally, there must be a 'struggle for life'. Again no selection effects would obtain if there were resources available that are sufficient to sustain any birth explosion.

Only after Darwin died and after the importance of the work of his contemporary Gregor Mendel was rediscovered the three conditions were fitted together in the so-called Modern Darwinian Synthesis. The work of Mendel facilitated a better understanding of the first two conditions that Darwin specified. Mendel pointed out the mechanisms and laws of inheritance and on the basis of his work it was found that the primary mechanisms responsible for variation are genetic recombination, in case there is sexual reproduction, and genetic mutations.

Given this reconstruction of evolutionary biology, it is tempting to argue that the idea of evolution by natural selection comprises the joint working of three sorts of mechanisms. The first sort of mechanism sees to it that variation is generated continuously. The second sort of mechanism accounts for genetic stability over time: this sort of mechanism sees to it that (at least part of) the present genetic material is preserved in subsequent generations (provided, of course, that the organisms in question succeed in reproducing themselves). The third sort of mechanism is responsible for differential reproduction over time: the genetic material of the reproductively more successful will tend to replace that of the less successful ones.

Some biologists (and philosophers of biology) treat only the latter sort of mechanism as indicating natural selection proper (see, for example, Sober, 1984), whereas others (see, for example, Dennett, 1995) take natural selection to be the combined working of the three sorts of mechanisms. At any rate, it is illuminating, I think, to distinguish sharply between the first and the third sort of mechanism, as they steer processes of evolution in opposite directions. The first sort of mechanism takes care of divergent evolution, while the third sort leads to convergent evolution. The first sort of mechanism incessantly produces new genetic material that the third sort of mechanism incessantly decimates. The third sort of mechanism works as a filter or screening device. Its operation involves a negative causal feedback loop: the genes that program organisms in a reproductively successful way expand in the population's gene pool at the cost of the genes that program organisms in a less successful way.[6]

Now, what is the relevance of all this for economics? The second subcategory within the 'orthodox' group of economists that I identified in Section 2 seem to hold that Darwinian evolution is in a strict and literal sense relevant for economics. After all, they argue, individual economic agents are organisms belonging to some species that have evolved under pressure of natural selection some 1.7 billion years ago. In particular, they seem to endorse the view that members of *homo sapiens* pass their preferences genetically over to their offspring and that in the course of the evolution of our species some preferences have won out over others.

Other proponents of evolutionary theorizing seem to opt for a less literal and more metaphorical use of Darwin's basic ideas. As we have seen, someone like Hayek argues that we should go back to the Darwinians-before-Darwin: Mandeville, Ferguson, Hume and Smith. What they showed us, Hayek has repeatedly argued, is that social order can evolve spontaneously. Social order is always the product of human action, but need not be the result of human design. Mutually beneficial institutions can be the unintended consequences of the unconcerted actions taken by many individuals. The processes of spontaneous evolution that may lead to such consequences are clearly not of a biological, but of a cultural type. Nevertheless, it can be argued that all of the three sorts of mechanisms that produce evolution by natural selection have counterparts in Hayek's conception of cultural evolution (see Vromen, 1995, chapter 8). First, the role of gene recombination and mutation in producing variation is taken here by experimentations by individual economic agents who try to improve their position. Second, just as descendants inherit their genes from their ancestors, so can individuals imitate ideas, concepts and modes of conduct from their teachers, mentors and 'cultural heroes'. And, third, the

---

[6]. Sometimes, the first sort of mechanism is said to entail the working of a positive feedback loop in the sense that deviations from some equilibrium reinforce themselves.

counterpart of natural selection as a screening device in biological evolution is adaptive, trial-and-error learning.[7]

The selection arguments of Alchian, Friedman and Becker entail a notion of economic evolution that is more akin to the Darwinian account of evolution by natural selection than to Hayek's or other accounts of cultural evolution.[8] Reproductive success in biological evolution may depend on a number of things such as the (relative) aptitude to gather food, (relative) invulnerability to climatic changes, (relative) invulnerability to predators, (relative) fertility and so on. All these factors can be generalized by saying that the reproductive success in biological evolution depends on (relative) access to resources (or energy) (see Ghiselin, 1974). Likewise, Alchian *cum suis* argue that reproductive success in economic evolution depends on (relative) access to money, as a generalized resource. The general idea is that in a market economy, firms that succeed in making (positive) profits accumulate resources that they can use for investments and expansion, whereas firms that suffer losses cannot but contract. An important difference with the complete Darwinian account of evolution by natural selection is, of course, that firms do not leave offspring (at least not literally). In fact, with the exception of Alchian, these authors have nothing to say about economic 'inheritance' and 'variation'.[9]

So much on the 'ancestors' of the present interest in evolutionary theorizing in economics. What about current attempts at evolutionary theorizing and modelling? Almost all attempts seem to draw inspiration from Nelson and Winter's seminal *An Evolutionary Theory of Economic Change* (1982). What does their notion of economic evolution amount to? They take over the general idea of Alchian *cum suis* that differential profitability of firms in an industry accounts for differential expansion of their market shares in the industry. *Ex post* competition decides upon the viability of firms. This idea can be found back in their formal models under the heading of selection effects. But unlike Alchian *cum suis* they take

---

[7]. It can be argued that imitation is part of social learning: if individuals are trying to improve their position, they are likely to imitate others only if others are successful on their standards and they are likely to prolong the imitation only if it does reasonably well on their standards. For this reason, trial-and-error learning can be said to comprise imitation.

[8]. Similar accounts of cultural evolution are given in Cavalli-Sforza and Feldman (1981) and Boyd and Richerson (1985). See also Dawkins (1976) for the notion of a meme as the cultural analogue of gene.

[9]. The biological notions of 'species' and 'speciation' do not seem to have a real analogue in economics either.

effort to identify an economic analogue of 'genes'. In Nelson and Winter's view, routines play the same role in firms as genes do in organisms: they first of all instruct or program the behaviour of firms. And, second, although the routines of a firm are not transmitted to descendants (for there are none), they do establish a stable, if not inert, identity of the firm over time. Thus Nelson and Winter account for the 'inheritance', identity-preserving part of the Darwinian scheme. But what about routine mutations, the mechanisms that produce variations in routines?

At this juncture Nelson and Winter depart from the orthodox Darwinian scheme by assuming that 'mutations' in routines are not blind, but goal-directed. 'Mutations' in routines are called innovations by Nelson and Winter, and in their view they occur as a conscious and deliberate attempt to enhance the profitability of firms. When profits fall below some critical threshold, firms are assumed to engage in a search for better, more profitable routines.[10] Once more profitable routines are found, they become part of the standard operating procedures of the firm. It is for these reasons that Nelson and Winter call their evolutionary theory Lamarckian rather than Darwinian: in their theory search is failure-induced and acquired new routines are 'inheritable'.

As I have argued elsewhere (Vromen, 1995, chapter 6), however, the typical explanatory structure of Nelson and Winter's evolutionary theory and models is brought out much more clearly by saying that two separate mechanisms are working side by side than by saying that there is just one Lamarckian mechanism operating. In Nelson and Winter's view, processes of economic evolutionary change are driven by the joint operation of a selection and an adaptive learning mechanism. In their formal models the effects of these mechanisms are dubbed selection and search effects respectively. As we have already seen, selection effects are due to differences in profitability among the firms in an industry. Search effects are produced by attempts of individual firms to improve their profit record. Herbert Simon's notions of bounded rationality, satisficing and, especially, procedural rationality are central to understanding Nelson and Winter's view on search processes. The main idea is that firms stick to routines as long as following the routines yield satisfactory results (that is, as long as they exceed some aspiration level). Only if profits fall below aspiration levels firms are enticed to search for better routines. Simon's notion of procedural rationality is invoked to argue that search activities are also guided by (higher-order) rules or routines. What is more, Simon's 'procedural rationality' also comprises the idea that the new routines firms come up

---

[10]. Notice that in this respect, Nelson and Winter's evolutionary theory resembles Hayek's.

with are most of the time (re)combinations of their old ones. Thus, although search efforts may change the operating characteristics of firms considerably over time, firms can be said to retain their specific identities.

Here, I venture, we hit on a distinguishing feature not only of Nelson and Winter's evolutionary theory, but of evolutionary theorizing and modelling in economics in general: the identities of economic agents are constituted by the rules that govern their behaviour. This feature can be detected in different guises in the various attempts at evolutionary theorizing and modelling that have been undertaken so far. In the evolutionary models of technological innovation that followed Nelson and Winter's pioneering attempts, for example, one of the key ideas is that firms have their own specific technological trajectories, paradigms or regimes (the pioneering attempt is Dosi, 1982). Firms cannot change their technologies overnight, but are more or less tied to them. Similarly, one of the central assumptions in standard evolutionary game theory is that agents are characterized by their fixed, unalterable behavioural strategies. In attempts to apply evolutionary game theory to account for a Hayek-type of cultural, spontaneous evolution of conventions and institutions it is assumed that the behaviour of individual agents is constrained by rules of conduct.

This feature of rule-governed economic behaviour has often been contrasted by evolutionary economists with a supposedly opposite assumption in neoclassical economics: the assumption that economic agents are unconstrained and have unbounded powers to respond in a flexible and optimal way to changes in circumstances. As argued in Section 2, however, it is not at all clear that (all) neoclassical economists subscribe to this assumption. To some neoclassical economists their assumption of rational individual behaviour does not entail any claim as to the reasoning processes individual agents are going through (see also Binmore, 1994). Conversely, the assumption of rule-governed behaviour does not by itself preclude the possibility of flexible and optimal behaviour. 'Rule-governed behaviour' does not necessarily mean that rules fix the standard operating behaviour of economic agents once and for all. For, as in Nelson and Winter's evolutionary models, the agents' rules may include higher-level rules that guide changes in their standard operating behaviour.

What the evolutionary assumption of economic agents following their own rules does contrast with, I think, is with the 'representative agent' type of neoclassical analysis. This 'typological' mode of thought is replaced by 'population' thinking in evolutionary theorizing (see Metcalfe, 1989). Instead of assuming from the outset that one equilibrium type of agent can stand for the whole industry (population), evolutionary theorizing starts with the assumption that initially there typically is diversity or variation in the rules of behaviour that agents follow. This diversity would persist *ad infinitum* if it would not be impinged upon by two contrary evolutionary forces. One force is analogous to natural selection in evolutionary biology in that it tends to delimit the diversity or variation by elimination of less successful rules. The other, opposite force tends to enlarge the diversity or variation by generating new rules. The outcomes of the combined workings of these forces depend among other things on their relative strengths. Processes of economic evolution may come to rest in equilibria (or stationary points). But they may also be out-of-equilibrium all of the time. Or along the way new equilibrium states may emerge.[11]

What distinguishes evolutionary theorizing from neoclassical economics, I think, is not so much its theoretical results as its theoretical aim, outlook and assumptions. Evolutionary theorizing in economics aims at enhancing our understanding of processes of economic change by modelling the interplay of the evolutionary forces or mechanisms that steer these processes. As I hope to have made clear, it is not that evolutionary economists envisage evolutionary forces or mechanisms that no economist has recognized before. Quite on the contrary, ever since Smith these forces and mechanisms have been with us. They have been part and parcel even of *appreciative* (or working paper) orthodox neoclassical theory (see Nelson and Winter, 1982; Winter, 1991; Nelson, 1995). What is new is that in evolutionary theorizing these forces and mechanisms are no longer lurking at the background. They are put centre stage.

In order to make the workings of the forces and mechanisms formally tractable, evolutionary economists have to look for 'nonstandard' mathematical techniques. At present several mathematical techniques are available that seem to be suited to model evolutionary economic processes explicitly. Our understanding of the mathematics of nonlinear dynamic systems and chaos theory has improved considerably over the last decades. The same can be said of the mathematics of Markov chains and evolutionary game theory. And the use of computer simulations, for example in 'Artificial Life' projects using genetic algorithms, is also intensifying rapidly. Some evolutionary economists tend to treat such nonstandard mathematical techniques as the hallmark of evolutionary economics. Some even seem to go as far as to identify evolutionary economics with the use of one particular mathematical technique. In my opinion, this does not make sense. There is no point to first combatting the theoretical dogmatism of neoclassical economics and then trying to reinstall a new dogmatism. We should not put the cart before the horse. I wholeheartedly subscribe to

---

[11]. See, for example, the growing literature on self-organization, dissipative structures and bifurcations that is inspired by the work of Prigogine and Stengers (1984).

Arthur's warning that it is the problem at hand (and not the latest technique that has sprung from the mathematics department) that should guide our choice of mathematical techniques (in Day and Chen, 1993, pp. 319–20).

The theoretical aim to analyse evolutionary forces and mechanisms explicitly reflects a quest for realism that, I think, is indicative of evolutionary economists (see, for example, Mäki, 1989; Lawson, 1989; Foss, 1994). Evolutionary economists are not only interested in theoretical results or outcomes (that can or cannot be confirmed in empirical tests), as instrumentalists typically are, they also want to understand the processes that lead to the results. And they typically hold that processes of economic change really are fuelled by the evolutionary forces and mechanisms that they model. This explains that evolutionary economists believe that our understanding of economic reality is deepened by evolutionary models even in cases when evolutionary models reproduce 'standard neoclassical results'. Indeed it is sometimes argued by evolutionary economists that it is precisely one of the merits of evolutionary modelling that it allows for a systematic and solid examination of the claim of neoclassical economists like Alchian and Friedman that evolutionary economic processes lead to 'standard neoclassical results'. To be more precise, evolutionary modelling allows us to identify the necessary conditions that are to be met in reality for standard neoclassical results to obtain. Thus conceived, evolutionary models are claimed to be part of a general theory of economic change of which neoclassical theory is a special case.

Evolutionary economics is not done full justice, however, by arguing that it makes a better understanding possible of the phenomena that are addressed by neoclassical theory. Phenomena that fall outside the scope of neoclassical economics come within sight when the evolutionary outlook is adopted. These phenomena include research and development activities by firms and technological innovations that spring from them, and the evolution of conventions, institutions and preferences (for more on this see Nelson, 1995). In so far as these phenomena play any role in neoclassical analyses, they are treated as exogenous variables. In general it can be said that evolutionary economics typically tries to endogenize changes in variables and parameters that are treated as exogenous shocks in neoclassical economics.

4 PUZZLES

The idea that individual economic agents display rule-governed behaviour is central, we have seen, to evolutionary economics. This idea seems to be diametrically opposed to the idea that is often ascribed to neoclassical economists: individual economic agents are rational decision-makers. The latter assumption has been a target of criticism from its inception. The main thrust of the criticisms has been, it seems, that in the latter idea economic agents are portrayed as smarter and more autonomous than they actually are. In evolutionary economic theories and models individual economic agents seem to be taken to be less smart and less autonomous that they seem to be in rational choice theories. But do not evolutionary theories and models draw an opposite, but equally unrealistic caricature of economic behaviour? Don't they picture economic agents as being too dumb and too much in the iron grip of forces and influences that they cannot control?[12]

The first thing to note is that modelling the behaviour of economic agents as rule-governed behaviour does not necessarily imply that the modellers in question hold that the behaviour of individuals is caused (or determined) by rules. Modelling economic behaviour as rule-governed behaviour is compatible with the view that economic agents are engaged in reasoning processes before making their choices. This is the mirror image of the fact that neoclassical economists need not be committed to the view that economic agents really go through the reasoning processes that their assumptions suggest. Revealed preference theory and von Neumann–Morgenstern cardinal utility theory, for example, can be said to be entirely silent on the issue of what goes on in processes of decision-making (see Binmore, 1994). To put it bluntly, mindless rule-following behaviour can be accounted for in rational choice theories and, *vice versa*, rational calculative behaviour can be modelled as rule-governed behaviour.

What this makes clear, I think, is that a theorist's (or observer's, or third person's) point of view should be distinguished from an agent's (or participant's or first person's) point of view. Whether an agent is involved in routine behaviour or thinks things through before acting may be not that important to a modeller. A modeller may be interested mainly or only in regularities in overt behaviour, and not in what is behind the behaviour. As long as the behaviour of the agents exhibits some consistency over time, it can be accounted for in either way: either as utility-maximizing behaviour or as rule-governed behaviour. But from an agent's point of view, it makes quite a difference whether she handles things in a routine fashion or considers all alternatives available, weighs their costs and benefits, and so on, before making up her mind.

The claim of evolutionary economists that economic agents display rule-governed behaviour goes often further, I submit, than just claiming that, from a theorist's point of view, it is more convenient to model consistent

---

[12]. These questions also bother Hodgson (1993) in the final part of his book.

behaviour as rule-governed behaviour than as utility-maximizing behaviour. Many evolutionary economists seem to hold that economic agents do behave in a routine way most, if not all of the time. Nelson and Winter, for example, go at great lengths to argue that firm behaviour is more the result of following routines than of case-by-case rational decision-making. It is for this reason that they prefer to model firm behaviour as rule-governed behaviour over modelling it as profit-maximizing behaviour. Again this can be related to the inclination of evolutionary economists to adopt a realist stance. If rules are the dominant determinants of behaviour, so the argument seems to go, then rules should be represented in modelling behaviour.

But does the idea that rules are the dominant determinants of economic behaviour really accord with the self-understanding of economic agents? Don't we (and we include managers of firms) think of ourselves mainly as the authors of the drama of our own lifes? We seem to be convinced that we choose our own path of life within the confines set by our own limitations and environmental constraints. If this is our self-understanding, shouldn't we conclude that rules are not dominant determinants of our behaviour? I think that this conclusion is unwarranted for several reasons.

First, although some rules of behaviour may have come into existence because we consciously decided to install them, after their installation the rules may acquire a life of their own. That is to say, after their inauguration following the rules is not reconsidered on a case-by-case basis in each and every instance in which they are taken to be applicable. Following the rules may get habituated and become a routine affair. This view runs as a common thread from Machlup (1946) to contemporary thinkers as Heiner (1983) and Vanberg (1993). As it is assumed that the inauguration of rules is chosen rationally at some *meta*level, this view still is very much in line with the tradition of rational choice models in economics.

In the second place, it may also be the case that rules pervade our behaviour in much more profound ways and that we are simply unaware of it. In other words, we cannot rule out the possibility that our self-understanding is at least partly incorrect. Perhaps we suffer from self-deception. Maybe it only appears to us that most of what we do is consciously chosen by us. Perhaps we do more often react to stimuli in a habitual, routine and semi-automatic way than we think or like to think. Everyone knows the temptation to indulge in rationalizations: to come up with reasons to explain retrospectively what we did (or what we did not do), whereas in fact no deliberation at all preceded our acting (or non-acting).

Our resistance against the idea that our behaviour is to a large extent governed by rules may also be related to our conviction that we have 'free will'. As Dennett (1995, p. 366) remarks, our self-understanding of autonomous beings having 'free will' is inextricably tied up with the notion of self-control. For (almost) all we have done, the doctrine of 'free will' implies, we could have acted differently. Not some rules (or habits, customs, conventions, norms, institutions, genes, memes or what have you) are in charge, 'we' are in charge. The problem here is with the 'we': who is supposed to have 'free will'? If we assume, for the sake of argument, that we do (almost) all we do deliberately, then we do what we do because we have certain goals, beliefs and expectations. To say then that we could have acted otherwise, is to say that we could have desired, believed or expected other things than we actually did. It is easy to think of other desires, beliefs and expectations we could or would have had, had the external circumstances been different. But this does not seem to capture the spirit of the free will doctrine. Its spirit is done more justice, I think, by something like the following: given the same circumstances, we could have had other desires, beliefs and expectations than we actually did, if only we had wanted it.

We then can ask ourselves why we wanted to have the desires, beliefs and expectations that we actually had. With respect to our desires, this amounts to the question: why did we want what we wanted? If we insist that at this level we also have free will, then we can ask again: why did we want to want what we wanted? And so on all the way up, *ad infinitum*.[13] This would clearly lead to an infinite regress. At each level we would have to ask why we wanted to have the wants that we, according to the free will doctrine, have at that level. This also implies that we cannot speak of our deepest, ultimate motives, feelings and dispositions. For to claim that we have free will at all of these levels would be to claim that not only our 'superficial' wishes and desires, but also our deeper motives, feelings and dispositions are the result of our own design. Who would be prepared to defend such a claim?[14] Recall that even reputed defenders of neoclassical analysis such as Becker, Hirshleifer, Coase and Demsetz hold that our basic preferences are not chosen by us, but are moulded in processes of natural selection.

Whether our ultimate motives are shaped by biological forces or not, it seems highly implausible that they are chosen by us. But also at more 'superficial' levels it seems that what we want, desire and aspire to be is moulded at least to some extent by our memes, conventions, customs and

---

[13]. For a similar argument, see 'The myth of volitions', pp. 62–8 in Ryle (1949).

[14]. Such a claim would be defended only by someone who would believe in 'absolute agenthood', as Dennett (1984, p. 84) calls it.

the like. In so far as our ultimate motives and our aspirations, wants and desires can be said to be substantial parts of our identities, it seems that our identities cannot be separated from such rules. If this is right, then we could still maintain that 'we', and not some external social influences are in charge. But we should not forget then that the 'we' includes or incorporates prevailing rules (see also Dennett, 1995, p. 367). Rules thus exert their influence on behaviour indirectly: through the determinants of purposeful, intentional action.

Another interesting way to reconcile the idea that we are purposefully acting individuals with the idea that rules are dominant determinants of our behaviour is suggested by Hayek and Simon. It may come as a surprise that Hayek and Simon are taken together here as having similar ideas on the issue at stake. I do not want to suggest Hayek's and Simon's ideas on human behaviour are identical.[15] But I do maintain that they share one core idea: in their goal-directed actions, individuals are led by rules. Most of the time the rules in question are tacit ones that are followed unconsciously. In Hayek's view, rules delimit the range of options that purposefully acting agents take into consideration. Such negative rules, as Hayek calls them, mitigate the cognitive demands on purposeful acting agents. Negative rules do not perform this function because agents call them into existence to do just that. They evolve spontaneously and function implicitly. The agents may well be unaware of such rules. They may well think that they truly optimize and that no such negative rules are in play.

Simon holds that intentionally acting individual agents hold on to rules as long as they yield satisfactory results. If rules fail to yield satisfactory results, then search for better rules is triggered. Search activities, of course, are goal-directed actions *par excellence*. But in Simon's view, search activities are also led by higher-order rules (see also Cyert and March, 1963 on this). Simon takes such higher-order rules to function as (positive) heuristic devices. They make search selective rather than random. Thus even creative and innovative action are rule governed in Simon's view.[16] What is more, Simon argues, the new rules that searching agents come up with are most of the time recombinations of old ones. Taken together, Simon's ideas foster the impression that genuine novelty does not come about. Or to put it more precisely, not only are new rules taken to be produced by

---

[15]. One important difference between the two, of course, is that Simon is preoccupied with individual behaviour, whereas Hayek focuses on coordination problems of interacting individuals.

[16]. Indeed, Simon (1992) goes as far as to argue that, Popper's warnings notwithstanding, there is such a thing as a 'logic of discovery'.

invoking old (higher-order) ones, they are also believed to be assemblages of old (first-order) ones.

This does not mean, however, that the emergence of new rules is a deterministic, predictable process in Simon's view. Even if old (higher-order) rules were to function as unequivocal instructions in the production of new rules (and if we knew these old rules), we would still not be able to predict precisely what new rules will come about.[17] For we simply cannot predict what situations and circumstances the searching agents will come across. This leads Nelson and Winter, who as we have seen take Simon's ideas over in their entirety, to build in stochastic elements in their evolutionary modelling of search effects. It would be presumptuous for evolutionary economists to claim, I think, that they could predict inventions. Although they can claim to have a better understanding of the mechanisms that prompt and guide Research and Development activities than mainstream economists, concerning the results and findings of these activities they are in the same position as economists of other trades: they can only stab in the dark. Related to this is Ulrich Witt's distinction between pre-revelation and post-revelation analysis (see, for example, Witt, 1993). Evolutionary economists are as bad in anticipating genuine novelty as any other economist, Witt argues, but they may be better in post-revelation analysis; the analysis of how innovations spread or disseminate over industries and markets.

Here we seem to hit on limits of the view that rules are dominant determinants of economic behaviour. Saying that rules are dominant determinants of economic behaviour holds out the promise, it seems, that as soon as we know the rules economic behaviour is predictable (at least to some extent). But there seem to be clearly instances of economic behaviour, like inventions of new production techniques, that are not predictable even though we may find rules that guide search for them. It is only fair to add, however, that the unpredictability of certain types of human action poses an even more severe problem to neoclassical economists. Since unpredictability of economic behaviour implies that some observed consistency in behaviour can be upset at any moment, neoclassical economists may be forced to revise their ascriptions of utility-functions over and again. What is worse, contrary to evolutionary economists neoclassical economists do not seem to have much to say about the mechanisms that prompt search activities and the mechanisms that take care of the spread of innovations over industries.

---

[17]. As argued by many (see, for example, Winter, 1986, and Loasby, 1991) it is more likely that higher-order rules do not really unequivocally instruct search processes, but that they merely set the agenda.

What we have seen in this section is that the idea that is characteristic of evolutionary economics, namely that the behaviour of economic agents is rule governed, does neither necessarily imply that economic agents are dumb nor that they are not engaged in purposeful action. Or, to put it somewhat differently, reasonable goal-directed behaviour can be said to be rule governed in several ways. By moulding wants, desires and aspirations, rules can be said to have an impact on the determinants of intentional actions. And rules may also provide the (positive) heuristics for learning and search behaviour. The idea that economic behaviour is rule governed should not be taken to imply, however, that future economic behaviour is predictable. In particular, even though rules may be discerned that explain when economic agents engage in search behaviour and how they conduct their search activities, recognition of such rules falls short of predicting what new rules searching agents come up with. It is a notorious feature of evolutionary thinking, both in biology and in economics, that it is better at giving *ex post* explanations than at giving *ex ante* predictions.

5 PROSPECTS

Which ways will evolutionary economics be going? Of course, just as evolutionary economics is not able to predict what future tracks the economy will take, so are we not able to predict what future tracks evolutionary economics will take. Given the achievements of evolutionary economists so far and present activities in the field, it may nevertheless be possible to engage a little bit in extrapolation.

It cannot be claimed that the current insight that 'institutions and history matter in economic life' is exclusively due to evolutionary theorizing and modelling. This would be too much honour for evolutionary economics. But it can be maintained, I think, that evolutionary economics has contributed much to our understanding of exactly how institutions and history can and do matter in economic life. The post-Nelson and Winter literature on technological regimes and paradigms point out ways, for example, in which firms can be caught in their own firm-specific routines. And the accounts of the spontaneous evolution of conventions that make use of evolutionary game theory make clear how the establishment of shared rules of conduct can enhance the welfare of all who are involved.

The very same accounts also shed some light on how history may matter. As the notion of technological paradigms already suggests, if the present and future performance of firms is really determined to a great extent by routines that have been built up in the past, then this may imply lock-in in inefficient paths of behaviour if, for example, conditions change considerably. Path dependencies and lock-in effects can also be accounted for in the applications of evolutionary game theory to institutional change.[18] In fact, evolutionary game theory is apt to illustrate these phenomena in a very lucid way (see, for example, Friedman, 1991). Evolutionary game theory makes clear, for example, that there is a vast number of games (including the famous Hawk–Dove game) in which there is only one suboptimal (or inefficient) Evolutionarily Stable Strategy (ESS). Lock-in in such ESSs can be avoided only if the strategy set is extended by the emergence of a completely new strategy in the population. For other types of games it can be pointed out that there are multiple ESSs (or attractors), at least some of them being suboptimal and each having its own zone of attraction. It then crucially depends on 'accidental' starting conditions what ESS will be reached. In case suboptimal ESSs have large zones of attraction, the population has a high probability of converging on (and consequently being locked-in in) a suboptimal ESS.

What the foregoing also makes clear, I think, is that different techniques may be used to model the same ideas and insights. At present there seems to be a wide gap between those who are running computer simulations in the post-Nelson and Winter era and those who are developing evolutionary game theory further. The two strands seem to evolve completely independent of each other. This does not seem to stem only from ignorance of each other's work. It also seems to stem from a strong mutual dislike of the broader theoretical traditions in which the modelling techniques currently figure. No doubt, those working on evolutionary game theory are much closer to mainstream neoclassical thought than those who are inspired by Nelson and Winter. But it does not make sense, I think, to completely disregard each other's work on such grounds. Such parochialism on both sides is more likely to be detrimental than conducive to the further development of evolutionary economics. Generally speaking, I think that evolutionary economists should not throw out the baby with the bathing water, as Lipsey puts it (in Day and Chen, 1993, p. 317). They should rather retain elements and tools of mainstream economics that are useful for their own purposes.

Evolutionary economists have contributed to our understanding of how institutions and history matter in economic life, as we have just seen. In doing so, they have discovered that the mental processes economic agents go through also matter in economic life. They found out that the courses that processes of economic evolution take depend on how economic agents

---

[18]. The issues of path dependency and lock-in effects have been introduced by Paul David and Brian Arthur. See, for example, Arthur (1994).

learn from their own experiences and those of others. Thus, understanding learning behaviour appears to be central to understanding processes of cultural and (socio-)economic evolution. Understanding learning behaviour in turn requires an understanding of the mental processes learning agents go through: when do agents stick to their prevailing (first-order) routines?, when do they engage in search activities?, how do they search for better routines?, and so on. To say that evolutionary economists have come to acknowledge that mental processes matter does not mean, however, that they know exactly how they matter. Of course, as we have seen in the previous section many evolutionary economists draw on Simon's ideas on procedural rationality and selective search. But these ideas only present the beginnings and perhaps the general framework of a more profound understanding of mental processes. If we really want to understand processes of cultural and (socio-)economic evolution more thoroughly, we have to pursue Simon's line of research further and go into more detail.

It is doubtful whether we can learn a lot from the notions of natural selection and evolution in biology here. Simon seems to be convinced that human learning closely resembles natural selection (see Simon, 1983, p. 40). But the dissimilarities between human learning and natural selection may be far greater than their similarities. As we have seen in Section 3, (at least) three types of mechanisms can be said to be involved in biological evolution: one relating to the generation of new variation in genetic material, one relating to the inheritance or replication of existing genetic material and one pertaining to the selection of the 'fitter' material. In fact the puzzle that occupied us in Section 4 relates to the question how analogues of the second and first type of mechanisms work in (socio-)economic and cultural evolution. We have seen how the firmly rooted idea that we are goal-seeking and searching individuals can be reconciled in various ways with the characteristic idea of evolutionary economists that economic behaviour (including search behaviour) is rule-governed. But this does not mean, of course, that we have more than a dim understanding of how, exactly, existing rules are replicated and new rules are generated in (socio-)economic and cultural evolution. Whereas we have a fairly accurate and precise understanding of replication in Mendelian genetics, we do not know much yet of transmission of behavioural rules via imitation. Simon's contention that new rules emerge in a similar 'combinatorial process' as genetic recombination seems to be highly speculative at best.

It is doubtful whether the analogue of the third type of mechanism, the selection mechanism proper, fares better in this respect. The analogue of natural selection in cultural evolution was identified in Section 3 as adaptive or trial-and-error learning. But while some objective, or at least intersubjective standard for natural selection can be identified, this is doubtful for trial-and-error learning. In natural selection the idea simply is that the genetic material of the organisms that happen to have a fitness lower than the population-weighted average will be wiped out in the population's gene pool. What analogue of population-weighted average fitness as 'executioner' is there in cultural evolution? The problem is that such an intersubjective standard may be lacking altogether. Each and every individual agent may have his or her own standard, since each individual may value outcomes differently. The fact that in biological natural selection there is an intersubjective standard allows evolutionary game theorists to describe the behaviour of the population over time in terms of the so-called replicator dynamics. Early attempts to apply evolutionary game theory to cultural evolution simply postulated that cultural evolution could be described by the very same replicator dynamics. But unless some substitute intersubjective standard is found in cultural evolution, this postulate is hanging in the air (see, for example, Crawford, 1991).

What is badly needed, then, is a better insight into the mechanisms of cultural evolution (provided there are such).[19] Although there are several interesting pioneering attempts (see, for example, Cavalli-Sforza and Feldman, 1981; Lumsden and Wilson, 1981; Boyd and Richerson, 1985), much remains to be done.

6 CONCLUSIONS

Evolutionary economics is not, or at least need not be, antagonistic to everything neoclassical economics stands for. No doubt there are branches of evolutionary economics that are alien to neoclassical economics in respect of their theoretical outlook, the phenomena that are dealt with and the theoretical results that are reached. But there are also branches that are much closer to neoclassical economics. We have seen that in one of these latter branches it is argued by Alchian, Friedman and Becker that, appearances notwithstanding, the typical neoclassical theoretical results are not really the result of rationally deliberating individuals, but of competitive 'natural selection'. Their selection argument was surely meant to be a defence of neoclassical analysis against what they took to be misguided

---

[19]. Another crucial issue is how biological and cultural evolution interfere with each other. As Selten (1991) argues, it may be important here to distinguish different time spans: as cultural evolution is thought to proceed faster than biological evolution, in analyzing processes of cultural evolution interferences by processes of biological evolution may be abstracted from.

criticisms raised by the so-called antimarginalists. They wanted to point out that because of ongoing processes of competitive 'natural selection', the mental processes that businessmen go through do not matter.

It is a little bit of irony that now, some four decades later, we can observe that their argument had unintended consequences. Instead of entertaining evolutionary ideas as merely afterthoughts, they are now widely modelled and studied explicitly. What the studies made clear already is that in investigating processes of economic evolution we cannot get around analysing mental processes of searching individuals. Precisely the issues that the proponents of the selection argument wanted to dispense with have resurfaced again. Only time will tell whether progress will be made in analysing mental processes in more detail and, if so, whether it will undermine or underscore neoclassical results.

REFERENCES

Alchian, A.A. (1950), 'Uncertainty, evolution, and economic theory', *Journal of Political Economy*, **58**, 211–21.

Arthur, W.B. (1994), *Increasing Returns and Path Dependence in the Economy*, Ann Arbor: University of Michigan Press.

Becker, G.S. (1962), 'Irrational behavior and economic theory', *Journal of Political Economy*, **700**, 1–13.

Becker, G.S. (1976), 'Altruism, egoism and genetic fitness: economics and sociobiology', *Journal of Economic Literature*, **14**, 817–6.

Binmore, K. (1994), *Game Theory and the Social Contract (part I): Playing Fair*, Cambridge: MIT Press.

Boulding, K.E. (1981), *Evolutionary Economics*, Beverly Hills: Sage.

Boyd, R. and P.J. Richerson (1985), *Culture and the Evolutionary Process*, Chicago: University of Chicago Press.

Cavalli-Sforza, L.L. and M.W. Feldman (1981), *Cultural Transmission and Evolution*, Princeton: Princeton University Press.

Coase, R.H. (1978), 'Discussion', *American Economic Review (Papers and Proceedings)*, **68**, 244–5.

Crawford, V.P. (1991), 'An "evolutionary" interpretation of Van Huyk, Battalio and Beil's experimental results on coordination', *Games and Economic Behavior*, **3**, 25–59.

Cyert, R.M. and J.G. March (1963), *Behavioral Theory of the Firm*, Englewood Cliffs: Prentice Hall.

Darwin, C. (1959), *The Origin of Species by Means of Natural Selection*, London: Watts.

Dawkins, R. (1976), *The Selfish Gene*, Oxford: Oxford University Press.

Dawkins, R. (1986), *The Blind Watchmaker*, Harlow: Longman.

Day, R.H. and P. Chen (1993), *Nonlinear Dynamics and Evolutionary Economics*, New York/Oxford: Oxford University Press.

Demsetz, H. (1988), *Ownership, Control and the Firm*, Oxford: Basil Blackwell.

Dennett, D.C. (1984), *Elbow Room: The Varieties of Free Will Worth Wanting*, Oxford: Clarendon Press.

Dennett, D.C. (1995), *Darwin's Dangerous Idea: Evolution and the Meanings of Life*, London: Allen Lane, The Penguin Press.

Dosi, G. (1982), 'Technological paradigms and technological trajectories', *Research Policy*, **11**, 147–62.

Dosi, G., C. Freeman, R. Nelson, G. Silverberg and L. Soete (eds) (1988), *Technical Change and Economic Theory*, London: Pinter.

Fisher, R.A. (1930), *The Genetic Theory of Natural Selection*, Oxford: Clarendon Press.

Foss, N.J. (1994), 'Realism and evolutionary economics', *Journal of Social and Evolutionary Systems*, **17**, 21–40.

Frank, R.H. (1988), *Passions within Reason*, New York: W.W. Norton.

Friedman, D. (1991), 'Evolutionary games in economics', *Econometrica*, **59**, 637–66.

Friedman, M. (1953), *Essays in Positive Economics*, Chicago: University of Chicago Press.

Ghiselin, M.T. (1974), *The Economy of Nature and the Evolution of Sex*, Berkeley: University of California Press.

Hansen, R.G. and W.F. Samuelson (1988), 'Evolution in Economic Games', *Journal of Economic Behavior and Organization*, **10**, 107–38.

Hayek, F.A. (1964), 'Kinds of order in society', *The Individualist Review*, **3**, 3–12.

Hayek, F.A. (1978), *New Studies in Philosophy, Politics, Economics and the History of Ideas*, London: Routledge & Kegan Paul.

Heiner, R.A. (1983), 'The origin of predictable behavior', *American Economic Review*, **73**, 560–95.

Hirshleifer, J. (1977), 'Economics from a biological viewpoint', *Journal of Law and Economics*, **20**, 1–52.

Hirshleifer, J. (1978), 'Competition, cooperation, and conflict in economics and biology', *American Economic Review*, **68**, 238–43.

Hirshleifer, J. (1982), 'Evolutionary models in economics and law: cooperation versus conflict strategies' in R.O. Zerbe (ed.), *Research in Law and Economics*, **4**, Greenwich: JAI Press.

Hodgson, G.M. (1993), *Economics and Evolution: Bringing Life Back into Economics*, Cambridge: Polity Press.

Khalil, E.L. (1992), 'Economics and biology', *Methodus*, **4**.

Langlois, R.N. (1986), 'Rationality, institutions, and explanation' in R.N. Langlois (ed.), *Economics as a Process*, Cambridge: Cambridge University Press.

Latsis, S.J. (1976), 'A research programme in economics' in S.J. Latsis (ed.), *Method and Appraisal in Economics*, Cambridge: Cambridge University Press.

Lawson, T. (1989), 'Abstraction, tendencies and stylised facts: a realist approach to economic analysis', *Cambridge Journal of Economics*, **13**, 59–78.

Loasby, B.J. (1991), *Equilibrium and Evolution*, Manchester: Manchester University Press.

Luce, R.D. and H. Raiffa (1957), *Games and Decisions*, New York: Dover.

Lumsden, C. and E.O. Wilson (1981), *Genes, Mind, and Culture*, Cambridge: Harvard University Press.

Machlup, F. (1946), 'Marginal Analysis and Empirical Research', *American Economic Review*, **36**, 519–54.

Mäki, U. (1989), 'On the problem of realism in economics', *Richerche Economiche*, **43**, 176–98.

Malthus, T.R. (1798), *An Essay on the Principle of Population*, London: Johnson.

Maynard Smith, J. (1982), *Evolution and the Theory of Games*, Cambridge: Cambridge University Press.

Menger, C. (1985), *Investigations into the Method of the Social Sciences with Special Reference to Economics*, New York: New York University Press.

Metcalfe, J.S. (1989), 'Evolution and economic change' in A. Silberston (ed.), *Technology and Economic Progress*, Basingstoke, Hampshire: Macmillan Press.

Nelson, R. (1995), 'Recent Evolutionary Theorizing about Economic Change', *Journal of Economic Literature*, **39**, 48–90.

Nelson, R. and S.G. Winter (1982), *An Evolutionary Theory of Economic Change*, Cambridge: Belknap Press of Harvard University Press.

Prigogine, I. and I. Stengers (1984), *Order out of Chaos*, London: Heinemann.

Ryle, G. (1949), *The Concept of Mind*, London: Hutchinson.

Saviotti, P.P. and S.G. Metcalfe (1991), *Evolutionary Theories of Economic and Technological Change*, Chur/Reading: Harwood Academic Publishers.

Schaffer, M.E. (1989), 'Are profit-maximizers the best survivors?', *Journal of Economic Behavior and Organization*, **11**, 29–45.

Schotter, A. (1981), *The Economic Theory of Social Institutions*, Cambridge: Cambridge University Press.

Schweber, S. (1968), 'Darwin and the political economists: divergence of character', *Journal of the History of Biology*, **13**, 195–289.

Selten, R. (1991), 'Evolution, learning and economic behavior', *Games and Economic Behavior*, **3**, 3–24.

Simon, H.A. (1976), 'From substantive to procedural rationality' in S. Latsis (ed.), *Method and Appraisal in Economics*, Cambridge: Cambridge University Press.

Simon, H.A. (1978), 'Rationality as a process and as product of thought', *American Economic Review*, **68**, 1–16.

Simon, H.A. (1983), *Reason in Human Affairs*, Oxford: Basil Blackwell.

Simon, H.A. (1992), 'Scientific discovery as problem solving' in M. Egidi and R. Marris (eds), *Economics, Bounded Rationality and the Cognitive Revolution*, Aldershot: Edward Elgar.

Sober, E. (1984), *The Nature of Selection*, Cambridge: MIT Press.

Sugden, R. (1986), *The Economics of Rights, Co-operation and Welfare*, Oxford: Basil Blackwell.

Vanberg, V.J. (1993), 'Rational choice, rule-following and institutions: an evolutionary perspective' in U. Mäki et al. (eds), *Rationality, Institutions and Economic Methodology*, London: Routledge.

Veblen, T. (1898), 'Why is economics not an evolutionary science?', *Quarterly Journal of Economics*, **12**, 373–97.

von Neumann, J. and O. Morgenstern (1944), *Theories of Games and Economic Behavior*, Princeton: Princeton University Press.

Vromen, J.J. (1995), *Economic Evolution: An Enquiry into the Foundations of New Institutional Economics*, London: Routledge.

Winter, S.G. (1964), 'Economic "natural selection" and the theory of the firm', *Yale Economic Essays*, **4**, 225–72.

Winter, S.G. (1986), 'The research programme of the behavioral theory of the firm' in B. Gilad and S. Kaish (eds), *Handbook of Behavioral Economics*, Greenwich: JAI Press.

Winter, S.G. (1991), 'On Coase, competence and the corporation' in O.E. Williamson and S.G. Winter (eds), *The Nature of the Firm*, Oxford: Oxford University Press.

Witt, U. (1993), 'Evolutionary economics: some principles' in U. Witt (ed.), *Evolution in Markets and Institutions*, Berlin: Springer Verlag.

4. Evolutionary Economics and the Theory of the Firm: Assessments and Proposals for Research

Nicolai J. Foss[1]

1 INTRODUCTION

In his 1967 Presidential Address to the American Economic Association, Fritz Machlup assessed the contemporary debate on the theory of the firm, specifically the critique levelled by a number of economists against the neoclassical theory of the firm. His conclusion essentially was that managerialist and behaviouralist theories of the firm were not competitors to the neoclassical theory of the firm – at most, they were complementary to it. Machlup's perfectly valid reasoning centred around the simple point that since these theories were concerned with the firm at different levels of analysis – in particular, the role of the firm in neoclassical economics was simply to provide a necessary part of the analysis of market-level allocation – the theories did not have the same objects of explanation, and were, consequently, not theoretical competitors.

The behaviouralist theory of the firm that Machlup criticized was then unconnected to evolutionary economics (except for Winter, 1964), but today the connection has been made explicit by a number of evolutionary theorists (for example, Nelson and Winter, 1982; Loasby, 1991; Marengo, 1992). Thus, given the many strides forward that evolutionary economics has made since 1967, it would seem natural to inquire into whether we today have an evolutionary theory of the firm that is competitive relative to the neoclassical theory of the firm (bearing in mind that the neoclassical theory

[1]. The comments of Gabriel Benito, Jens Frøslev Christensen, Bo Eriksen, Kirsten Foss, Geoff Hodgson, Kenneth Husted, Brian Loasby, John Nightingale, Steen Thomsen, and Ulrich Witt are gratefully acknowledged. The usual disclaimer applies.

has changed since Machlup wrote, not the least into the modern contractual theory of the firm).

In a broad sense, a theory is 'competitive' relative to another theory to the extent that the theories in question address the same object of explanation with different explanatory apparatuses. Moreover, the hypotheses that underlie the alternative theories should have some implications where they are in opposition, and where it is, therefore, possible to discriminate between them. Examining the relations between evolutionary and neoclassical theories of the firm with an emphasis on whether they are competitive or complementary is the overall objective that inspires this paper, and I shall repeatedly return to it. My overall conclusion is roughly the following.

We now have a growing collection of evolutionary models and theories of firms' market behaviour, of their internal organization, of their boundaries and of their role as repositories of knowledge. Taken as a whole, this collection of theories has the same objects of explanation as modern neoclassical theories, plus it adds something, such as the role of firms as repositories of knowledge, a role that is not treated in neoclassical economics. Thus, the two sets of theories would indeed appear to be genuinely competitive. However, it is also possible to advance an argument that they are in fact complementary rather than competitive, since there certainly are differences in their primary theoretical perspectives.[2]

Moreover, we do not yet have a set of unifying principles that can connect the diverse evolutionary insights into firm organization, in the same manner that formal contractual economists can use incentive-compatibility issues to approach virtually any aspect of the firm. Thus, on basic conventionalist criteria, such as simplicity, rigour and unity, the neoclassical contractual literature on the firm is probably superior to the evolutionary theories.

The paper falls into three parts. First, I present what is essentially a survey of evolutionary economics, and the role of firms in evolutionary economics. In the second part of the paper, I discuss the relations between the evolutionary and the contemporary non-evolutionary theory of the firm, in particular Coasian contractual economics. I argue that in its present manifestation, the body of contractual theories of the firm is non-evolutionary. However, I also present a more conciliatory reading of the

---

[2].   For example, contracts and incentives *versus* knowledge-accumulation and utilization. However, as Ulrich Witt pointed out to me, theories that are seemingly complementary in this sense may still be competitive, namely by claiming different degrees of relevance for the object of explanation.

relation between the two sets of theories, and argue that some insights of contractual theories are complementary to evolutionary insights, and may be featured in a distinct evolutionary theory of the firm. This leads me, in the third part of the paper, to speculate on various research strategies that evolutionary economists may pursue when approaching the firm. For example, I shall argue that inspiration is likely to come from business economics.[3]

2 SOME BASIC EVOLUTIONARY IDEAS

2.1 Basic Ideas

Defining the meaning of 'evolutionary economics' is a venture fraught with dangers and uncertainties, to a large extent because of the plethora of meanings that have been ascribed to the term, and, indeed, still are. In his splendid doctrinal study, Geoff Hodgson (1993) identifies and discusses the many meanings that have been and are ascribed to evolutionary economics, ranging from the economics of Thorstein Veblen over Marshall to Austrian economics. In a later essay (Hodgson, 1994) and in his contribution to the present volume, Hodgson provides an expanded list of possible criteria for a theory being labelled 'evolutionary'. Thus, the most basic criterion is an *ontological* one, according to which the attempt to theorize the emergence of *novelty* in the economy is necessary (see also Witt, 1992; Foss, 1994b). The next criterion in Hodgson's hierarchical structure of criteria is methodological and refers to whether the theory under consideration is *reductionist* or not. Only then comes the third criterion, that of what is *the relevant metaphor* (for example, is it biology?). The final criterion is whether the theory is *gradualist* or not. These criteria are not all necessary. For example, conceptually a theory can be evolutionary in the sense of stressing a biological metaphor, the working of the selection mechanism (selecting over some pre-given variation), while neglecting or playing down the novelty creating mechanism.

Adherence to the use of relevant biological metaphors seems to be perhaps the dominant criterion for a theory to qualify as 'evolutionary'. As is well known, this has raised all sorts of questions relating to whether these

---

[3]. There has for almost two decades been influential and viable evolutionary theorizing within business studies, namely in the form of population and organization ecology studies (for example, Baum and Singh, 1994), and in some quarters of the organizational learning field (for example, March, 1991; Levinthal, 1992).

analogies are really proper on the domain of social science, a debate still raging today. One position is to sidestep the problems with the biological analogy, because they are not seen as deep problems; they are 'merely' problems of analogy – and a certain sloppyness is warranted here. However, it seems to be rather more acknowledged now that in fact similar causal patterns may be involved in economic and biological evolution (Silverberg, 1988, p. 532). To those who subscribe to this view, identifying precise counterparts (not 'analogies') to the mechanisms of biological evolution would seem more pressing.[4]

However, a too seldom noted problem is that the mechanisms of biological evolution are less than well understood.[5] For example, the unravelling of DNA has revealed the existence of control mechanisms, many of which may have implications for survival. The Fisher relation is for a single selection variable, whereas real biological systems are immensely complex. Conceptually, economic selection mechanisms could be more simple. At any rate, my own position is that too much energy has been invested in the search for precise analogies and isomorphism in the mapping from biological mechanisms to social mechanisms, and that our analogies – the triple notion of variety, heredity and selection – do have relatively precise and very useful connotations within economics.

The preference among the majority of contemporary evolutionary economists clearly seems to be to settle on a conception that 1) stresses the emergence of novelty, 2) is reductionist, and 3) utilizes biology as the relevant metaphor in a rather pragmatic way. Richard Nelson (1995, p. 54) probably sums up something close to consensus when he argues that

> The general concept of evolutionary theory ... involves the following elements. The focus of attention is on a variable or set of them that is changing over time

---

4. In connection with the selection analogy, there are the well-known problems that firms themselves choose and influence their selection environments, and that there may be more selection environments (for example, not only product markets, but also financial and factor markets). Traditionally, however, the deepest problems have been identified in connection with identifying the unit of selection and of accounting for 'reproduction' on the economic domain. According to standard evolutionary theory, the unit of selection has to possess some survival capability and some reproductive capability. In the context of economics, what is the unit of selection? Is it routines, as Nelson and Winter (1982) argue, or is it rather the firm, understood as a cluster of pooled knowledge assets, including routines, as other contributions (Chandler, 1992) may suggest? A sensible position, defended by Hodgson (1994), is that the unit of selection will vary with the focus or the level in the hierarchy of investigation.

5. Thanks to John Nightingale for informing me of the points in this paragraph.

and the theoretical quest is for an understanding of the dynamic process behind the observed change ... The theory proposes that the variable or system in question is subject to somewhat random variation or perturbation, and also that there are mechanisms that systematically winnow on that variation ... It is presumed that there are strong inertial tendencies preserving what has survived the selection process. However, in many cases there are also forces that continue to introduce new variety.

Thus, evolution is considered to concern transformation of a system through time, accomplished through the operation of the mechanisms of variation, selection and heredity.[6] In the following sections, I try to add more conceptual content to this overall structure.

2.2 Elements of the Evolutionary Research Programme

Let me here sum up, what I think are the 'hard core' and 'heuristic' propositions in the emerging evolutionary research programme (cf. Lakatos, 1970),[7] drawing on some recent key sources (Witt, 1992; Hodgson, 1993; Nelson, 1995). In contrast to standard practice in applications of the methodology of scientific research programmes to economics, I shall refrain from identifying a single model of behaviour as a hard core proposition. This is because no such model exists within contemporary evolutionary economics; indeed, evolutionary economics may be consistent with all sorts of behavioural models, including more limited versions of the constrained optimization model.[8]

---

[6]. It is possible to supplement this overall and rather uncontroversial conceptualization in many ways. For example, in a recent contribution, Esben S. Andersen (1994, pp. 1–2) argues that a 'viable' evolutionary research programme is not only characterized by the population perspective brought out in the Nelson quotation above, but is also (or rather, should be) strongly committed to a positive heuristic consisting of an empirical orientation, a mix of an algorithmic (simulation) and a formal approach, and an awareness of the doctrinal past, specifically to 'a "dialogue" with older, verbal studies of economic evolution' (such as Schumpeter's). Geoff Hodgson (1993) eloquently argues that evolutionary economics should adopt methodological organicism; I (Foss, 1994b) have argued that evolutionary economists should endorse the philosophical position of realism (for example, Bhaskar, 1978); and Ulrich Witt (1992) argues that the crucial concept in evolutionary economics is novelty, and that evolutionary analysis should centre around the emergence ('pre-revelation analysis' and spread ('post-revelation analysis') of novelties.

[7]. Nightingale (1994) and Knudsen (1995) present Lakatosian readings of evolutionary economics, differing slightly from the one sketched out here.

[8]. Thus, the important aspect of evolutionary change in a social-scientific context may not really be the inoptimality of behaviours *per se*, but rather inertia.

What matters is rather that agents in an evolutionary setting are not presumed to choose completely determinate responses to external stimuli. Thus, evolutionary economics, in my view, makes a break with situational determinism. Essentially, this is because agents are allowed to have a relatively rich internal make-up, consisting of various behavioural rules, heuristics, learning algorithms, and so on.

Following standard practice, I shall phrase the discussion in terms of (analogies to) the triple notions of variation, heredity and selection[9] – not necessarily because these concepts are indispensable in any discussion of economic evolution (they are not), but because of their expository advantages: it is possible to subsume most of the interesting characteristics of evolutionary explanation under these three concepts.

Variation

The right place to begin is probably with the ontological fact of variation among members of a population, understood as a collection of entities in competition with each other for resources (for example, firms in an industry). It is this essential ingredient of any evolutionary explanation that was suppressed by the emergence of the new value theory with its emphasis on uniform agents, only gradually re-emerging with the evolutionary rearguard actions of theorists such as Alchian (1950), Downie (1958) and Winter (1964). In fact, modern evolutionary economists think that the very *raison d'être* of evolutionary economics lies in its ability to 'explain the origin and consequences of diversity in behaviour' (Metcalfe, 1994, p. 328), an ability purportedly not possessed by contemporary orthodoxy.

Clearly, variation is both *explanandum* and *explanans* in evolutionary theories. In a population perspective, one wishes to account for (explain) existing variation in terms of (with the help of) the working of evolutionary mechanisms, including variation and the production of variation. To the extent that evolutionary explanation involves the explanation of the emergence of new variation, it involves theorizing novelty, both in its pre-revelation and in its post-revelation aspects (cf. Witt, 1992).

There are two easy ways of approaching novelty – both equally unsatisfactory: the first – neoclassical – approach is to suppress novelty, the second approach is to insist that it is so prevalent and radical that it ruins the idea of regularities on the social domain. This is the position that George Shackle was – rather unfairly – accused of occupying. The theoretical challenge, of course, is to identify and theorize novelty-producing

---

[9].   See Witt (1992) and Hodgson (1994) for discussions of the explanatory status of the triple notions.

mechanisms. And the theoretical problem is that this issue raises all sorts of difficult, more or less philosophical, questions relating to whether there is such a thing as an uncaused cause, what are the determinants of creativity, whether novelty by its nature defies the boundaries of formalization, and so on. The best we can do is probably to aim for multiple-exit models, in which behavioural characteristics and social institutions constrain the set of possible outcomes (see O'Driscoll and Rizzo, 1985).

Heredity: historical individuals
A second crucial proposition, and the one connecting to the heredity component of evolutionary explanation, is that agents are more than Popperian 'zeros' (Popper, 1967). That is to say, action is not best analysed as simply the application of a rationality principle to the logic of the situation. Rather, agents come equipped with an internal make-up consisting of decision rules ('theories') that may be changed, for example, in the face of refuting instances. In the context of the theory of the firm, this is accounted for by postulating that firms come equipped with, for example, 'routines' (Nelson and Winter, 1982) or 'competences' (Dosi and Marengo, 1993). Since the decision rules agents hold will seldom be the optimal ones (Nelson and Winter, 1982; Dow, 1987) and will change through learning, there will seldom be perfect environmental matching and decision rules will differ among agents.

The non-optimality of decision rules also has the important implication that behaviours cannot be deduced from simply observing the environmental signals (such as prices) that agents are exposed to (Nelson and Winter, 1982). In other words, single-exit modelling becomes problematical. A further implication is that coordination problems will, *prima facie*, loom larger in evolutionary economics than in neoclassical economics: since agents hold different theories, there can be no appeal to some generally shared grand theory that supplies the glue holding the system together (Loasby, 1991). We note in passing that this may have important implications for the theory of the firm. For example, it implies that firms may find a rationale in their ability to supply some shared vision (a 'culture') of the world to some subset of the economy's input-owners.[10] And it also implies that the pure coordination aspects of firm organization should not be sacrificed at the expense of incentive issues (more on this later).

---

[10]. For an elaboration of this point, see Kogut and Zander (1992) and Witt (1995). And for an argument that the provision of shared visions does not constitute an independent rationale for the firm, see Foss (1996).

Analogies to heredity are closely related to the proposition that in an evolutionary setting, agents are more than Popperian zeros. Heredity has not always been properly treated within evolutionary economics, perhaps because heredity in a social scientific context must have Lamarckian characteristics, that is to say, acquired knowledge can be 'inherited' through social mechanisms of knowledge transfer across generations. Thus, Alchian (1950) was taken to task by Edith Penrose (1952) for not incorporating a mechanism of inheritance.[11] The missing mechanism was explicitly supplied by Winter (1964)[12] in his identification of 'firm routines' as the relevant carriers of knowledge. Given variation and a mechanism introducing persistence, so that variation cannot be immediately changed through adaptation, we are ready to consider another indispensable part of evolutionary explanation.

Selection
The third important component of the evolutionary economic research programme is the dual claim that

- there exists a mechanism that sorts among members of a population (or some populations over other populations), and
- that this mechanism sorts on the basis of some criterion/criteria that connects to realized behaviours.

Generally, selection is defined as differences in survival rates. In the context of evolutionary economics, this sorting mechanism manifests itself in, for example, differential growth rates of firms.

It was the mechanism of selection that was highlighted in Alchian's classic 1950 article more than the other mechanisms of evolutionary change. Alchian recognized that it is possible to move from individual actions to aggregate outcomes in a distinctly evolutionary way by claiming that the

---

[11]. A mistake also committed by Milton Friedman (1953) in his application of evolutionary reasoning.

[12]. And implicitly by Penrose herself, namely in her 1959 conceptualization of the firm as a bundle of accumulating and idiosyncratic knowledge resources. Thus, in spite of her harsh critique of evolutionary explanations in economics (Penrose, 1952), her own discussion of (differential) firm growth and the causes of firm growth is perfectly consistent with an evolutionary explanation.

market adopts instead of firms adapting.[13] Thus, rather than an invisible hand, there may be a pair of invisible feet, prodding the ill-adapted. And he used this to demonstrate that the usual qualitative results of comparative–static price theory may in fact be obtained by means of essentially evolutionary reasoning.

Since Alchian, a rejection of comparative statics has in fact been a characteristic of evolutionary economics as an explicitly causal–genetic approach.[14] This is not to say that evolutionary economics is simply neoclassical economics with an attached account of the causal forces that moves an industry from one equilibrium to another, constructed by substituting some full rationality and/or auctioneer assumption by competitive mass behaviour (but for such a story, see Nelson and Winter, 1982, chapters 7 and 8). In many evolutionary models, equilibrium – for example, the state defined by the Fisher equation's asymptotic end state – is not necessarily a feature, since all sorts of change mechanisms may disrupt the path to an equilibrium.

The above discussion of the criteria of evolutionary explanation put some loose restrictions on what we should understand by 'an evolutionary theory of the firm', that is to say, on the nature of the *explanans* we utilize for approaching the firm.

For example, it is apparent that very 'thin' conceptualizations of the firm, such as the conceptualization of the firm in standard 'Marshallian' price theory or in general equilibrium theory, cannot qualify in any sense as an evolutionary theory: such conceptualizations do not incorporate, for example, any mechanisms of heredity, basically because firms are treated as Popperian zeros without any internal structure.

---

[13]. Alchian (1950, p. 22) illustrates this by means of the following example:

Assume that thousands of travellers set out from Chicago, selecting their roads completely at random and without foresight. Only our 'economist' knows that on but one road are there any gasoline stations. He can state categorically that travellers will *continue* to travel only on that road; those on the other roads will soon run out of gas ... The correct direction of travel will be established. As circumstances (economic environment) change, the analyst (economist) can select the type of participants (firms) that will now become successful; he may also be able to diagnose the conditions most conducive to a greater probability of survival.

[14]. Followers of Georgescu-Roegen may wish to connect this rejection to time irreversibility. Foss (1994b) takes a methodological point of view and connects the rejection of comparative statics to the realism versus instrumentalism debate, that is to say, the debate on whether the aim of science is the identification and theorizing of real generative mechanisms or prediction. As I argue, evolutionary economics is, and has historically been, much more committed to a realist methodology than neoclassical economics has.

A less trivial question, however, is whether or to what extent 'thicker' theories of the firm – such as Coasian theories, managerial theories, behaviouralist theories, resource-based theories, and so on – may qualify as evolutionary or at least as broadly compatible with evolutionary thinking. As I argue in the following sections, evolutionary economists have in fact borrowed their conceptualization of the firm from behaviouralist organization theory. On the side of contractual theories of the firm, Oliver Williamson (1985) explicitly draws on the behaviouralist heritage, while other contributors occupy an orthodox neoclassical position (for example, Alchian and Demsetz, 1972). This indicates a problematic relation between evolutionary theories and contractual theories of the firm.

3 FIRMS IN EVOLUTIONARY ECONOMICS

3.1 Some Historical Observations

To begin with, we may note that evolutionary economics has a pre-history that is intimately associated with the theory of the firm. At least two important, and related, doctrinal incidents make this clear.

The first refers to the fate of Alfred Marshall's industrial analysis. Marshall sought to incorporate variety as a critical dimension in his explanatory apparatus. His concept of industry equilibrium, which combined a population of disequilibrium firms with industry level supply-demand equilibrium is a reflection of Marshall's attempt to analytically approach variety. In order to bridge the firm level and the industry level, Marshall invented the concept of the representative (average) firm. As is well known, this concept was severely criticized and was, if not entirely abandoned, transformed into something very far from Marshall's intentions: in the hands of Arthur Pigou and Joan Robinson, Marshall's disequilibrium firm was transformed into the uniform equilibrium firm.

This seemingly subtle change in fact had the effect of suppressing all of that in Marshall's thought that had an evolutionary or developmental character (O'Brien, 1984). In terms of the doctrinal history of evolutionary economics, it is hard to underestimate the importance of this episode (Foss, 1994d). The advent and complete triumph of the new value theory over the older Marshallian approach was the decisive event cementing maximization, equilibrium, complete uniformity, and single-exit modelling as the essentials of neoclassicism; all principles that represent the complete denial of the central principles of any evolutionary economics.

The second, and probably better known, episode is the profit maximization controversy, involving in its first rounds such illustrious figures as Fritz Machlup (1946), Milton Friedman (1953), Armen Alchian (1950) and Edith Penrose (1952), continuing with the seminal work of Sidney Winter (1964, 1971, 1975), and later with the joint work of Richard Nelson and Sidney Winter (1982).

It is seldom recognized that these two incidents are closely related. Thus, Nelson and Winter, their many references to Schumpeter notwithstanding, are in reality much more Marshallian than Schumpeterian. Their emphasis on incremental innovation and routinized firm behaviour, as well as the use of an industry equilibrium concept that features a population of heterogenous disequilibrium firms is straight out of *Principles of Economics* rather than out of *The Theory of Economic Development*.[15]

Let us also here note another historical parallel: in their modern manifestations, evolutionary economics and the contractual theory of the firm emerge at almost the same time, namely at the beginning of the 1970s (Farrell, 1970; Nelson and Winter, 1973; Alchian and Demsetz, 1972; Williamson, 1971). However, in spite of their simultaneous emergence, the two streams of research have made relatively little contact,[16] no doubt because of the much more loyal attitude that the contractual theory of the firm has had relative to neoclassical economics.

Given the fact that key episodes in the history of evolutionary economics have been relating directly to the theory of the firm, one could perhaps entertain the expectation that the theory of the firm would be one of the most highly developed subject areas within evolutionary economics. Moreover, there is also an important substantial reason for the expectation

---

[15]. The direct connection between Marshall and Nelson and Winter appears in the neglected work of Jack Downie (1958) which combined an explicit population perspective with Marshallian ideas. On Downie, see Nightingale (1993).

[16]. But see Winter (1993) for an explicit attempt to incorporate important aspects of Williamson's explanatory apparatus into evolutionary economics. Williamson himself relies on rather crude evolutionary arguments when defending his transaction costs economics: 'Transaction costs economics ... maintains that later, if not sooner, inefficiency in the commercial sector invites its own demise ... The economizing to which I refer operates through weak-form selection – according to which the fitter, but not necessarily the fittest, in some absolute sense, are selected' (Williamson, 1993, p. 126). Rather than an attempt to combine transaction cost and evolutionary arguments, this defence amounts essentially to much the same point that Friedman (1953) made: that the role of selection forces, adaptive dynamics, and so on can be neglected, precisely because selection forces can be relied upon to produce the efficient results (that is, transaction cost minimizing governance structures).

that the theory of the firm should occupy a central place in evolutionary economics: firms and firm behaviours directly relate to the central mechanisms of evolutionary change. Thus, firms may be seen as embodying relevant units of selection, such as routines (Nelson and Winter, 1982), they may represent the hereditary component which is so crucial in any evolutionary explanation, differences between firm routines and revealed firm behaviour are important sources of variety, and competitive firm behaviour constitutes much of the selection environment confronting firms.

In spite of this, however, I think it is fair to say that within evolutionary economics the theory of the firm has not been given attention on a par with the attention given to, for example, technological change. That firms are normally featured in evolutionary economic theory – with the possible exception of extremely abstract and aggregate theory – as agents of change, embodiments of productive knowledge, and representations of diversity in microbehaviours does not fundamentally challenge this observation: what is key is that firms are not featured in these stories for their own sake, as it were, but as intermediate steps in the explanatory logic. Thus, the role of firms in most of evolutionary economics is not fundamentally different from the role of firms in standard neoclassical economics – they are part of the *explanans,* not of the *explanandum.*

In fact, it could be argued that there is no evolutionary theory of the firm – depending on precisely what one understands by 'a theory of the firm'. For example, if what is meant is a theory that addresses the existence, boundaries and internal organization of the firm, then in this understanding – prevalent within modern contractual economics (Holmström and Tirole, 1989) – there is no established evolutionary theory of the firm.

However, there has lately been some evolutionary work on aspects of firm organization, dealing in particular with internal organization, the boundaries of the firm, and firms as repositories and generators of productive knowledge. Particularly pertinent here is the work carried out by Gunnar Eliasson (1990), Brian Loasby (1991), Luigi Marengo (1992), Bruce Kogut and Udo Zander (1992), Richard Langlois (1992), Nicolai Foss (1993), and Ulrich Witt (1995).

More generally, one is also comforted by the observation that the theorists more responsible than anyone else for turning the attention of modern economists towards evolutionary economics and for reforming evolutionary economics, Richard Nelson and Sidney Winter, are both increasingly directing their interests towards the firm rather than the industry level (for example, Nelson, 1991, 1992; Winter, 1988).

Although evolutionary economists' interest in the firm may, however, be rising in terms of the number of articles that are published on the subject, these contributions do not have a large share in the expanding output of evolutionary economics. For corrobation one may consult, for example, the house journal of the Schumpeter Society, *Journal of Evolutionary Economics*. The attention paid to firms and firm organization here is scant indeed. In fact, the relative attention paid to firm level phenomena may in fact have been shrinking during recent years in favour of the investigation of highly aggregate and formal non-linear models of growth, foreign trade, technological change, and much else – a rather ironic development, since the modern formal evolutionary economics was conceived with primary reference to firm (and industry) dynamics (Winter, 1964; Farrell, 1970; Nelson and Winter, 1973).

There may be many reasons for the lack of a distinct theory of the firm within modern evolutionary economics. Arguably, this may have to do with the fact that many modern evolutionary economists, whether they are right or wrong, view Joseph Schumpeter as a patron saint – and Schumpeter simply had rather little to say about the firm.

Another, and perhaps more convincing reason, lies in the population-ecological orientation of modern evolutionary economics. For example, Nelson and Winter's 1982 book is essentially a story about what happens to an industry's population of firms, not about individual firms *per se*. In such a story, it is not necessary to say much about the firm, for exactly the same reason that it is not necessary to say much about the firm in neoclassical price theory. In both cases, the firm is a step in the mental apparatus constructed for analysing industry level phenomena (Machlup, 1967). In short, the primary attention on phylogenesis on the economic domain rather than on ontogenesis accounts for the relative neglect of the firm.

3.2 Why an Evolutionary Approach to the Firm?

The question contained in the heading of this section can be addressed in several ways. The first, and trivial, is simply to say that the firm is empirically so important (for example, in terms of the percentage of total transactions that it has handled inside firms, or, in terms of firms' importance to economic growth, and so on) that an evolutionary economics as a quite natural matter should have something to say about it (cf. Winter, 1990, p. 273). Less trivially, some conceptualization of firms is necessary in evolutionary theories of higher-level economic phenomena. For example, an evolutionary theory of industry and economy-wide technical change requires propositions about firm behaviour as important elements of the *explanans*. Finally, it may be asserted that there are aspects of firms that are better addressed by an evolutionary logic than by a neoclassical one.

We may also ask what it is that we want from an evolutionary theory of the firm. Grand questions in this regard are: Why do firms differ?; How does it matter?; How should it be theoretically approached (cf. Nelson, 1991). Somewhat more specifically, we may ask empirically motivated questions such as

- Why do we observe such a wide dispersion of returns among firms, even within the same industry? (cf. Rumelt, 1984)
- Why is this dispersion seemingly persistent? (ibid.)
- Why do firms exhibit different rates of growth?
- Why do firms, even within the same industry, have different boundaries, strategies, organizational structures, and so on?

Note that these questions concern variety and/or dynamics. Not surprisingly, they are all questions that the simple neoclassical theory of the firm is unable to satisfactorily address and answer. By this I mean that to the extent that differences among firms are admitted, these differences are rationalized by pointing to some initial – and therefore essentially unexplained – differences in endowments (including information), and barriers to imitation (that is, prohibitive costs of information, patent rights, and so on) sustain these differences. Thus one can have an equilibrium with firms of different efficiency, yielding different returns, which are then interpreted as rents (Lippman and Rumelt, 1982). This is an interesting line of research, but it does not capture all, or even the most important aspects of, sustained inter-firm differences. Rather, theoretical answers may turn on the essentially evolutionary notions of firms as knowledge-bearing, learning, and novelty creating entities, that is to say, on the notion of the firm as endogenously creating its productive opportunity set (Penrose, 1959, p. 1).

The following sections consider such theoretical answers. I here draw an overall distinction between firms in phylogenetic theories of economic evolution, that is, theories that are concerned with the evolution of a population of firms, and ontogenetic theories of the firm, that is, theories of the evolution of individual firms. While the firm is part of the *explanans* in the first type of theory, it is *explanandum* in the second type.

3.3   Firms in Phylogenetic Economic Evolution

On the face of it, the role of firms in phylogenetic economic evolution seems to be as restricted as the role of firms in traditional neoclassical microeconomics. As Nelson (1992, pp. 166–7) admits:

the treatment of firms in our models [that is, Nelson and Winter (1982), NJF] and in neoclassical ones is similar in many respects. Our interest is in what happens to variables defined at the level of an industry or economy. The only attributes that are modelled are those that bear on these matters.

However, there are in fact some differences between neoclassical and evolutionary industry-level analysis with respect to how the firm is conceptualized.

First, the population orientation of phylogenetic evolutionary models means that there cannot be any representative firms; there is just a distribution of different firms and it is meaningless to single any of them out as 'representative'.[17] This is in contrast to neoclassical analysis in which any firm may be taken to be representative, simply because firms are essentially uniform. Moreover, what individual firms do matters in models such as those in Nelson and Winter (1982). This is because firms are modelled as making 'draws' from a probability distribution of technical advances. Thus, best-practice technology at any time can be seen as having been found by particular firms, which means that fully understanding the dynamics of the Nelson and Winter models requires a description of what particular firms did (Nelson, 1992, p. 167).

Moreover, firms in evolutionary phylogenetic models, such as the Nelson and Winter models, are less anonymous than neoclassical firms, because they come equipped with different decision rules, whereas neoclassical firms are only hard-wired with maximization as a decision rule. Interestingly, it is essentially the population logic, with its emphasis on variation, that produces a need for a less stylized view of the firm. Nelson and Winter (1982) construct this less stylized view by suggesting an 'organizational genetics', where firms' hierarchically arranged routines are the relevant genotypes. Organizational structure, degree of diversification, revealed firm performance, and so on, thus correspond to the phenotype, that is, the outward manifestation of the firm-specific knowledge coded in routines.

Nelson and Winter (1982) devote two chapters (4 and 5) to developing the notion of routines as parts of a wider theory of organizational knowledge; an analysis that is firmly grounded in behaviouralist organization theory, but adds to this an elaborate analysis of the notion of tacitness as it connects to organizational knowledge. According to Nelson and Winter, routines emerge through experiences of particularity. They code

---

[17]. As a historical aside, it may be suggested that it was precisely the difficulties of giving meaning to representativity within a population perspective that caused the problems that Marshall's concept of the representative firm met with, even among sympathetic interpreters.

organizational knowledge, and are history-bound, socially produced and reproduced, and rigid. Their presence introduces path-dependence and inflexibility on the cost side, while introducing specialization advantages and cohesiveness on the benefit side. The conceptualization of the firm that emerges from Nelson and Winter's two chapters is one of a body of idiosyncratic and productive knowledge which is implemented in productive tasks through existing routines.

Although they are fascinating, and representing analyses in their own right, Nelson and Winter's two chapters merely function to create a foundation for asserting a certain rigidness of firm reactions. Moreover, they also serve to rationalize variety in terms of unit costs (see also Metcalfe, 1994), and therefore differences in revealed competitive advantages. In sum, routines (and similar notions) are essentially a shorthand for a much more complex set of behaviours (Nelson and Winter, 1982, p. 15), but play the role of introducing the hereditary component that is necessary in an evolutionary explanation. Nevertheless, the Nelson and Winter conceptualization of firms is considerably richer than the neoclassical conceptualization, and implied promises for further work. Moreover, the notion suggests that firms may have several traits of selective significance, and that these traits need not be aligned. As we shall see, this is indeed a crucial objection to, for example, the idea that the only criterion of selective success is transaction cost minimization. In order to better understand this, we have to make the individual firm the explicit object of analysis.

3.4 Firms in Ontogenetic Economic Evolution

Evolutionary theories that are explicitly concerned with analysing the individual firm, rather than firm populations, industries or the economy, are 'ontogenetic' theories. By this is meant that they are concerned with the evolution of the individual 'organism'; for example, they inquire into the 'unfolding process' (Penrose, 1959, p. 1) of firm growth.

There has traditionally been a rather sharp distinction between ontogenetically oriented approaches to the firm in which the firm is factored in its own right, and phylogenetically oriented studies in which firms are factored because they embody mechanisms of heredity, variety and variety creation but where the analytical attention is towards the industry level. Of course, the difference in terms of the anonymity with which firms are described is to a large extent a matter of the difference in terms of level of analysis. Sometimes, however, one also sees the distinction phrased as a matter of a deep and clear-cut difference between the study of the adoption on the part of economic system or the study of individual adaptation. This is pretty much what separated Armen Alchian (1950) and Edith Penrose

(1952), with the latter insisting on a substantial measure of intentionality and rationality in the economic process.

However, the distinction between economics as either the study of systemic adoption or the study of individual adaptation is a false one. Selection is perfectly consistent with intentionality and rationality, with carefully chosen strategies and with adaptation – if not with perfect adaptation.[18] What matters in terms of the working of the basic evolutionary mechanisms is differential firm growth.

Moreover, the evolutionary argument that firms are inert does not amount to the proposition that firms are completely unable to change. Rather, it is a much more subtle argument that some parts – perhaps the crucial ones – are much less likely to change rapidly in response to outside changes than other parts. It is widely recognized that the resources that matter the most for firm success – such as technological competencies, culture, reputation, and so on – are best viewed as 'stock variables' that can only be gradually changed by appropriately chosen input flows (Dierickx and Cool, 1989).

Thus, there is nothing wrong in principle with positing the simultaneity of ontogenesis and phylogenesis on the social domain; they 'simply' constitute a hierarchy of processes (cf. Simon, 1962). In simpler words, the interaction of phylogenesis and ontogenesis on the social domain implies a two-level theory, one encompassing both the firm level and the industry (or technology) level. Because of the explanatory and modelling complexity involved in constructing an adequate two-level theory, we are far from possessing such a theory in any full-fledged form.[19] The best way forward may be to go on developing ontogenetic theories of the firm, and hope for the emergence of attempts in constructing two-level theories at a later date.

At any rate, there are many reasons for being interested in ontogenetic theories. By focusing on the unfolding process of the growth of the individual firm, an ontogenetic story of firms better allows us to understand why firms differ, giving us an improved basis for discussing how such differences matter (cf. Nelson, 1991). That is, we are more detailed and explicit about a necessary element in the overall evolutionary explanation.

This is not necessarily to say that the fundamental evolutionary mechanisms are inapplicable to the organizational level. On the contrary, Herbert Simon (1962) long ago explicitly tied organization-level learning

---

[18]. For a discussion of some of the philosophical issues involved here, see Hodgson (1993, chapter 14).

[19]. However, the work of Daniel Levinthal (1992) and of Michael Tushman and his colleagues (for example, Anderson and Tushman, 1990) may be cited as constructive attempts.

dynamics to evolutionary theory by arguing that processes of search and discovery can be conceptualized in terms of variety and selection. Thus, it is not necessarily sloppy terminology to say of a firm that it is 'evolving' rather than 'developing'.[20]

With respect to work on what I here call ontogenetic evolutionary theories, two main streams of research are identifiable. The first one is an organizational learning approach that has been inspired by the Nelson and Winter treatment of organizations, making more explicit the behaviouralist components of that analysis. Important contributions within this stream of research have been made by James March (1991), Luigi Marengo (1992), and Massimo Warglien (1995), among others. Brian Loasby's 1976 classic on *Choice, Complexity and Ignorance* may also be placed within this category. This approach is explicitly process oriented (because of the emphasis on learning), and in its recent manifestations it is much given to the method of computer simulation. A recent study by Luigi Marengo (1992) exemplifies this approach.

Taking his cues from Cyert and March (1963), Marengo is particularly interested in the coordination of individual learning processes inside the firm, and how a stock of organizational knowledge emerges from the interaction of these learning processes. In his simulation model, agents do not have any prior knowledge of the environment they are facing and they do not possess a shared partition of the states of the world (that is, there is no common knowledge).

Such a shared partition is, however, necessary for coordination – for example, understanding the demand of the exogenous market and coordinating this with the different shops inside the firm – to take place. And, in fact, as demonstrated by Marengo's simulations, coordination emerges gradually and spontaneously, as agents interact under given organizational structures and under the impact of given environments. Thus, spontaneous order (to borrow Hayek's [1973] terminology) may arise within the planned order of the firm.

This is an important evolutionary contribution towards better understanding the more 'emergent' aspects of the internal organizations of firms, something about which contemporary orthodox theory is almost entirely silent. Moreover, it goes a long way in accounting for the ultimate sources of firm heterogeneity: because of the role of random influences and the path-dependent nature of collective learning processes, these are particularly likely to be the key causal forces behind the emergence of essential variation among firms.

---

[20]. See Nelson (1995, pp. 55–6) for a pertinent discussion of this point.

The other dominant approach to firm evolution is the competence (or capability) approach. This is perhaps less process oriented and more concerned with the properties of the products of learning processes. Thus, competencies, as products of prior learning, are analysed in terms of, for example, their content of tacit knowledge, the extent to which they involve complementarities between firm resources, and so on.

Whereas the organizational learning approach is directly associated with organization studies, the competence approach has had a leaning towards the firm strategy field.[21] This is not surprising, since there is a close connection between the various properties of competencies and their ability to generate and sustain a rent-yielding capacity when deployed to a product market; for example, properties of competencies, such as tacitness and complexity, help sustain competitive advantage. Going back to the (process-oriented) work of Edith Penrose (1959), recent contributions to the competence approach encompass Teece (1982), Rumelt (1984), Wernerfelt (1984), Barney (1991), Langlois (1992), Foss (1993), and Montgomery (1995).

One may conclude from this brief presentation that the organizational learning and the competence approach are complementary: the one investigating learning process, the other one investigating the properties of the products of these processes. However, it is somewhat problematic to make a sharp distinction between the process and the content of learning, a point repeatedly emphasized in Nelson and Winter's (1982) critique of traditional choice theory. Thus, in the end both perspectives conceptualize firms essentially as 'problem-solvers' (Loasby, 1976, 1991; Dosi and Marengo, 1993), where the problems to be solved may include, but certainly are not restricted to, finding organizational forms that economize with transaction costs.

To sum up on this section, an ontogenetic perspective on the firm breaks with the relative anonymous portrayal of the firm contained in phylogenetic evolutionary stories. In an ontogenetic perspective, one possible understanding of what an evolutionary theory of the firm amounts to is a theory that explains the structure and the behaviour of the firm as emergent results of the dynamics of interaction among agents within the firm and interaction among the firm and its environment. By focusing on the development of ontogenetic theories of the firm, it may also be possible to build theoretical alternatives to contemporary neoclassical theories of the firm, such as the contractual theories. I turn to a discussion of the relation between contractual and evolutionary theories of the firm in the following section.

---

[21]. And here it is often referred to as 'the resource-based approach' (Wernerfelt, 1984).

4 CONTRACTUAL AND EVOLUTIONARY THEORIES OF THE FIRM: CONTRASTS AND COMPLEMENTARITIES

To recapitulate, the evolutionary view of the firm is that the firm is, first and foremost, a repository of knowledge. This knowledge, in turn, is generated, reproduced, and augmented through the application of problem-solving skills and behavioural rules. It is thus social, has a large tacit component, involves both production and organization elements, makes the firm path-dependent and essentially different from other firms. Moreover, to the extent that this stock of knowledge is characterized by superior efficiencies it may yield (scarcity) rents when deployed to product markets. In order to examine the relations between this view of the firm, and the one that is dominant on the mainstream scene, I plan to briefly discuss the Coasian or contractual theory (or, rather theories) of the firm[22] and its relation to evolutionary theories of the firm.

4.1 The Contractual Approach

The contractual approach to the firm begins, of course, with Coase (1937). Coase's insight was that in order to address not only the existential issue, but also the efficient boundaries and the internal organization issues, one had to add the concept of transaction cost to the price-theoretical apparatus. The internalization of some relevant transactions because of their high market transaction costs rendered the existence of firms intelligible; appealing also to the costs of internal governance helped explain the efficient boundaries of the firm and the firm's organization.

After three decades of relative neglect, the Coasian analysis was given a new lease of life by Alchian and Demsetz (1972) and Williamson (1975). These are the two early classical contributions to the contractual perspectives, and just as they both grew out of Coase's original contribution, they themselves have given birth to diverging branches within the overall contractual perspective.[23] An overall perspective on this branching is to say that the Alchian and Demsetz analysis and those contributions that have

---

[22]. Milgrom and Roberts (1988) and Holmström and Tirole (1989) are excellent surveys.

[23]. Williamson has consistently emphasized the differences between his own approach and the approach pioneered by Alchian and Demsetz (for example, Williamson, 1985, chapter 1). See also Alchian and Woodward (1988) for an explicit distinction between 'the moral hazard approach' and 'the asset specificity approach'. For a philosophically oriented discussion of the 'two Coasian traditions', see Foss (1994a).

taken their lead from Alchian and Demsetz (such as Cheung, 1983) are characterized by a quite orthodox neoclassical approach.

The theorizing of Williamson and those inspired by him is in contrast characterized by the import of a number of non-neoclassical concepts and insights, the Simonian concept of bounded rationality being the most obvious example. While these two contractual approaches have isolated almost the same questions from the original Coasian analysis – what is the precise nature of transaction costs? how are they best to be operationalized? what determines the size of hierarchical costs? and so on – they have given rather different answers.

In Alchian and Demsetz's (1972) original analysis the existence of the firm was explainable in terms of the incentive problems that arise when team production is combined with asymmetrical information and opportunistic proclivities. Shirkers do not bear the full social cost of their actions, and viable shirking is the result. This, of course, is a classical prisoners' dilemma type of interaction. The way to internalize these externalities is to implement the institutional structure known as the 'classical capitalist firm', characterized by the existence of a monitor-residual claimant with whom other input owners enter into contracts. Market forces then guarantee efficient monitoring of team production via the incentive structure confronting the monitor-residual claimant. Viable firms are those that succeed in minimizing the (metering) costs involved in monitoring team production. A number of analytical addenda to this basic theory have been presented, most conspicuously in the development of the modern formal principal–agent theory.

All these refinements of the nexus of contracts approach came at a cost, however. Though the basic claim was present in Alchian and Demsetz's (1972) original discussion, it became clear that within this tradition the very concept of the firm was difficult to uphold. What we ordinarily refer to as 'a firm' is simply a complex set of market contracts (Cheung, 1983), only distinguished from ordinary spot market contracts by the continuity of association among input owners. Not only was 'the firm' not qualitatively different from markets in terms of exit costs (Alchian and Demsetz, 1972), but driving the (in itself sensible) methodological individualist notion, that the firm is not an individual, to its extreme meant that, for example, notions such as 'the firm's strategy' became difficult to give any analytical meaning.

Given this, it comes as no big surprise that nexus of contracts theorists, Eugene Fama (1980) and Steven Cheung (1983) call for an abandonment of the concepts of 'the entrepreneur' and 'the firm', respectively.

In the same way that the nexus of contracts approach seems to have increasingly centred around one central analytical concept, the cost of metering quality of goods and services, the contractual approach associated with Williamson (1985) has increasingly focused attention on one central character: asset specificity. The tussle for rents in bilateral monopoly situations characterized by asset specificity, opportunism and bounded rationality is the driving force behind firms's integration activities. It is, in other words, costly bargaining games that underlie the existence of the firm and its efficient boundaries.

As indicated by Grossman and Hart's (1986) refinement of this mode of analysis, it is not really the contractual 'ink costs', and not even the appropriation potential relating to the rents from specific assets that underlies integration *per se*. It is rather the mutual desire to implement efficient (really, second-best) investment incentives that determines to whom the ownership rights ('residual rights') – that is, the right to determine and control the use of (physical) assets in circumstances not spelled out in the contract – will be allocated. Thus, the Grossman and Hart (1986) theory, like all other contractual theories, views the firm as first and foremost a structure of property rights and incentives, as embodied in explicit and implicit contracts. To the extent that agents are allowed to hold different representations (theories) of the world, this diversity only influences economic organization because it creates potential agency problems.

Having given an outline of evolutionary and contractual theories of the firm, it is time to begin discussing their relation. I suggest to conduct this discussion in terms of the contrasts between the theories, their different objects of explanation, and their possible complementarities.

4.2 Contrasts

It is immediately apparent that there are many and deep-seated contrasts between evolutionary and contractual theories of the firm. For example, the comparative static method of the contractual approach clashes directly with the resolute rejection of comparative statics in evolutionary economics. Thus, there is a *prima facie* case for considering the two sets of theories theoretical competitors. This is not only because the explanatory apparatuses are different, but also because the two sets of theories have different and rival implications.

For example, Williamson rather explicitly argues that transaction cost minimization is the relevant criterion of survival. Although there is little reason to doubt that transaction cost properties is one trait of selective significance, Williamson's view is much too simple. Evolutionary economics emphasizes that although particular constellations of incentives (Holmström and Milgrom, 1994) is an aspect of the firm, the firm is also a structure of hierarchical and nested information flows, and a structure of productive knowledge, residing in competencies. Moreover, the kind of organizational theory that has traditionally influenced evolutionary economics emphasizes the political nature of the firm. Thus, at least the following are relevant 'traits':

- Incentives, or, the allocation of property rights in explicit and implicit contracts;
- Information flows (systems);
- Competencies (of a largely social and tacit nature);
- Political aspects (the internal power structure).

In an evolutionary perspective, these 'traits' of the firm may all have some selective significance. Moreover, they may interact in various ways – introducing 'epistatic effects' (Kauffman, 1993) – and this interaction may also have fitness implications.[24] Of course, this in itself introduces additional variety among a population of firms. But, more importantly, it also indicates the possibility that not all of the organization's traits are necessarily equally conducive to long-term survival. For example, a firm with very strong transaction cost properties may have inferior properties in terms of learning competencies (and vice versa[25]). Thus, there is no guarantee of a perfect alignment between the various traits, that is, aspects of the organization (Levinthal, 1992).

To continue with the contrasts, one of the favourite charges against contractual theories has been that they – much in contrast to evolutionary theories – 'neglect technology' (for example, Englander, 1988). Unless substantially modified, this assertion is plainly wrong. Clearly, the focus on team production and asset specificity in contractual theories means that technology is not neglected in the contractual approaches *per se*. And as Jensen and Meckling (1979) made clear from the nexus of contracts perspective and Grossman and Hart (1986) from the asset specificity position, the allocation of rights matters a great deal for investment

---

[24]. Perhaps rather counterintuitive ones. For example, there is no *a priori* guarantee that, say, two fit traits create a fitter combination, or that the combination of relatively unfit traits necessarily produces an unfit combination.

[25]. In fact, much can be said in favour of the (old) view that there is a trade-off between the provision of incentives and learning. For example, while diversity of behaviours and preferences leads to agency problems, diversity also fosters learning (cf. Loasby, 1991). For a splendid treatment of the related trade-off between 'exploitation' and 'exploration', see March (1991).

incentives, and hence for technology. Thus, the charge of neglecting technology clearly has to be modified.

The modified charge then is that contractual theories largely neglect technology in its knowledge form. The predominant tendency is either to identify technology with only artifacts, such as technological 'hardware', or to make individuals the ultimate repositories of technological knowledge, as for example in Williamson's concept of human asset specificity. The embodiment of technology in routines (Nelson and Winter, 1982) or competencies does not enter the argument. This is what Winter (1982) means when he observes that the firms of the contractual perspectives 'are held together *only* by the thin glue of transaction cost minimization' (p. 75; my emphasis).

The tendency is, furthermore, to pursue static (comparative) analysis of alternative contractual forms in terms of their efficiency properties, holding technology constant. The underlying assumption is, in other words, that technology – as well as the menu of inputs and outputs more generally – is given through some process that is historically and logically prior to the issue of the organization of economic activities. The economic problem, then, centres around combining given inputs in a way that minimizes transaction costs, given technology. Innovation, the creation of markets, learning within and between firms and other evolutionary pet themes are either side-stepped or implicitly taken to be unimportant to economic organization.

Taking the transaction – not competencies, routines or bundles of such – as analytical unit implies that the contractual perspectives have difficulties understanding the firm as a distinct historical entity (Chandler, 1992). Individual transactions are not the prime vehicles of historicity; it is the firm's competence endowment that is relevant here. But the contractual perspectives generally have room for only human capital in their explanatory apparatus – not for the social capital of intersubjectively shared and practised competencies.

One consequence of this is that the contractual perspectives lose sight of the sources of firms' competitive advantage, and, therefore, of the content of their strategies. Contractual approaches are capable of addressing the integration strategies that may support competitive advantage; but they have nothing to say about why firms pursue different generic strategies and the competence endowments that may allow them to do so. In short, they have little to say about variety and the sources of variety.

4.3 Objects of Explanation

To be fair, much of the above does not necessarily amount to a diagnosis of failure on the part of contractual theories of the firm. For example, these theories are not really designed to explain, for example, the sources of firms' competitive advantages. This may lead us to reconsider the question of whether evolutionary and contractual theories are competitive or whether their relations are more in the nature of complementarity. Bearing this in mind, the table below identifies the key objects of explanation of evolutionary theories of the firm on the one hand, and neoclassical theories (including contractual theories) of the firm on the other hand.

The table conveys the impression that there is in fact a strong case for regarding evolutionary and neoclassical theories of the firm as competitors – they are rival theories that address the same objects of explanation (the exception being knowledge accumulation). Moreover, with respect to some objects of explanation, such as internal organization or the boundaries of the firm, the theories have different and rival implications; for example, evolutionary work on the firm considers coordination problems as crucial here (Marengo, 1992; Langlois, 1992), whereas these are played down in the orthodox, contractual literature.

For example, Kogut and Zander (1992), Foss (1993) and Langlois and Robertson (1995) argue that firms, because of the huge tacit component of competencies, usually know more than their contracts can tell – which may lead to communication problems with suppliers. Excessive communication costs may lead to the internalization of the relevant transactions. This basic story has nothing to do *per se* with misaligned incentives in already established relations, but rather centres around the more basic coordination problem of getting people on the same wavelength, as it were.

Similarly, the work of Marengo (1992) does not directly appeal to misaligned incentives, but instead highlights other types of coordination problems as more basic for an understanding of internal organization. Thus, there is in fact evolutionary work on firm organization that is genuinely rival to neoclassical work on the same subject.

However, the schema disguises something. For example, in a broader view, evolutionary theory of the firm is weak with respect to the standard questions of transaction cost economics: how are the existence and the boundaries of firms to be rationalized? Since these are not (yet) established research questions within the evolutionary theory of the firm, we only have a few contributions here, not in any way comparable to the richness and rigor of the contractual perspective. This makes it more pressing to speculate on relations of complementarity between evolutionary and neoclassical, primarily contractual, theories of the firm. In the next section,

I present a more conciliatory reading of the relation, stressing complementarity.

Table 4.1   Key objects of explanation of evolutionary and neoclassical theories of the firm

Object of explanation	Evolutionary theories of the firm	Neoclassical theories of the firm
Internal organization	March (1991), Marengo (1992): spontaneous emergence of coordinative competencies	Principal–agent theory: optimal incentive schemes
Existence and boundaries	Langlois (1992), Kogut and Zander (1992), Foss (1993), Teece et al. (1994): the firm is a response to non-incentive related coordination and communication problems	Transaction cost theory, for example, Williamson (1985) and incomplete contract theory, for example, Grossman and Hart (1986): the firm is a particular constellation of property rights over physical assets
Knowledge accumulation and strategy	Penrose (1959), Nelson and Winter (1982), Montgomery (1995): the firm is a cluster of knowledge assets, and articulates its strategy on this basis	Knowledge accumulation not treated. Strategy only deals with product markets (New IO). Strategy is a matter of tactical ploys
Industry-level analysis	Nelson and Winter (1982), Metcalfe (1994). The firm is a relatively anonymous bundle of routines	Standard microeconomics. The firm is a completely anonymous production function

4.4 Points of Complementarity

As has been made clear from a well-known debate on explanation in the social sciences, it is possible to associate at least two, quite different, meanings with 'a theory of phenomenon X'. One of these, the 'genetic' approach, accounts for the existence of X – let us say, a firm – in terms of its history of emergence. The other approach, the 'teleological' (functionalist or intentionalist) approach, accounts for the existence of a firm in terms of its good consequences for the involved actors. Transaction cost theories of the firm are either functionalist (for example, Williamson's theory) or intentionalist (for example, principal–agent theory or incomplete contract theory).

However, normally a social phenomenon can only be fully comprehended if its history of emergence is factored in the explanation. Otherwise, the 'explanation' will easily degenerate to mere description of the thing to be explained, the explanandum. For example, we should only be fully able to understand why a particular firm has diversified in the way it has by incorporating its prior development of competencies in the explanatory apparatus (Penrose, 1959). In contrast, evolutionary theories of the firm lie clearly within the genetic approach.

However, there is no need to strictly oppose a genetic and a functionalist approach; in some circumstances, the two approaches are complementary. For example, it is widely recognized that some genetic story of the emergence of, for example, an institution is necessary in order to render legitimate a functionalist approach to the explanation of the existence of that institution.

As previously argued (Foss, 1994c), transaction cost economics as a basically functionalist theory 'needs' genetic evolutionary theory for this reason. Functionalist explanation is legitimate only to the extent that a causal feedback mechanism/process can be specified, one that shows how agents can maintain an institution/organization over time when the beneficial consequences are unanticipated (Elster, 1983). One such mechanism is natural selection (ibid.), so this variation on the explanation/process theme, too, suggests the necessity of integrating evolutionary insights with transaction cost economics, so that a more satisfactory functional-evolutionary mode of explanation may be reached.

There are, however, other reasons why the contractual approach needs evolutionary economics; or, to phrase the issue somewhat differently, why it may pay off as a research strategy to combine propositions from the two sets of theories. Here are some of these reasons.

Important explananda

One reason for bringing together hitherto separately existing theories is that they somehow complement each other, and that the emerging unified theory thus possesses greater problem-solving power than any of the two theories in isolation. Moreover, there exist objects of explanation that cannot be fully approached by any of the two theories in isolation, but need a combined theory. Such objects of explanation could be, in arbitrary ranking, the influence of path-dependence on economic organization, the influence of changing industry structure on economic organization, entrepreneurship and economic organization, the organization of technological changes, and so on. Intuitively, such objects cannot be fully comprehended by the contractual approach or by evolutionary economics alone, but in some sense need them both for a satisfactory explanation.

What can legitimately be taken as given?

In the analysis of the competitive firm of conventional price theory, inputs, outputs and technology are taken as given, and the economic problem has to do with combining them in a profit-maximizing manner given prices. The economic problem in the firm of transaction cost economics is not substantially different from this; here the economic problem has to do with combining inputs in a transaction cost minimizing way, given contractual hazards. Implicit in this is that outputs, inputs and technology are given through some process that is logically and historically prior to the issue of the organization of economic activities.   This is what Williamson (1985, p. 84) means when he says that the presumption that 'in the beginning there were markets' informs the transaction cost perspective.

To abstract from this process is grossly inadequate if technological changes – changes in the menu of inputs, outputs, and technology – significantly influence economic organization, for example, because they influence transaction and information costs (cf. North, 1990). Understanding variations in economic organization would then presuppose understanding of variation in technology, and so on.

Moreover, technological changes are fundamentally injected into the economic system in the form of transactions, so that the organization of technological changes is not, in principle, out of the reach of theories of economic organization. But that would seem to necessitate some story about the emergence of technological changes as part of the explanatory task. That story is supplied by evolutionary theories (Nelson and Winter, 1982).

The implicit presence of change in contractual theories

In, for example, Williamson's (1985) theory of economic organization, concepts such as complexity, uncertainty, asymmetric information, opportunism, incomplete contracts, and frequency are crucial. Other theories, such as Alchian and Demsetz's (1972) theory of team production as the basis of the firm, operate with a more narrow menu of determinants of economic organization. However, all contractual theories, whatever their differences may be, utilize concepts – uncertainty, incomplete contracts, asymmetric information – the meaning of which is only fully comprehensible against the background of an economic reality characterized by change. In other words, change is implicitly seen as necessary to make sense out of these theories. And the theories that explain economic and technological change are evolutionary theories.

However, clearly not all kinds of change may be relevant to economic organization. An important distinction relates to whether change and the consequences of change are anticipated or not. Normally, anticipated change and anticipated consequences will not influence economic organization, since no transaction or information cost will change.

But we have it from Hayek that 'It is ... worth stressing that economic problems arise always and only in consequence of change' (1945, p. 82). And we have it from Coase (1937) (paraphrasing Knight) that the firm would not arise in the absence of 'uncertainty', and that one aspect of the efficiency of the firm has to do with its flexibility in adjusting to certain kinds of unanticipated change. As Coase observed, interesting contracts were not only long in duration but also open-ended, because it is usually too costly or epistemically impossible to specify all future contingencies.

This is a theme that has been comprehensively addressed by Oliver Williamson and incomplete contract theorists such as David Kreps (1992) and Sanford Grossman and Oliver Hart (1986). As these writers make clear, some notion of unanticipated change, as embodied in the notion of an incomplete contract, is necessary to make economic sense out of the institution known as the firm.

In the formal manifestations of this idea, agents are however typically portrayed as so clever that they can design *ex ante* contracts that can efficiently handle unanticipated future change, so that later revisions of contracts are not necessary. Characteristically, Kreps' (1992) title to his formal modelling of this is '*Static* Choice in the Presence of Unforeseen Contingencies' (my emphasis). Dow (1987) argues that it is logically problematic to claim that agents can rationally *ex ante* design efficient responses to future unanticipated change, since one can only adjust efficiently to something that is foreseen.

Wherever that may lead us, at least it seems warranted to conclude that in order to make sense out of economic organization – at least of a non-trivial sort – the concept of unanticipated change should be included in the analysis. And that concept is supplied by evolutionary economics; it has in fact been argued to be the concept that ultimately sets evolutionary economics apart from neoclassical economics (Foss, 1994b; Witt, 1992). The concept of unanticipated change is, however, not a part of standard neoclassical economics, probably because it makes analysis of the efficiency properties of institutions and allocations hard and is troublesome to reconcile with maximizing behaviour (Kreps, 1992).

In a way, the above reasoning implies a very conciliatory reading of the relation between the contractual and the evolutionary view of the firm, namely that they are largely complementary, and that research may therefore centre on combining propositions from the two approaches.

An important example of such research is the work of David Teece (1982, 1986), who has combined insights from contractual and evolutionary economics in his attempt to address efficient diversification (1982) and the innovation boundaries of the firm (1986).

Much more ambitiously, Douglass North (1990) has combined insights from contractual economics with insights from evolutionary economics in his attempt to seek an institutional answer to the causes of the wealth of nations. Clearly, this is a promising research avenue, as may be signalled by the conferment of the Nobel Prize to North. It is also one that has been endorsed by the prominent contractual economists Paul Milgrom and John Roberts (1988). As they argue

> The incentive based transaction cost theory has been made to carry too much of the weight of explanation in the theory of organizations. We expect competing and complementary theories to emerge – theories that are founded on economizing on bounded rationality and that pay more attention to changing technology and to evolutionary considerations (p. 450).

Thus, research on how the contractual perspective complements the evolutionary perspective (and vice versa) is, if not an established area of research within the theory of the firm, then at least seen as a promising avenue of research. However, it may also be possible to develop the theory of the firm along more directly evolutionary lines, lines that do not directly draw on contractual economics.

5 EXPANDING THE EVOLUTIONARY THEORY OF THE FIRM: A MENU OF RESEARCH STRATEGIES

As I argued above, one way of expanding the explanatory potential of evolutionary economics is to tie it more explicitly to neo-institutional economics of the transaction cost variety.[26] Thus, evolutionary theories of the firm may be seen as complementary to contractual theories of the firm, for example because they supply the emphasis on idiosyncratic production and organization knowledge that is so badly missing in modern contractual theories.

However, evolutionary purists may protest against a too close association with neo-institutionalism, finding this body of theorizing too reductionist, static and efficiency oriented. They might have a point; but their protests should only be taken seriously to the extent that it is possible to expand the problem-solving capacity/domain of application of the evolutionary theory of the firm in other ways (that is, by not leaning on neo-institutionalist theories). Here is a brief, not at all exhaustive, and strongly speculative list of possible research avenues with respect to carrying further evolutionary work on the firm.

Develop an improved micro-analysis of competence

Because of the need to better understand the firm's 'hereditary system' and how this constrains firm behaviour, there is a need for exploring the implications and the processes of emergence and reproduction of competence.[27] Important work in this direction has been done by Pavel Pelikan (1989), whose work, however, mostly centres on comparative systems issues and the interplay between firms and capital markets (see also Eliasson, 1990). Inspiration for developing a micro-analysis of competence is particularly likely to come from management theorists (for example, Hedlund, 1994), since the notions of competence and organizational learning have for long enjoyed much attention within management studies. In general, a better understanding of competence and its influence on economic organization is likely to be a multi-disciplinary affair, requiring, for example, insights from social psychology and artificial intelligence research (Kogut and Zander, 1992; Witt, 1995).

---

[26]. Another variety of neo-institutionalism is the work on the emergence of norms and conventions, much of which explicitly draws on evolutionary game theory. For an assessment of the relation between this work and evolutionary economics, see Nelson (1995). For some actual modelling exercises on norms from an explicit evolutionary economics position, see Andersen (1994).

[27]. Chandler (1992, p. 99) concurs: 'evolutionary theory raises significant questions for study. How precisely were the learning processes carried out? How and why did industry-specific and particularly company-specific characteristics vary? ... What were the contents of the routines developed to evaluate and capture new markets and move out of old ones?'

Develop the notion of the firm as option-providing institution
Brian Loasby (1976, 1991, 1993) has developed a unique perspective on economic organization that in many ways dovetails with evolutionary perspectives on the firm. Drawing on many influences, particularly post-Marshallian and Austrian economics, Loasby suggests to think of economic organization in terms of the provision of flexibility. Thus, whereas markets supply options for future contracts, firms provide contracts for future options. Although this is an example of an incomplete contract logic, the thrust is completely different from the thrust of standard contractual economics. Incomplete contracts are interesting, not because of the room they provide for opportunistic behaviour, but because they represent the proper contractual structure around partly unpredictable learning processes. Thus, in line with the competence theme, the firm may in this reading be seen as providing options for mutual learning. This provides one way of thinking in a disciplined way about the firm as an evolutionary learning machine.

Develop a better understanding of epistatic effects in firms
From an evolutionary perspective, the firm is an entity that solves productive and organizational problems from a distinct competence basis and with the application of distinct heuristics. However, firms are also contractual, political, cultural, and so on, entities. In other words, there are many relevant traits of the firm – 'relevant' in the sense of possessing selective significance.

The problem with much of evolutionary economics is that it has focused on only one or two of these traits, and much the same can be said of the contractual theory of the firm. This is unfortunate, since we have many reasons to expect that these traits interact in various ways, that is to say, that epistasis takes place. For example, a firm with superior transaction cost properties may have inferior properties in terms of exploration and experimenting (and conversely). On the other hand, there may be positive epistatic effects between, say, competencies and cultures. Work aiming at understanding such effects may start with the NK model in Kauffman (1993), partly designed to understanding epistatic effects in a biological context (see also Levinthal, 1992).

To which extent may evolutionary economics provide independent rationales for economic organization?
For example, to which extent may the evolutionary conceptualization of production and production and organization knowledge – as reflected in the notion of competence – account for the variety of economic organization, independently of considerations of misalignment of incentives. In other

words, to which extent may the pure coordination and learning aspects of production be used as independent rationales for economic organization? Is it possible to construct a story of the existence of the firm on this basis? Of its boundaries? And so on (see Foss, 1995a). In spite of the existence of a few contributions (discussed in Section 4.3), this a much under-researched area in the evolutionary theory of the firm. However, since issues are the crucial ones in modern neoclassical theories of the firm, a genuinely competitive evolutionary theory of the firm has to address them in convincing ways.

6 CONCLUSIONS

In conclusion I return to where I began: to Fritz Machlup (1967) and his assertion that the non-neoclassical approaches to the firm of his time were not really competitive with the neoclassical theory of the firm, but rather complementary. Do we now – almost three decades after Machlup wrote and after much evolutionary work on the theory of the firm – have an evolutionary theory of the firm that is competitive with neoclassical theory?

The answer is either a qualified 'no' or a qualified 'yes', depending on which criteria one deems important. Yes, we do have a collection of evolutionary theories of the firm that are different in terms of the underlying explanatory apparatus, have different implications relative to the neoclassical theories of the firm, and are therefore genuinely competitive with these. The 'qualified no' response turns on two observations. First, in terms of basic conventionalist criteria such as explanatory elegance, rigor, simplicity, degree of formalization, and so on, there is no evolutionary theory of the firm that is comparable to the best contractual work (such as Holmström and Milgrom, 1994). Moreover, the theories should rather be seen as complementary, since modern neoclassical theories of the firm mostly concentrate on the contractual structure of the firm, whereas evolutionary theories mostly concentrate on knowledge accumulation and utilization.

However, in the last analysis, the crux of the matter is the relation between evolutionary economics and neoclassical economics (cf. Dosi and Marengo, 1993). This is so, because work on the theory of the firm is derived from more fundamental propositions at the core of the evolutionary or neoclassical research programmes. And it is precisely because the core of particularly neoclassical economics seems to be (slowly) changing that it is so hard to venture any guesses on the future relation between evolutionary and neoclassical theories of the firm.

It is hard to deny that the research frontier of neoclassical economics has, on the whole, become increasingly open to insights that traditionally belong to evolutionary approaches. For example, many neoclassical economists and game theorists (for example, Radner, Aumann, Binmore) now take seriously the notion of bounded rationality, so that there is now a possibility for a crucial broadening of the behavioural repertoire of neoclassical economics. In fact, recent work in organizational economics would seem to indicate the necessity of such a broadening, since, for example, a sound understanding of the nature of the firm seems to necessitate that unanticipated changes be incorporated in the analysis (through the notion of incomplete contracts) (Kreps, 1992).

Non-maximizing modes of behaviour and unanticipated changes have been among the hallmarks of evolutionary economics (Nelson and Winter, 1982; Witt, 1992). To the extent that these notions are beginning to be taken seriously in neoclassical economics, it is the nature of orthodoxy that is changing, and changing towards something like the metaphysics that underlie evolutionary economics. This metaphysics is one that sees the economic world as fundamentally open-ended, and the future as emerging more or less unpredictably out of the creative choices of men (Foss, 1994b). It is on this basis that evolutionary, Austrian and post-Keynesian economists for a long time have complained that neoclassical economics is fundamentally static: it operates within a deterministic world in which everything is settled from the beginning.

This complaint may have lost some of its force in the face of the many recent attempts to incorporate path dependence under the umbrella of formal neoclassical economics, on strategic complementarity, the application of the mathematical theory of chaos to economics, and so on. If, however, the charge of being 'too static' is to be interpreted to mean that neoclassical economics continues to be equilibrium oriented, then in this sense neoclassical economics is surely 'static'. As Nelson and Winter (1982, p. 8) note: 'although it is not literally appropriate to stigmatize orthodoxy as concerned only with hypothetical situations of perfect information and static equilibrium, the prevalence of analogous restrictions in advanced work lends a metaphorical validity to the complaint'.

The issue of 'analogous restrictions' may or may not be thought to be the fundamental division. However, the general expansion of the interest of neoclassical economists in incorporating notions such as path dependence and broadening the behavioural foundation of neoclassical economics, combined with the growing formalizing evolutionary economics may indicate the possibility of some convergence between these hitherto separately developed perspectives. And then we might witness the development of a theory of the firm that combines the best of the contractual approach with the best of the evolutionary approach.

REFERENCES

Alchian, A.A. (1950), 'Uncertainty, Evolution, and Economic Theory', in idem.

Alchian, A.A. (1977), *Economic Forces at Work*, Indianapolis: Liberty Press.

Alchian, A.A. and H. Demsetz (1972), 'Production, Information Costs, and Economic Organization', in A.A. Alchian (1977).

Alchian, A.A. and S. Woodward (1988), 'The Firm is Dead; Long Live the Firm', *Journal of Economic Literature*, **26**, 65–79.

Andersen, E.S. (1994), *Evolutionary Economics*, London: Pinter.

Anderson, P. and M.L. Tushman (1990), 'Technological Discontinuities and Dominant Designs', *Administrative Science Quarterly*, **35**, 604–33.

Barney, J.B. (1991), 'Firm Resources and Sustained Competitive Advantage', *Journal of Management*, **17**, 99–120.

Baum, J.A.C. and J.V. Singh (eds) (1994), *Evolutionary Dynamics of Organizations*, New York: Oxford University Press.

Bhaskar, R. (1978), *A Realist Theory of Science*, London: Harvester Wheatsheaf.

Chandler, A.D. (1992), 'Organizational Capabilities and the Economic History of the Industrial Enterprise', *Journal of Economic Perspectives*, **6**, 79–100.

Cheung, S.N.S. (1983), 'The Contractual Nature of the Firm', *Journal of Law and Economics*, **26**, 1–22.

Coase, R.H. (1937), 'The Nature of the Firm', *Economica*, **4** (n.s.), 386–405.

Cyert, R. and J.G. March (1963), *A Behavioral Theory of the Firm*, Englewood Cliffs: Prentice-Hall.

Dierickx, I. and K. Cool (1989), 'Asset-Stock Accumulation and Sustainability of Competitive Advantage', *Management Science*, **35**, 1504–11.

Dosi, G. and L. Marengo (1993), 'Some Elements of An Evolutionary Theory of Organizational Competences', in R.W. Englander (ed.) (1993), *Evolutionary Concepts in Contemporary Economics*, Ann Arbor: The University of Michigan Press.

Dow, G. (1987), 'The Function of Authority in Transaction Cost Economics', *Journal of Economic Behavior and Organization*, **8**, 13–38.

Downie, J. (1958), *The Competitive Process*, London: Macmillan.

Eliasson, G. (1990), 'The Firm as a Competent Team', *Journal of Economic Behavior and Organization*, **13**, 275–98.

Elster, J. (1983), *Explaining Technical Change*, Cambridge: Cambridge University Press.

Fama, E. (1980), 'Agency Problems and the Theory of the Firm', *Journal of Political Economy*, **88**, 288–307.

Farrell, M. (1970), 'Some Elementary Selection Processes in Economics', *Review of Economic Studies*, **37**, 305–19.

Foss, N.J. (1993), 'The Theory of the Firm: Contractual and Competence Perspectives', *Journal of Evolutionary Economics*, **3**, 127–44.

Foss, N.J. (1994a), 'The Two Coasian Traditions', *Review of Political Economy*, **5**, 35–61.

Foss, N.J. (1994b), 'Realism and Evolutionary Economics', *Journal of Social and Biological Systems*, **17**, 21–40.

Foss, N.J. (1994c), 'Why Transaction Cost Economics Needs Evolutionary Economics', *Revue d'Economie Industrielle*, **64**, 7–26.

Foss, N.J. (1994d), 'The Biological Analogy and the Theory of the Firm', *Journal of Economic Issues*, **28**, 1115–36.

Foss, N.J. (1996), 'Knowledge-Based Theories of the Firm', *Organization Science*, **7**, 470–6.

Friedman, M. (1953), 'The Methodology of Positive Economics', in idem. (1953), *Essays on Positive Economics*, Chicago: University of Chicago Press.

Grossman, S.J. and O.D. Hart (1986), 'The Costs and Benefits of Ownership', *Journal of Political Economy*, **94**, 671–719.

Hayek, F.A. von (1945), 'The Use of Knowledge in Society', in idem. (1948).

Hayek, F.A. von (1948), *Individualism and Economic Order*, Chicago: University of Chicago Press.

Hayek, F.A. von (1973), *Law, Legislation, and Liberty, Vol. 1: Rules and Order*, Chicago: University of Chicago Press.

Hedlund, G. (1994), 'A Model of Knowledge Management and the N-Form Corporation', *Strategic Management Journal*, **15**, Special Issue, 73–90.

Hodgson, G.M. (1993), *Economics and Evolution: Bringing Life Back Into Economics*, London: Polity Press.

Hodgson, G.M. (1994), 'The Evolution of Evolutionary Economics', *The Scottish Journal of Political Economy*, **42**, 469–90.

Holmström, B.R. and J. Tirole (1989), 'The Theory of the Firm', in R. Schmalensee and R.D. Willig (eds) (1989), *Handbook of Industrial Organization*, Amsterdam, North-Holland.

Holmström, B.R. and P. Milgrom (1994), 'The Firm as an Incentive System', *American Economic Review*, **84**, 972–91.

Jensen, M.C. and W.H. Meckling (1979), 'Rights and Production Functions: An Application to Labor-managed Firms and Codetermination', *Journal of Business*, **52**, 469–506.

Kauffman, S.A. (1993), *The Origins of Order: Self-Organization and Selection in Evolution*, New York: Oxford University Press.

Knudsen, C. (1995), *Economic Methodology*, London: Routledge.

Kogut, B. and U. Zander (1992), 'Knowledge of the Firm, Combinative Capabilities, and the Replication of Technology', *Organization Science*, **3**, 383–97.

Kreps, D.M. (1992), 'Static Choice in the Presence of Unforeseen Contingencies', in Partha Dasgupta et al. (eds) (1992), *Economic Analysis of Markets and Games: Essays in Honor of Frank Hahn*, Cambridge: MIT Press.

Lakatos, I. (1970), 'Falsification and the Methodology of Scientific Research Programmes', in idem. (1978), *Falsification and the Methodology of Scientific Research Programmes*, Cambridge: Cambridge University Press.

Langlois, R.N. (1992), 'Transaction-Cost Economics in Real Time', *Corporate and Industrial Change*, **1**, 99–127.

Langlois, R.N. and P.L. Robertson (1995), *Firms, Markets, and Economic Change: A Dynamic Theory of Business Institutions*, London: Routledge.

Levinthal, D. (1992), 'Surviving Schumpeterian Environments: An Evolutionary Perspective', *Industrial and Corporate Change*, **2**, 427–43.

Lippman, S.A. and R.P. Rumelt (1982), 'Uncertain Imitability: An Analysis of Interfirm Differences in Efficiency under Competition', *Bell Journal of Economics*, **13**, 418–38.

Loasby, B.J. (1976), *Choice, Complexity, and Ignorance*, Cambridge: Cambridge University Press.

Loasby, B.J. (1991), *Equilibrium and Evolution*, Manchester: Manchester University Press.

Loasby, B.J. (1993), 'Understanding Markets', mimeo, University of Stirling.

Machlup, F. (1946), 'Marginal Analysis and Empirical Research', *American Economic Review*, **36**, 519–54.

Machlup, F. (1967), 'Theories of the Firm: Marginalist, Behavioral, Managerial', in idem. (1978), *Methodology of Economics and Other Social Sciences*, New York: Academic Press.

March, J.G. (1991), 'Exploration and Exploitation in Organizational Learning', *Organization Science*, **2**, 79–87.

Marengo, L. (1992), 'Structure, Competence, and Learning in an Evolutionary Model of the Firm', *Papers on Economics and Evolution*, edited by the European Study Group for Evolutionary Economics, Freiburg.

Metcalfe, J.S. (1994), 'Competition, Fisher's Principle and Increasing Returns in the Selection Process', *Journal of Evolutionary Economics*, **4**, 327–46.

Milgrom, P. and J. Roberts (1988), 'Economic Theories of the Firm: Past, Present and Future', *Canadian Journal of Economics*, **21**, 444–58.

Montgomery, C.A. (ed.) (1995), *Resource-Based and Evolutionary Theories of the Firm: Towards a Synthesis*, Boston: Kluwer.

Nelson, R.R. (1991), 'Why Do Firms Differ, and How Does It Matter?', *Strategic Management Journal*, **14**, 61–74.

Nelson, R.R. (1992), 'The Role of Firms in Technical Advance: A Perspective from Evolutionary Theory', in G. Dosi, R. Giannetti and P.A. Toninelli (eds) (1992), *Technology and Enterprise in a Historical Perspective*, Oxford: Clarendon Press.

Nelson, R.R. (1995), 'Recent Evolutionary Theorizing About Economic Change', *Journal of Economic Literature*, **33**, 48–90.

Nelson, R.R. and S.G. Winter (1973), 'Toward an Evolutionary Theory of Economic Capabilities', *American Economic Review*, **63**, 440–9.

Nelson, R.R. and S.G. Winter (1982), *An Evolutionary Theory of Economic Change*, Cambridge: Bellknap Press of Harvard University Press.

Nightingale, J. (1993), 'Solving Marshall's Problem with the Biological Analogy: Jack Downie's Competitive Process', *History of Economics Review*, 20, 74–95.

Nightingale, J. (1994), 'Situational Determinism Revisited: Scientific Research Programmes in Economics Twenty Years On', *Journal of Economic Methodology*, 1, 233–52.

North, D.C. (1990), *Institutions, Institutional Change, and Economic Performance*, Cambridge: Cambridge University Press.

O'Brien, D.P. (1984), 'The Evolution of the Theory of the Firm', in F.H. Stephen (ed.) (1984), *Firms, Organization, and Labour*, London: Macmillan.

O'Driscoll, G.P. and M. Rizzo (1985), *The Economics of Time and Ignorance*, Oxford: Basil Blackwell.

Pelikan, P. (1989), 'Evolution, Economic Competence and Corporate Control', *Journal of Economic Behavior and Organization*, 12, 279–303.

Penrose, E.T. (1952), 'Biological Analogies in the Theory of the Firm', *American Economic Review*, 52, 804–19.

Penrose, E.T. (1959), *The Theory of the Growth of the Firm*, Oxford: Oxford University Press.

Popper, K.R. (1967), 'The Rationality Principle', in D. Miller (ed.) (1990), *A Pocket Popper*, Glasgow: Fontana Press.

Rumelt, R.P. (1984), 'Towards a Strategic Theory of the Firm', in Richard B. Lamb (ed.) (1984), *Competitive Strategic Management*, Englewood Cliffs: R.D. Irwin.

Silverberg, G. (1988), 'Modelling Economic Dynamics and Technical Change: Mathematical Approaches to Self-Organization and Evolution', in G. Dosi, C. Freeman, R. Nelson, G. Silverberg and L. Soete (eds), *Technical Change and Economic Theory*, London: Pinter.

Simon, H.A. (1962), 'The Architecture of Complexity', *Proceedings of the American Philosophical Society*, 106, 467–82.

Teece, D.J. (1982), 'Towards an Economic Theory of the Multiproduct Firm', *Journal of Economic Behavior and Organization*, 3, 39–63.

Teece, D.J. (1986), 'Profiting From Technological Innovation', in M.L. Tushman and W.L. Moore (eds) (1988), *Readings in the Management of Innovation*, Cambridge: Ballinger Publishing Company.

Teece, D.J., G. Dosi, S.G. Winter and R.P. Rumelt (1994), 'Toward A Theory of Corporate Coherence', *Journal of Economic Behavior and Organization*, 23, 1–30.

Warglien, M. (1995), 'Hierarchical Selection and Organizational Adaptation', *Industrial and Corporate Change*, 4, 161–86.

Wernerfelt, B. (1984), 'A Resource-Based View of the Firm', *Strategic Management Journal*, 5, 171–80.

Williamson, O.E. (1971), 'The Vertical Integration of Production: Market Failure Considerations', *American Economic Review*, 61, 112–23.

Williamson, O.E. (1975), *Markets and Hierarchies*, New York: The Free Press.

Williamson, O.E. (1985), *The Economic Institutions of Capitalism*, New York: Free Press.

Williamson, O.E. (1993), 'Transaction Cost Economics and Organisation Theory', *Industrial and Corporate Change*, **2**, 107–56.

Winter, S.G. (1964), 'Economic Natural Selection and the Theory of the Firm', *Yale Economic Essays*, **4**, 225–72.

Winter, S.G. (1971), 'Satisficing, Selection, and the Innovating Remnant', *Quarterly Journal of Economics*, **85**, 237–61.

Winter, S.G. (1975), 'Optimization and Evolution in the Theory of the Firm', in R.H. Day and T. Groves (1975), *Adaptive Economic Models*, New York: Academic Press.

Winter, S.G. (1982), 'An Essay on the Theory of Production', in S.H. Hymans (ed.) (1982), *Economics and the World Around It*, Ann Arbor: University of Michigan Press.

Winter, S.G. (1988), 'On Coase, Competence, and the Corporation', *Journal of Law, Economics, and Organization*, **4**, 163–80.

Winter, S.G. (1990), 'Survival, Selection, and Inheritance in Evolutionary Theories of Organization', in J.V. Singh (ed.) (1990), *Organization Evolution: New Directions*, London: Sage.

Witt, U. (1989), 'Subjectivism in Economics: A Suggested Reorientation', in K.G. Grunert and F. Ölander (eds) (1989), *Understanding Economic Behavior*, Dordrecht: Kluwer.

Witt, U. (1992), 'Evolutionary Concepts in Economics', *Eastern Economic Journal*, **18**, 405–20.

Witt, U. (ed.) (1993), *Evolutionary Economics*, London: Edward Elgar.

Witt, U. (1995), 'Imagination and Leadership – The Neglected Dimension of an (Evolutionary) Theory of the Firm', unpublished ms.

5. Neo- and Post-Schumpeterian Contributions to Evolutionary Economics

Esben Sloth Andersen

[S]tudents who attempt to act upon the theory that the most recent treatise is all they need will soon discover that they are making things unnecessarily difficult for themselves. Unless that recent treatise itself presents a minimum of historical aspects, no amount of correctness, originality, rigor, or elegance will prevent a sense of lacking direction and meaning from spreading among the students or at least the majority of students. This is because, whatever the field, the problems and methods that are in use at any given time embody the achievements and carry the scars of work that has been done in the past under entirely different conditions. (Schumpeter, 1954, p. 4)

1 INTRODUCTION: SCHUMPETER VERSUS NEW EVOLUTIONARY ECONOMICS

Important parts of the heterodox economics of technical change and of the more encompassing, model-building evolutionary economics have hitherto considered the relationship to the Schumpeterian heritage as a nearly self-evident fact. Empirically oriented researchers have invoked 'Schumpeter hypotheses' to delineate areas of study like the innovativeness of small and large firms (Kamien and Schwarz, 1982) and the importance of supply- and demand-side factors in innovation (Rosenberg, 1982). Theoretically oriented researchers like Nelson and Winter (1982) and Dosi (1988; 1990) have seen Schumpeter as the economist who had most clearly delineated the area that they were trying to model. For instance, Nelson and Winter (1982, p. 39) said that 'we are evolutionary theorists *for the sake* of being neo-Schumpeterians – that is, because evolutionary ideas provide a workable approach to the problem of elaborating and formalizing the Schumpeterian view of capitalism as an engine of change'. They also state that 'the term "neo-Schumpeterian" would be as appropriate a designation for our entire approach as "evolutionary"'.

Since these statements were made, a rapid expansion has taken place with respect to Schumpeterian scholarship and to evolutionary-economic modelling. Especially after the centenary celebration of Schumpeter's birth in 1983 an extensive literature has emerged, and now we have biographies like Swedberg (1991), bibliographies like Augello (1990), collections of papers like Wood (1991), and even an International Schumpeter Society that publishes a series of selected conference papers as well as the *Journal of Evolutionary Economics*. With respect to evolutionary approaches to economics the change has been even more significant as can be seen from, for example, the paper collection by Witt (1993), the reference work by Hodgson, Samuels, and Tool (1994), and the review by Nelson (1995). In contrast to older types of evolutionary-economic thinking, many of the modern contributions are characterized by the use of formal modelling and/or computer simulation. This is not least the case for researchers who emphasize their relationship to Schumpeter. Some of these contributions try to develop an evolutionary growth theory (see Silverberg and Verspagen in the present volume), but the neo- and post-Schumpeterian model builders cover a larger set of issues centred around the notion of Schumpeterian competition (Winter, 1984; Silverberg, Dosi and Orsenigo, 1988; Kwasnicki, 1992; Chiaromonte and Dosi, 1993; Silverberg and Verspagen, 1994).

In this new situation Hodgson has challenged the original perception of the relationship between Schumpeter and the parts of evolutionary economics which have referred to his name. According to Hodgson (1993, p. 149) 'the invocation of Schumpeter's name by the new wave of evolutionary theorists in the 1980s and 1990s is both misleading and mistaken'. The invocation seems to build on 'superficial similarities' while 'at a deeper theoretical level there is a complete divergence'. Hodgson finds this divergence especially in the basic ideas about the role of the selection mechanism in the evolutionary process. While the new evolutionary modellers from Nelson and Winter to Dosi and Silverberg base their models on a selection mechanism which is analogous to biological selection, Schumpeter 'eschewed the natural selection analogy for economics and adopted an entirely different conception of evolution ... more economic revolution than economic evolution' (Hodgson, 1993, 149f.). Another problem, emphasized by Hodgson in the present volume, is that the self-proclaimed Schumpeterians are anti-reductionist while Schumpeter embraced the reductionist programme and invented the term 'methodological individualism'. These and several other distinctions seem to demonstrate that 'selectionist evolutionary modelling in economics' should be considered as having 'much more to do with Veblen and the "old" institutionalism than with Schumpeter himself' (Hodgson, 1993, p. 150).

Hodgson is not the only researcher who observed that there is a certain discrepancy between Schumpeter's work and the later use of it. For instance, Rosenberg (1986, 197 f.) has remarked that the

> Schumpeterian renaissance ... has, so far, been an excessively partial one. That is, it has confined itself to a rather restricted portion of a much larger body of thought. ... [M]any of Schumpeter's contributions to economic and social thought remain neglected – even by people who would not shrink from the label 'Neo-Schumpeterians'.

Furthermore, Freeman (1990, p. 28) pointed out that there is a major difference with respect to Schumpeter's strategy of relating to general equilibrium theory: 'it was Schumpeter's misfortune that he attempted to marry it [the general equilibrium theory] with his own theory of dynamic destabilizing entrepreneurship'.

The present paper takes Hodgson's challenge, together with the more widespread uneasiness, as an opportunity for rethinking the relationship between Schumpeter's evolutionary works and the large subset of model-building evolutionary economics that has a self-declared relationship to Schumpeter.[1] The underlying method is inspired by Schumpeter (1954, pp. 39–45) who put much emphasis on the distinction between the vision and the analytical tools of great economists. In the present case the vision is Schumpeter's preliminary idea of the functioning of the process of economic evolution while the analysis is performed by means of concepts and formalized models. A basic proposition of the paper is that Schumpeter's originality and his importance to evolutionary modelling to a large extent lies in the fact that he acknowledged that he had a 'tool problem', that is he lacked relevant analytical tools for clearly expressing his view of economic evolution. Although Schumpeter's attempts to solve his tool problem was not satisfactory for himself, and although Schumpeter even lacked the tools for expressing the research agenda clearly, he provided modern researchers with a rich problem area (as we shall see in Section 2). Since present-day evolutionary modellers are to an increasing extent able to solve Schumpeter's tool problem (as suggested in sections 3–4), it is not at all unwarranted by them to invoke his name.

The propositions of a tool problem for evolutionary thought and of the increasing ability of evolutionary modellers to overcome this problem help to clarify many of the real and apparent contradictions between Schumpeter and the more or less Schumpeterian evolutionary model building. Section

---

[1]. In this endeavour the emphasis is put on other aspects of Schumpeter's work than is done in Swedberg (1991), cf. Andersen (1993).

2 examines how Schumpeter's evolutionary analysis was influenced by two factors: the anti-evolutionary context in which it was developed and the inadequate analytic tools available to him. These backgrounds help to explain many of Schumpeter's paradoxical statements as well as his affinity with Walras and his conflict with Marshall. In Section 3 core elements of the contribution of Nelson and Winter and other evolutionary modellers are treated as a potential solution to Schumpeter's tool problem and to the Schumpeter–Marshall conflict on the character of the evolutionary process. This is followed up in Section 4 that presents a sketch of a combined (post-) Schumpeter–Marshall strategy for evolutionary modelling. Such a strategy is important because evolutionary-economic modellers who deal with 'Schumpeterian competition' seem to be neo- or post-Marshallians just as much as they are neo- or post-Schumpeterians. To acknowledge this fact and to try to bridge the gap between Schumpeterian and Marshallian modes of thinking about evolutionary phenomena are major challenges for neo- and post-Schumpeterian types of evolutionary-economic modelling.

2 SCHUMPETER AND THE TOOL PROBLEM

In order to respond to Hodgson's challenge, it is important to place Schumpeter's evolutionary thought in its proper context. This context can be understood in terms of the 'long waves' in the application of evolutionary modes of thinking in economics and in other social sciences. Sanderson (1990, p. 2) has summarized one of the (very long) waves of evolutionary thinking within the social sciences as follows:

> The heyday of evolutionism was in the second half of the nineteenth century, for it was then that the doctrines of Morgan, Tylor, Spencer, Marx, and others were produced. This 'golden age' of evolutionary social science came rather suddenly to an end shortly after the turn of the century, however, and the first decades of the twentieth century represented a sort of 'dark age' for evolutionism.

During this 'dark age' evolutionary thinking was 'severely criticized ... as an outmoded approach that self-respecting scholars should no longer take seriously'. However, Sanderson points out that the situation finally began to change: 'By the 1930s some scholars were beginning to take evolutionism seriously again, and by the 1940s an "evolutionary revival" was well under way'.

This summary of a long wave in evolutionary thought helps to explain the cautious attitude of many economists working with evolutionary problems in the first half of this century. For example, it helps us to understand Schumpeter's remarks that 'the evolutionary idea is now discredited in our field' and that he does not endorse 'unscientific and extra-scientific mysticism' and 'dilettantism'. Schumpeter's conclusion is that 'we must be careful with the phenomenon [of evolution, *dem Entwicklungsphänomen*] itself, still more with the concept in which we comprehend it, and most of all with the word by which we designate the concept and whose associations might lead us astray in all manner of undesirable directions' (Schumpeter, 1934, 57f. [supplemented by Schumpeter, 1926, p. 88]). Read in the context of a downswing of evolutionary thought, these and other remarks of Schumpeter get a different meaning than when this context is left out of consideration (as is largely the case in Hodgson, 1993). For instance, Schumpeter emphasizes wisely that although 'it may be ... that certain aspects of the individual enterprise system are correctly described as a struggle for existence, ... no appeal to biology would be of the slightest use' (Schumpeter, 1954, p. 789). Behind this statement is not only the methodological distinction between the context of discovery (where any analogy or metaphor can be used) and the context of justification (where only economic facts and economic logic matters). There is also a long history of misuse of biological analogies.

One careful way of formulating the problem of evolution is to put it within a clear-cut economic setting: the Walrasian system or, rather, a radical reinterpretation of this system (Schumpeter, 1908; 1912, chapter 1). The choice of this semi- or pseudo-Walrasian setting (see Andersen, 1992) is not primarily a matter of professional tactics. It also relates to two of Schumpeter's deep-felt convictions. First, he thought that a full-fledged understanding of the process of economic evolution must include innovation as taking place in discrete steps; to implement this idea it seems a good idea to superimpose innovative entrepreneurship upon a Walrasian system reinterpreted as a routine-following set of economic agents who in some ways or another have found an equilibrium state. Second, Schumpeter's preference for the formalism of Walras is related to his theory of the development of the science of economics. Economic thought as such does not make progress, but 'economic theory is a box of tools' and the development of new tools 'poses and solves problems for which older authors could hardly have found answers even if they had been aware of them' (Schumpeter, 1954, pp. 15, 39). The problem for economists who have been arguing about economic evolution and even formulated 'visions' about the evolutionary process is that they have not been supported by adequate analytic tools. One of the most ambitious goals an economist can set to himself is to change this situation.[2]

In retrospect, it is obvious that Schumpeter failed in finding a fully adequate set of tools for the formulation and analysis of problems relating to the processes of economic evolution. Especially during his work with his book on *Business Cycles* (1939) it became clear that his early hopes concerning the formalization of evolutionary dynamics did not succeed because their basic character made his 'theories so refractory to mathematical formulations' (Schumpeter, in Swedberg, 1991, p. 230). One of the consequences of this was 'that his ardent support of mathematics in economics drove his students away from the fields of intellectual endeavor that made his own work so significant, and produced many results that he considered sterile' (Smithies, 1951, p. 14). Against this background, it is not difficult to understand why the old Schumpeter wanted to present his ideas in terms of case studies rather than in relation to formal analyses (Schumpeter, 1949) – even though the latter was his basic ambition (dating back to Schumpeter, 1908). His lifelong search for different ways of formulating his evolutionary vision, however, has left a huge material for his followers. Furthermore, Schumpeter's formulation of and confrontations with the tool problem of evolutionary analysis brings us a long way in clarifying many problems, including the wave form of evolutionary thinking in economics,[3] the role of Schumpeter in the history of economic thought and analysis (only indirectly touched upon in Schumpeter, 1954), and the relationship between Schumpeter and 'neo-Schumpeterian' evolutionary-economic modellers. In short, it helps to place much of present-day evolutionary modelling in a broader context. In order to see this we have

---

2. The success in such an endeavour is in no way guaranteed, but experiments with evolution-oriented tool-making seems worth a try: 'Das Faszinierende an der Wissenschaft ist im Grunde nur der Spass, den man hat, wenn man tut, was beste Autoritäten für unmöglich erklären; nur die Jagd nach solchen Gelegenheiten ist etwas wert'. (Schumpeter, 1932, p. 608)

3. The present paper concentrates on the 'long wave' which includes the turn of the century. But we also find a tool problem in the early upswing in the discussion of economic evolution which include the contributions of Adam Smith and other representatives of the Scottish Enlightenment. While Smith was in many ways treating the evolutionary-economic process, Ricardo and most of his followers concentrated on the easily formalizable but non-evolutionary part of his argument. Even Smith himself seems to some extent to have started this development. In Kaldor's (1972, p. 1240) stylized version of the story, Smith starts his *Wealth of Nations* with a fruitful discussion of the division of labour; but after that 'his interest gets bogged down in the question of how values and prices of products and factors are determined'. The more formalistic followers were quick to recognize which part of the argument could be supported by the available analytic tools.

to consider the history of economic thought from a very different angle than we find in Schumpeter's *History of Economic Analysis* and also very different from the ones presented in more specialized accounts (like Hodgson, 1993).

To demonstrate the relevance of the invocation of Schumpeter's work for modern evolutionary modellers, it is helpful to consider Schumpeter's context somewhat closer. Here Marshall becomes important as a would-be evolutionary thinker influenced by Hegel and Spencer (Hodgson, 1993, chapter 7; Groenewegen, 1995, 166f.). Actually, large parts of Marshall's *Principles* (1949) and *Industry and Trade* (1919) can be read as preliminary sketches of analyses of the evolutionary process. But when it came to the fulfilment of these more or less explicit promises, Marshall and most of his contemporaries tended to give up. This was the theme of a *fin-du-siècle* debate which included Veblen's (1898) famous paper: 'Why is Economics not an Evolutionary Science?' In this and other papers (1899–1900) Veblen primarily accused the formalized apparatus of marginalist economics of hindering evolutionary modes of thinking. But this is a one-sided explanation. Veblen's account (and Hodgson, 1993) ignores that the primary problem for Marshall, Böhm-Bawerk (1921), and several others was a lack of adequate analytic tools for treating the complex processes of evolution. By keeping their references to the evolutionary process in the revised editions of their works they emphasized the research task for the new generation (Marshall, 1898) but at the same time they introduced apparent inconsistencies into the formalized parts of their comparative-static argument.

Schumpeter's first book (1908) was designed to clear up this intellectually confusing situation. His main result was a kind of impossibility theorem: the core of the neoclassical apparatus cannot treat the process of economic evolution. This conclusion neither means that neoclassical tools should be dropped (they have important applications) nor that evolutionary phenomena should be abandoned. Evolutionary phenomena were confronted in Schumpeter's second book (1912) which was designed to demonstrate that an intellectually respectable theory of economic evolution (*Entwicklung*) can be developed (even) if we take a (pseudo-) Walrasian economic system as the point of departure. The alternative starting points in Marshall and Böhm-Bawerk were abandoned both because the task was to overcome the confusion created by their mixed character and because Schumpeter wanted to include discrete innovations rather than a theory of incremental change (which is contrary to their incrementalist evolutionary theories). Thus the Schumpeterian theory was formulated as an explicit (but rather incomplete) alternative to the dominant 'Marshallian theory of evolution' (Schumpeter, 1954, p. 1165). In a certain sense this theory sees economic evolution as 'organic growth' (Marshall, 1898, 42f.) in analogy with 'the gradual organic growth of a tree' (Schumpeter, 1934, p. 216).[4] Schumpeter (1939, p. 203) considered this 'picture of a steady march of progress to be misleading' since 'evolution is lopsided, discontinuous, disharmonious by nature' (Schumpeter, 1939, p. 102). To emphasize the essence of his own evolutionary vision, Schumpeter developed a theory which removed the gradualist and adaptive aspects from the focus of attention and (like Kuhn, 1970, with respect to scientific evolution) emphasized the incommensurability between old and new as a core characteristic of his concept of innovation. At the same time Marshall's 'manager' was transformed into a routine-following agent while the creative tasks were left to the Schumpeterian entrepreneur.

When studying Schumpeter's work we should use his own distinction between the analytic tools available to him and his evolutionary vision which to some extent became distorted by being expressed in terms of these tools. More specifically, Schumpeter formulated his evolutionary theory in connection to a (pseudo-) Walrasian framework: a routine-based circular flow of economic life. This framework is first challenged by an innovative entrepreneur; then swarms of entrepreneurs force the non-innovative entrepreneurs to adapt; finally everything settles down to a new routine-based circular flow.[5] This scheme, however, does not imply that Schumpeter thinks the new circular flow evolves directly out of the initial innovation (as Hodgson, 1993, p. 43, seems to suggest). Schumpeter's sole reliance on innovation rather than selection should instead be seen as reflecting the inadequate tools available to him. Given these tools (including a rough reinterpretation of Walras), Schumpeter chose to focus on an important aspect of his vision: that innovations are not (always) random variety to be selected, but (sometimes) powerful ways of restructuring the selection environment. He even chose to define an innovation as being successful, because in this way he was relieved from the trouble of studying all the

---

4. Schumpeter, (1939, p. 203) talks of this as a 'definite theory of economic evolution ... the Marshall–Moore theory of organic growth'. In a much-too-short form Schumpeter (1954, 892f.) has described this kind of evolutionary theory in the following way:
    [P]opulation increases, accumulation proceeds; markets widen in consequence; and this induces internal and external economies (cost-reducing improvements in the organization and technique of production). To these effects we must add those of non-induced or revolutionary inventions that just happen ... All this does not go fundamentally beyond J.S. Mill or even A. Smith. In particular, this progress is thought of as a continuous and almost automatic process that does not harbor any phenomena or problems of its own.

5. See the reconstruction in Andersen (1994, chapter 2).

unsuccessful innovative attempts. But this is obviously not a full demand specification for evolutionary models in the Schumpeterian tradition.

With the benefit of hindsight we can see that Schumpeter's connection to Walras and the radical split between the Marshallian approach and the Schumpeterian approach is unfortunate, not least because it tends to force the modern researcher to choose between different hypotheses which all appear to reflect aspects of the real process of economic evolution. One example is that Schumpeterian consumers have to be persuaded of the advantages of a product innovation by the Schumpeterian entrepreneurs while Marshallian decision-makers are normally able to judge the quality of a modified product or a modified process. In the Marshallian approach there is no need for a concept of innovation since economic evolution can be studied in terms of gradual quality improvements (called 'incremental innovations' by neo-Schumpeterian researchers) while the Schumpeterian approach focuses on significant innovations and leaves the realm of quality improvements to the routine-based behaviour of Schumpeterian managers.

At the time when Schumpeter (1927; 1928; 1934; 1939) presented his evolutionary ideas to an English-speaking audience, the Marshallian approach to economic evolution was under heavy attack. It was primarily Sraffa (1926) who provoked the end to the influential Marshallian blend of evolutionism and comparative-static analysis. This 'crowding out' of evolutionary perspectives from economics is an implicit but central theme in Shackle's *The Years of High Theory: Invention and Tradition in Economic Thought 1926–1939* (1967).[6] In these years Schumpeter went, once more, against the stream. On the one hand, he (for example, 1933) welcomed and supported the new wave of formalism within the core areas of economic theory, and implicitly he probably also welcomed the disintegration of the Marshallian blend of economics. On the other hand, he stubbornly proceeded in publishing his verbose accounts of his version of the evolutionary dynamics of capitalism. This apparently paradoxical double strategy can be explained by Schumpeter's hope that one day the mathematicians and econometricians would help him in articulating a more satisfactory version of his evolutionary theory. The present paper suggests, in contrast to Hodgson, that modern evolutionary modellers may come up with a delayed fulfilment of Schumpeter's hope.

---

[6]. Parts of this process is described in Foss (1991).

3 EVOLUTIONARY MODEL BUILDING AND SCHUMPETERIAN COMPETITION

The preceding account of Schumpeter's trouble with the available tools for expressing his evolutionary vision as well as his tendency to overdramatise the gap between his own and Marshall's evolutionary theories give many suggestions for the evaluation of the relationship between Schumpeter and 'neo-Schumpeterian' model builders.[7] Schumpeter's deep-felt tool problem is an obvious starting point for modern tool-makers who immediately remark that 'the intellectual coherence and power of thinking about Schumpeterian competition have been quite low, as one would expect in the absence of a well-defined theoretical structure to guide and connect research' (Nelson and Winter, 1982, p. 29). The mutual recognition of the tool problem does not make such a statement an expression of hostility. On the contrary, as we saw in the quotation in Section 1, Nelson and Winter (1982, p. 39) 'are evolutionary theorists *for the sake* of being neo-Schumpeterians'. The Schumpeter–Marshall relationship is somewhat more tricky for 'neo-Schumpeterian' modellers. One the one hand, Schumpeter's routine behaviour and his discrete innovations are much easier to handle than Marshall's incrementalist and flexible account of business behaviour. On the other hand, the Schumpeterian entrepreneurs tend to emerge out of nothing, so to say, while Marshallian business firms are more stable and predictable entities. The solution seems to be some sort of combination in which established firms are also able to show innovative behaviour. This solution was actually proposed by Schumpeter himself in his *Capitalism, Socialism, and Democracy* (1950) that deals with the more or less

---

7.   Although the relationship between evolutionary modellers and Schumpeter has been given priority, it is not the only one which can be studied. Nelson and Winter (1982, pp. 33–45) give credits to many of the authors who stuck to evolutionary perspectives during the dark ages for evolutionary thought. Schumpeter gets special attention but it is also suggested that 'our evolutionary theory is closer to the original Marshallian doctrine than is contemporary orthodoxy' (Nelson and Winter, 1982, p. 45). Furthermore, Adam Smith, Marx, Simon, Penrose, Chandler, and many others are mentioned. Only the American institutionalist economics in the tradition of Veblen and Commons are largely missing (see, however, Nelson and Winter, 1982, p. 404). This may explain why the notion of 'evolutionary economics' (invented by Veblen, 1898) is missing in the book. (The notion of 'evolutionary economics' however pops up in the index of Nelson and Winter, 1982, p. 432.) The recognized 'antecedents' of the Nelson and Winter theory are mainly the more or less heterodox economists who have admitted that they faced a tool problem. The institutionalists seem largely to have been denying the need for a formal foundation of evolutionary theorizing, and this might explain some of the background for Nelson and Winter's relationship to them.

permanent innovative activities of 'big business' (without any reference to Marshall). The solution has later been known as Schumpeter Mark II, while the young Schumpeter put much emphasis on the emergence of new firms based on a single innovation (Mark I).[8] It could just as well be called a preliminary Schumpeterian–Marshallian synthesis.

Nelson and Winter proposed a solution to the tool problem that met widespread attention when they rewrote several earlier articles and formulated a research programme in their book *An Evolutionary Theory of Economic Change* (1982). The principal contributions of Nelson and Winter (1982, p. 19) and their followers are based on the assumption that the 'verbal account of economic evolution seems to translate naturally into a description of a Markov process – though one in a rather complicated state space'. At a certain point in time, *t*, the state of the evolutionary process of an industry is described by the capital stock and the behavioural rules of each firm. This state is used for determining the short-term behaviour of the industry as well as the new capital stock and the new behavioural rules of each firm at time *t* + 1. It is the shift in behavioural rules which gives the overall evolution the character of a stochastic Markov process. When this process of state transformation is defined, it is relatively easy to translate it into computer models and simulations. This translation is, however, not purely trivial. The reason is that the translation into a programming language makes it possible to treat some of the intricacies of evolutionary mechanisms which were not clearly dealt with (or even imagined) in the original verbal-style account of the evolutionary process. For instance, we do not have to concentrate on the fact that firms are 'naturally selected' by the economic system (as emphasized by Alchian, 1950); we can also consider many details relating to the fact that firms are influencing their own destiny by modifying their own behaviour through search for and selection of new technologies (or broader: new modes of behaviour).

Through their work Nelson and Winter demonstrate the possibility of overcoming the basic difficulty in studying evolutionary processes, namely the need to combine elements which are normally considered as belonging to quite different areas of investigation. These elements are the processes of

---

8. Schumpeter's (1912; 1934) first theory of economic evolution (Mark I) is based on innovative entrepreneurship of a radical form: a discrete innovation that is introduced by 'new men' in 'new firms'; but the entrepreneurs are only able to perform a single innovation; afterwards they become 'mere managers'. Schumpeter's (1950) revised theory (Mark II) allows for more routinized innovative activities: large corporations may have emerged from single entrepreneurial acts, but they are transformed so that they are able to perform successive innovations. The innovative and imitative activities of such corporations are easier to model than single-act entrepreneurship.

transmission, variety creation, and selection; or more specifically: Simon's work on rule-based behaviour (Nelson and Winter, 1982, chapters 4–5), Nelson's and other Schumpeter-related work on invention and innovation (Nelson and Winter, 1982, chapter 11), and Alchian's and Winter's work on 'natural selection' (Nelson and Winter, 1982, chapter 6). Such a combination presupposes two opposing capabilities: an ability to cope with a wide variety of elements, and an ability to cut out the details and integrate the elements into an initially crude conception of an evolutionary process. The computer helps to organize this synthesizing exercise to the very last steps since 'the simulation format does impose its own constructive discipline in the modelling of dynamic systems: the program must contain a complete specification of how the systems's state at $t + 1$ depends on that at t and on the exogenous factors, or it will not run'. (Nelson and Winter, 1982, 208f.) By taking this process to a preliminary conclusion, Nelson and Winter provide a constructive proof of the existence of relatively interesting evolutionary-economic models. At the same time they give an explanation of the weaknesses of the informal approaches to evolutionary processes: these processes are normally so complex that it is nearly impossible to master them intellectually by means of the methods of the old evolutionary modes of thinking.

To see to which extent the Nelson and Winter framework helps to overcome the problem, we shall shortly consider their model of Schumpeterian competition which may be considered as their standard model type (Nelson and Winter, 1982, chapters 12–14), but we could also have considered the works of some of their followers (like Silverberg, Dosi and Orsenigo, 1988; Kwasnicki, 1992; Chiaromonte and Dosi, 1993; Silverberg and Verspagen, 1994). The typical Nelson and Winter model deals with the evolution of the production techniques and other behavioural rules of an industry producing a homogeneous product (see also Andersen, 1994, chapter 4). From the very beginning it is important to note that this model of Schumpeterian competition is just one simple example of a 'vastly larger' class of Markov models (Nelson and Winter, 1982, p. 407). But Nelson and Winter claim that such a simplistic model helps to clarify some of Schumpeter's thoughts. The model describes how the state of the industry in the next period is found when the state (capital stock and productivity) of the present period is given. First, the present state is used to define a short-term economic process in the industry whereby market shares, price, and profits of firms are found.[9] The simplicity of the solution depends on the firm's use of fixed (or evolving) rules for output determination and on the exogenous specification of the demand side of the model as well as of the factor markets. Second, the investment decision is treated in a simplified way.[10] Firms expand their capacity in relation to their profitability – partly with the help of banks. However, the expansion of firms with a particularly large market share is constrained by the fact that the effect of expansion on the market price is taken into account. Third, the processes of innovation and imitation is treated somewhat more thoroughly.[11] These processes are specified along the lines of Schumpeter Mark II in which the firms are continually searching for new production techniques and for copying the production techniques of their oligopolistic competitors. The simplicity of the solution depends on the firm's use of fixed (or evolving) rules in determining the R&D expenditure, and on the fixed 'landscapes of search' (with global or localized possibilities of search). Another contribution to the simplicity comes from the assumption that an innovation can immediately be applied throughout the firm, and this gives increasing returns to the application of innovations.

[9]. Summary of the short-term part of the model: the production capacity of each firm is physical capital times the capital coefficient. Output of each firm is decided by simple capacity utilization rules of firms. The aggregate output of the industry faces exogenously given demand conditions which together give the market-clearing price of the product. For each firm we calculate the turnover and then find the net profit by deducting capital depreciation, variable production costs, and R&D expenditure.

[10]. Summary of the investment part of the model: the only way to reduce productive capacity is through the process of physical depreciation. The firm's investment is delimited by its financial constraint which is determined by the net profit. The firm's desired net investment depends on the ratio of output price to unit costs and a target mark-up factor which is an increasing function of the firm's market share. The adjusted physical capital stock is available to the firm from the beginning of the next period.

[11]. Summary of the innovation/imitation part of the model: the innovation and imitation costs are given by the R&D rules of firms. The probability of success in innovation and imitation depends on the respective search costs and the difficulty of innovation/imitation in the industry. An imitative success means that the firm gets access to the best-practice technique in the industry. The outcome of an innovative success depends on the character of technical change in the industry ('science based' or 'cumulative technology'). The attempts to improve productivity end with a comparison between the capital coefficients obtainable by the technique inherited from the last period and the outcomes of imitative and innovative search; the technique with the best productivity is chosen. If the technique is changed, it will determine the capital coefficient for the next period (disembodied technical change).

In this model of Schumpeterian competition it is the combined result of innovation, imitation, and investment that determines the change in the market shares of firms during a simulation run (Nelson and Winter, 1982, chapters 12–14). The innovation behaviour tends to increase concentration while imitation and the monopolistic behaviour of large firms serve to constrain the rate of concentration. The question is, of course, how much this market process has to do with Schumpeter's work. A quick answer is that it is less designed to rethink Schumpeter's broad ideas of a self-transforming capitalist market process than the so-called Schumpeter hypothesis that a concentrated market structure is the precondition for rapid technological change. Through Nelson and Winter's analysis and simulations this Schumpeter hypothesis is refuted since the chain of causation runs in the opposite direction, that is from the exogenous conditions of R&D and firm strategies via differential performance of firms to industry structure. However, this refutation leads Nelson and Winter to express a preference for a broader Schumpeterian approach (of *The Theory of Economic Development*). This broader approach is especially developed in a paper by Winter (1984) as well as in later works in the neo-Schumpeterian tradition. Here it is emphasized that Schumpeter thinks in terms of two modes of technical change and two corresponding types of behavioural rules. The 'entrepreneurial mode' can, for example, be specified by assuming that the search work is performed before entry to the industry. If the new firm becomes sufficiently large, it reaches a threshold which allows a basic change in behavioural rules. It enters the 'routinized-search mode' where it has succeeded in incorporating routinized search into its normal business activities.

This account can be expanded into a story of 'creative destruction' which would probably have pleased Schumpeter more than the exploration of the Schumpeter hypothesis. It is not least the possibility of a rough account of the exit and entry of firms which gives immediate credence to Nelson and Winter's (1982, p. 39) belief 'that he [Schumpeter] would have accepted our evolutionary models as an appropriate vehicle for the explication of his ideas'. There are two types of destruction of firms (Winter, 1984; and others): a firm can invest so little that it in the end fails with respect to a minimum capital stock level; and the perceived performance of the firm may fall below a critical negative level. The creation of firms that are new to the industry raises some more interesting problems. Instead of giving a full account of the Schumpeterian entrepreneur, we consider the profit-seeking activities of entrepreneurs who are not yet producing the product of the industry. The activities of these entrepreneurs can be described in terms of costly innovative and imitative search – just like the activities we find within the industry.

Taken as an aggregate, external entrepreneurs are involved in search activities (R&D) which will occasionally give sufficiently promising results with respect to the production technique of the industry under study. To study this industry from its initial creation we start the whole story with a founder, or *Gründer*, who is successful in his innovative search activities. In other words, he finds a production technique that allows him to produce a potential product, and he obtains some initial information about the potential price of the product as well as of production inputs. His decision to create the industry depends on expectation of a high profit rate (to overcome the initial costs of market creation), and if this profit rate is realized, it will induce him to make a rapid rate of capacity expansion when he has entered into the industry. For the *Gründer* and his first followers there are few incentives for costly R&D activities (Schumpeter Mark I). However, the expansion of the output of the industry will diminish profits and this will lead to negative evaluations of the performance of the firms. In the case of 'satisficing behaviour' this will lead to an increase in innovative and imitative search efforts of existing firms (Mark II). Firms who do not adapt to this change are likely to become bankrupt.

This basic study of evolutionary industrial dynamics can be related to many of Schumpeter's discussions. It can also be adapted to Marshall's (1949, 263ff.) idea of an industry as a forest of firms where young firms struggle upwards while some older firms become dominant before they succumb because of a lack of vitality. Further possibilities are explored in the post-Nelson and Winter literature mentioned above (see also Nelson, 1995). These studies include the consequences for diffusion of innovation of the introduction of vintages of capital and embodied technical change, the consequences of the introduction of learning by doing in existing lines of production, the path dependency of the evolutionary processes, the shift in technological regimes and market regimes, the evolution of rules of behavioural strategies like the R&D intensity of firms, and so on. Even the issues of entrepreneurial strategies of firms have been dealt with in some depths, although the basic tendency in the research has been to focus on industries or other populations of firms.

4 DELINEATING A SCHUMPETER–MARSHALL MODEL OF COMPETITION AND SPECIALIZATION

The modern attempts to clarify and model Schumpeterian competition do not cope with all of Schumpeter's tool problems. In this respect the remark by Rosenberg (1986, p. 197) about the Schumpeter renaissance as 'an excessively partial one' is still valid. If modern economists confine themselves to a limited set of Schumpeterian propositions, they are clearly confronted with decreasing returns in terms of interesting modelling results. However, the most important task is not to explore a few more of the many propositions that relate directly to the Schumpeterian vision of economic evolution. An even more important manifestation of Schumpeter's tool problems was his inability to express clearly and develop the relationship between his evolutionary ideas and the evolutionary ideas implicit in the works of economists like Walras, Böhm-Bawerk and Marshall. It would be a very important contribution if modern modelling could clarify these relationships. In this respect the task is not only to extend Schumpeter's attempt to formulate a demarcation in terms of the exogenously driven or the self-transforming character of the economic process. The tool problem facing Schumpeter was not only one of expressing this and other demarcations (emphasized by the taxonomic approach of Hodgson in the present volume) but even more one of lacking the means of expressing the complementarity between the different approaches.

As suggested earlier it might be especially fruitful to explore the Schumpeter–Marshall relationship.[12] In Schumpeter's work we find little direct support for this task. On the contrary, he asserts that Marshall's theory of economic evolution is 'unsatisfactory' and 'misleading' because Marshall has left out discrete innovations as an endogenous part of the economic process (Schumpeter, 1939, p. 203). However, a full picture of the economic process should, according to Schumpeter (1928, pp. 62, 68), not only include the 'primary', Schumpeterian phenomenon of the entrepreneur 'as the propelling force of the process' but also a large number of 'secondary phenomena' that were emphasized by Marshall. A model that includes both propellant (Schumpeterian) and propelled (Marshallian) activities would have been welcomed by Schumpeter; only the lack of sufficient analytic tools made him ignore the more or less automatic consequences of innovative entrepreneurship. In the following such a Schumpeter–Marshall model of competition and specialization is sketched in relation to current research (cf. Andersen, forthcoming; Andersen and Lundvall, 1995). The Schumpeterian aspect of the model includes discrete innovations and their difficult introduction into the economic system. The Marshallian aspect concerns increasing returns (to the application of innovations), externalities (spill-overs from innovation and the emergence of cost-reducing subsuppliers), and other aspects of industrial organization (problems of intrafirm and interfirm division of labour).

---

[12]. An early example of an attempted integration between Marshallian and Schumpeterian ideas is described by Nightingale (1993).

Such an evolutionary model that attempts to combine aspects of Schumpeterian and Marshallian analysis can start from Nelson and Winter's theory of the firm. This theory is much more complex than can be seen from the simplified version of firm behaviour applied in the standard model of Schumpeterian competition (see Section 3). According to the full theory (Nelson and Winter, 1982, chapters 4–5), each firm is based on a large number of interdependent routines that are performed by the workers. The exposition of the theory of the firm follows that of Schumpeter: it starts from an 'analogue of Schumpeter's "circular flow" at the level of the individual organization' (Nelson and Winter, 1982, p. 98); then the processes of change are introduced into this setting; finally the possibility of routines for making innovations is discussed. The conclusion of this analysis is 'that it is quite inappropriate to conceive firm behavior in terms of deliberate choice from a broad menu of opportunities for the organization. The menu is ... built into the firm's routines, and most of the "choosing" is also accomplished automatically by those routines' (Nelson and Winter, 1982, p. 134). For instance, the firm 'chooses' to apply its customary production technique, and it even uses routines for the determination of output, investment, and R&D expenditure.

In the Nelson and Winter model of Schumpeterian competition, all this intra-organizational diversity has been reduced to a single evolving production technique and a set of fixed parameters of decision-making.[13] But Nelson and Winter's own verbal account for intra-firm complexity can actually be used in the study of the creation of markets by firms which specialize as a consequence of the evolutionary process. This helps us to use Schumpeterian competition to develop Marshall's (1949, pp. 222–31) account for the emergence of 'industrial districts' as well as even broader issues of industrial dynamics (cf. Young, 1928; Stigler, 1951). The simplest way of formalizing Nelson and Winter's theory of the firm in a way that opens up for a subsequent specialization of firms is to consider the overall task of producing the product of the firm as consisting of a series of subtasks which can either be done in parallel or in series (Andersen, forthcoming; Andersen and Lundvall, 1995).[14]

---

[13]. One explanation for this reduction of complexity is that the environment of the industry (markets for products, factors, and finance) is highly simplified. Extra complexity with respect to the specification of firms would just make the model more confusing.

[14]. To simplify we assume that the different production tasks are performed by means of labour alone. For each task of a firm it has in each period a specific production technique which is characterized by its labour coefficient, that is the amount of labour needed in this task for the production of one unit of final output. The total amount of labour needed for

The firm-level dynamics of the Schumpeter–Marshall model can most easily be understood by reference to Adam Smith's (1976, 14f.) famous case of pin-making. The overall product defines the task of delivering a pin (or a package of pins). This task can be divided into numerous subtasks: the delivery of pin heads and pin bodies; the delivery of the tools of pin-making and even the innovative ideas for the improvement of pin-making. Each of these subtasks can be further divided into sub-subtasks, and this process can continue recursively. In such a task-oriented conception of production there are many possibilities of increasing returns (Vassilakis, 1987; Scazzieri, 1993), but the Schumpeter–Marshall model concentrates on the increasing (social) returns to the application of innovations (the given costs of an innovation are spread over a smaller or larger output). More specifically, the model deals with innovations which produce non-incremental increases in the labour productivity of performing individual tasks.

This apparently simple revision of the Nelson and Winter model of the firm is the starting point of the study of an industrial dynamics which differ radically from the standard model of Schumpeterian competition. In the standard Schumpeterian model the firms compete about exactly the same 'niche'. To avoid that only one firm will survive, several stabilizers are introduced into the model: price determination and external finance do not secure rapid elimination of weak firms; large firms deliberately restrain their expansion; imitation eases the survival of weaker firms. The introduction of such stabilizers allows an illuminating analysis of industrial concentration (Section 3). But in order to understand the long-term coexistence of radically different types of economic behaviour, we have to transcend this limited model of Schumpeterian competition. The introduction of a number of different productive tasks which can be innovated individually creates a multi-dimensional system of competition which allows the survival of a larger number of behavioural variants. The reason is that firms can specialize: when a firm has made an innovation with respect to one of its tasks, it decides whether or not to specialize in pursuing this task. If it does so, it exploits the innovation on a larger scale. However, it has a problem of creating a market for the intermediate product which is the output of its innovated task.

---

the production of a unit of output is simply the sum of the labour coefficients of all the *n* tasks of production. To keep the model of Schumpeter–Marshall competition as close as possible to the model of Schumpeterian competition, it is assumed that the overall number of workers and thus the aggregate output of the firm is constrained by its organizational capital (which is renewed in the same way as physical capital).

A process in which innovations with respect to individual tasks take place repeatedly gives rise to a complex and evolving industrial network of suppliers. This process can most easily be illustrated in relation to Adam Smith's story of pin-making. Assume that a large number of firms perform all the subtasks of pin-making. Then a firm makes a major process innovation with respect to the production of pin heads. This firm has two possibilities: it can use the innovation in relation to the part of its production which concerns pin-head making, or it can specialize in pin-head making and supply other firms with an intermediate product (pin heads). If the firm specializes in pin-head production, it may still have a heterogeneous process of production which includes tool-making as well as the application of tools in the making of pin heads. Thus an innovation may concern the process of making tools for pin-head production rather than the application of these tools. This means that a new decision has to be made: whether to become a specialized tool-maker or to apply the innovation within a mixed process of production. In this way the process of intra-firm division of labour may go on. The formalized version of the story includes discrete steps of market creation, the dynamics of intermediate industries, the interdependence of the different parts of the 'development block'[15] of pin-making, and so on. It can be used in the study of the many kinds of coordination problems which emerge during the vertical disintegration and partial reintegration of such a development block.

A simulation experiment with the Schumpeter–Marshall model starts with the specification of the different parameters and the initial values of the state variables. It is convenient to start in a state of the system which is steadily reproduced provided that no innovation takes place. In this steady state all the firms are performing all the tasks in-house. In this case the intra-firm division of labour could be ignored, and we would have exactly the same system as in the standard Schumpeterian model. However, as soon as an innovation occurs, it becomes obvious that the Schumpeter–Marshall model is distinguished from other evolutionary-economic models by the production graph which describes how the individual tasks are connected in series and parallel. To simplify the description of the outcomes of the simulation, it is convenient to split tasks into equivalence classes according to the number of steps they are removed from final consumption (as the Austrian economists have suggested). The finalization of the output of the sector is in class 1, the directly connected tasks are in class 2, and so on. During the simulation, the proportion of exchanged products which comes from each of these classes will vary. Initially, all traded products come from

---

[15]. To use Dahmén's (1991) concept of the interdependent dynamics of different industries.

firms related to class 1 where all employment is concentrated. Then the proportion of employment in firms related to higher classes increases because of vertical disintegration. Finally, the employment share of class 1 firms may increase (in a modelling set-up with a fixed or declining number of firms). The reason is primarily that firms with an increasing organizational capacity (that is employment capacity) will need to cover more and more tasks in order to fully exploit their capacity (and profit opportunities). The rate of change of the aggregate labour coefficient will more or less change in parallel with this process: an initial increase and later a possible decrease. However, the emergence of a structure characterized by larger firms increases the speed of exploitation of innovations, although it is only in extreme cases that a large-scale reintegration can function more effectively than innovation-driven specialization.

The strength of the Schumpeter–Marshall model is based on the fact that it combines the classical approach to the division of labour with the Schumpeterian notion of discontinuous innovation. The model demonstrates how specialization and innovation are closely connected. At the micro-level vertical specialization is a way in which a previously unspecialized firm can often increase the returns from its innovation. At a more aggregate level specialization can be demonstrated to be a way of increasing the speed of the diffusion of the innovation. But the most interesting result of the (repeated) process of specialization is the emergence of a complex inter-industrial system. This system is not only consisting of competing firms. It also implies the emergence of a system of 'species' or 'industries' – and thus it gives an answer to one of Mirowski's (1983) critiques of the model of Schumpeterian competition. The issue of the non-incremental emergence of species is closely related to Schumpeter's vision of evolution. It may imply an important step forward for evolutionary modelling which might become clearer if a comparison with the development of evolutionary biology is made: the present-day evolutionary modelling has several similarities with the formal evolutionary models by Fisher and Haldane of the 1930s. However, the practical importance and the widespread use of evolutionary biology came from the 1940s and onwards when a 'modern evolutionary synthesis' was made which combined formal analyses of the evolutionary micro-level with theories dealing with macro-evolutionary phenomena (Mayr and Provine, 1980). Here we need a whole new set of concepts which have some similarities with the concepts of the neo-Darwinian synthesis of evolutionary theory, genetics, and taxonomy – like 'isolating mechanisms', 'sympatric and allopatric speciation', 'founder principle', 'gene flow', 'isolate', 'stabilizing selection', 'taxon', and so on.

The economic analogies of all these concepts include a large degree of discontinuities and they might to some degree be inspired by Schumpeter.[16]

The potential fruitfulness of the Schumpeter–Marshall approach is not solely described by these grand issues. It can also serve as a starting point for the study of many problems of economic coordination. One set of these problems relates to standardization. As long as intermediate products are made as one of many production tasks within vertically integrated firms, there is no need for an economy-wide standard on how to perform the task. Thus a certain degree of heterogeneity with respect to the specification and costs is allowed to exist between the firms. When firms begin to specialize, this will disclose much of this heterogeneity. Standardization is an evolutionary process which includes a period with alternative proposals and incremental adaptations before the emergence of a standardized solution; later this solution might be challenged by product innovation. The basic characteristics of such a process can be characterized in relation to Smith's pin-making parable. Before inter-firm specialization of labour has taken place, each firm is free to choose its own way of fitting the results of the different tasks together. For instance, the necessary restriction for a feasible production process is mainly that pin heads and pin bodies fit together rather than that they individually have specified sizes. Thus each firm may have its own specification of pin heads. But as soon as pin-head producing firms starts to deliver to a customer, a problem emerges. Assuming that the pin-head specifications of the producer and the user differs, the pin-head

---

[16]. These formulations are an example of how an analogy can be used as a quick way of describing an idea. The same has been the case with respect to other uses of biological analogies by evolutionary-economic modellers. However, since there are so many possibilities to make analogies within the realm of economics and social sciences, the relation to biological metaphors are not a major issue. Most modellers do not emphasize the biological analogy although they exploit the tool-making performed in biology. They tend to agree with Schumpeter as well as Freeman (1992, p. 123) that an analogy may be a 'fertile source of new ideas and explanations' but 'it is important not to get carried away by evolutionary analogies and to mistake the analogy for the reality'. Often they use it more as a piece of pedagogics rather than as a guide for the modelling work. Even the one who contributed most to the analogy, Alchian, emphasized in his answer to Penrose's critique of his use of the analogy:

> The theory I presented stands independently of the biological analogy. ... In my original article every reference to the biological analogy was merely expository, designed to clarify the ideas of the theory. ... Readers of an earlier draft, containing no references to the biological similarity, urged that the analogy be included as helpful to the understanding of the basic approach. (Alchian, 1953, p. 601)

Similarly, Winter (1987) has tried to transcend the question of biological analogies. This is the reason why this part of Hodgson's challenge has not been directly confronted in the paper.

producer has to decide whether or not to reorganize his production. This problem will be more compelling when more customers are to be supplied. Either pin heads are to be produced in several batches or the new customers must be persuaded to accept the 'standardized' specifications of pin heads.

Another set of problems relates to product innovation. 'Product differentiation plays an important role in the histories of industries; to understand this fully, we need to admit more complexity to the demand side of markets in which our evolving firms operate' (Nelson and Winter, 1982, p. 408). Progress has been quite slow in this respect, although Gerybadze (1982, chapters 3–5) has made direct extensions of their model in this direction by studying the interaction of firms which sell and buy a certain type of product. The Schumpeter–Marshall model might change the situation. To do so, we shall be somewhat more precise in the definition of the quantity of intermediate products than we were when discussing standardization: the unit of an intermediate product is as equal to the amount of the product necessary for the production of a unit of final output. In other words, to produce one unit of final output, one unit of each of the intermediate products is necessary; only labour coefficients can be changed. An intermediate unit can, however, be of varying quality. A product innovation is a non-incremental change in the quality of an intermediate product. Such a product innovation implies that the buying of an intermediate product will not only substitute the labour previously engaged in the task(s) taken over by the intermediate producer but also some of the labour engaged in the task that uses the intermediate product. In this setting it is easy to define product innovation related to the producer and product innovation related to the user. An important coordination problem (formulated by, for example, Lundvall, 1992) emerges when the activities of the user are of potential importance for the producer's product innovation. One solution is to establish an innovative linkage between the two firms in a way which increases the productivity of the product-oriented R&D of the producer.

5 CONCLUSIONS

The starting point of the paper was Hodgson's criticism of the relationship between Schumpeter and 'neo-Schumpeterian' evolutionary modelling. The major conclusion from the analysis of different aspects of the relationship is that the invocation of Schumpeter's name by many modern evolutionary modellers is neither misleading nor mistaken. Although the relationship often appears to be based on a few Schumpeterian catchwords, there is deeper congruence. Like many modern modellers, Schumpeter emphasized the

conceptual and formal tools for expressing complex evolutionary processes, he preferred discrete to continuous change, he tried to introduce the evolutionary problems both in relation to standard economics and to a wealth of new ideas, and first and foremost he took the stand for the study of broad set of evolutionary processes at a time when the overwhelming viewpoint was that this was 'supremely intelligent after-dinner talk' (Lord Robbins, according to Elster, 1983, p. 112). For these and other reasons the relationship is likely to proceed for some time. However, if it continues to be based on a rather small set of topics taken from Schumpeter's most popular works, it cannot avoid decreasing returns. Therefore, a basic issue is whether and how the relationship can be renewed. The main suggestion of the paper is to develop a model which combines elements of the Schumpeterian model of evolution with elements of the Marshallian (and broader: the classical) model of evolution. This may look as 'localized search only in the near neighborhood of orthodoxy' (Mirowski, 1983, p. 766). But as it has been suggested above, such a localized search might lead to major novelties. It also helps to transcend Hodgson's taxonomic borderlines between different types of evolutionary theories.

REFERENCES

Alchian, A.A. (1950), 'Uncertainty, Evolution and Economic Theory', *Journal of Political Economy*, **58**, 211–21.

Alchian, A.A. (1953), 'Biological Analogies in the Theory of the Firm: Comment', *American Economic Review*, **43**, 599–603.

Andersen, E.S. (1992), 'The Difficult Jump From Walrasian to Schumpeterian Analysis', IKE Working Papers 78, Institute for Production, Aalborg University.

Andersen, E.S. (1993), 'Review of R. Swedberg: Schumpeter: A Biography', *Journal of Economic Literature*, **31**, 1969–70.

Andersen, E.S. (1994), *Evolutionary Economics: Post-Schumpeterian Contributions*, London: Pinter.

Andersen, E.S. (forthcoming), 'The Evolution of Economic Complexity: A Division-and-Coordination-of-Labour Approach', in E. Helmstädter and M. Perlman (eds), *Behavioral Norms, Technological Progress and Economic Dynamics: Studies in Schumpeterian Economics*, Michigan: Michigan University Press.

Andersen, E.S. and B.-Å. Lundvall (1995), 'National Innovation Systems and the Dynamics of the Division of Labour', paper presented at the third meeting of the Systems of Innovation Research Network, Söderköping Conference, 7–10 September 1995, Department of Business Studies, Aalborg University.

Augello, M.M. (1990), *Joseph Alois Schumpeter: A Reference Guide*, Berlin: Springer.

Böhm-Bawerk, E.v. (1921), *Positive Theorie des Kapitales. Zweite Abteilung, Erster Band von: Kapital und Kapitalzins*, 4th edn, Gustav Fischer, Jena.

Chiaromonte, F. and G. Dosi (1993), 'The Micro Foundations of Competitiveness and their Macroeconomic Implications', in D. Foray and C. Freeman (eds), *Technology and the Wealth of Nations: The Dynamics of Constructed Advantage*, London: Pinter, pp. 107–34.

Dahmén, E. (1991), *Development Blocks and Industrial Transformation: The Dahménian Approach to Economic Development*, ed. by B. Carlsson and R.G.H. Henriksson, Stockholm: Almquist & Wiksell.

Dosi, G. (1988), 'Sources, Procedures and Microeconomic Effects of Innovation', *Journal of Economic Literature*, **26**, 1120–71.

Dosi, G. (1990), 'Economic Change and Its Interpretation, or, Is There a "Schumpeterian Approach"?', in A. Heertje and M. Perlman (eds), *Evolving Technology and Market Structure: Studies in Schumpeterian Economics*, Ann Arbor, Mich.: University of Michigan Press, pp. 335–41.

Elster, J. (1983), *Explaining Technical Change: A Case Study in the Philosophy of Science*, Cambridge: Cambridge University Press.

Foss, N.J. (1991), 'The Suppression of Evolutionary Approaches in Economics: The Case of Marshall and Monopolistic Competition', *Methodus*, **3**, 65–72.

Freeman, C. (1990), 'Schumpeter's *Business Cycles* Revisited', in A. Heertje and M. Perlman (eds), *Evolving Technology and Market Structure: Studies in Schumpeterian Economics*, Ann Arbor, Mich.: University of Michigan Press, pp. 17–38.

Freeman, C. (1992), 'Innovation, Changes of Techno-Economic Paradigm and Biological Analogies in Economics', in C. Freeman (1992), *The Economics of Hope: Essays on Technical Change, Economic Growth and the Environment*, London: Pinter, pp. 121-42.

Gerybadze, A. (1982), *Innovation, Wettbewerb und Evolution: Eine mikro- und mesoökonomische Untersuchung des Anpassungsprozesses von Herstellern und Anwendern neuer Produzentengüter*, J.C.B. Mohr (Paul Siebeck), Tübingen.

Groenewegen, P. (1995), *A Soaring Eagle: Alfred Marshall 1842–1924*, Aldershot: Edward Elgar.

Hodgson, G.M. (1993), *Economics and Evolution: Bringing Life Back into Economics*, Cambridge: Polity.

Hodgson, G.M., W.J. Samuels and M.R. Tool (eds) (1994), *The Elgar Companion to Institutional and Evolutionary Economics*, Aldershot: Edward Elgar.

Kaldor, N. (1972), 'The Irrelevance of Equilibrium Economics', *Economic Journal*, **82**, 1237–55.

Kamien, M.I. and N.L. Schwarz (1982), *Market Structure and Innovation*, Cambridge: Cambridge University Press.

Kuhn, T.S. (1970), *The Structure of Scientific Revolutions*, 2nd edn, Chicago and London: University of Chicago Press.

Kwasnicki, W. (1992), *Knowledge, Innovation, and Economy: An Evolutionary Exploration*, Oficyna Wydawnicza Politechniki Wroclawskiej, Wroclaw (revised version will be published by Edward Elgar).

Lundvall, B.-Å. (1992), 'User-Producer Relationships, National Systems of Innovation and Internationalisation', in B.-Å. Lundvall (ed.), *National Systems of*

Innovation: Towards a Theory of Innovation and Interactive Learning, London: Pinter, pp. 45–67.

Marshall, A. (1898), 'Distribution and Exchange', *Economic Journal*, **8**, 37–59.

Marshall, A. (1919), *Industry and Trade: A Study of Industrial Technique and Business Organization; and their Influences on the Conditions of Various Classes and Nations*, 2nd edn, London: Macmillan.

Marshall, A. (1949), *Principles of Economics: An Introductory Volume*, reset version of 8th edn, Macmillan, Basingstoke and London.

Mayr, E. and W.B. Provine (eds) (1980), *The Evolutionary Synthesis: Perspectives on the Unification of Biology*, Cambridge, Mass. and London: Harvard University Press.

Mirowski, P. (1983), 'An Evolutionary Theory of Economic Change: A Review Article', *Journal of Economic Issues*, **17**, 757–68.

Nelson, R.R. (1994), 'Economic Growth via the Coevolution of Technology and Institutions', in L. Leydesdorff and P.v.d. Besselaar (eds), *Evolutionary Economics and Chaos Theory: New Directions in Technology Studies*, London: Pinter, pp. 21–32.

Nelson, R.R. (1995), 'Recent Evolutionary Theorizing about Economic Change', *Journal of Economic Literature*, **33**, 48–90.

Nelson, R.R. and S.G. Winter (1982), *An Evolutionary Theory of Economic Change*, Cambridge, Mass. and London: Belknap Press.

Nightingale, J. (1993), 'Solving Marshall's Problem with the Biological Analogy: Jack Downie's Competitive Approach', *History of Economics Review*, **20**, 75–94.

Rosenberg, N. (1982), *Inside the Black Box: Technology and Economics*, Cambridge: Cambridge University Press.

Rosenberg, N. (1986), 'Schumpeter and Marx: How Common a Vision?', in R.M. MacLeod (ed.), *Technology and the Human Prospect: Essays in Honour of Christopher Freeman*, Pinter, London and Wolfeboro, N.H., pp. 197–213.

Sanderson, S.K. (1990), *Social Evolutionism: A Critical History*, Cambridge, Mass. and Oxford: Basil Blackwell.

Scazzieri, R. (1993), *A Theory of Production: Tasks, Processes, and Technical Practices*, Oxford: Oxford University Press, Clarendon Press.

Schumpeter, J.A. (1908), *Das Wesen und der Hauptinhalt der theoretischen Nationalökonomie*, Leipzig: Duncker & Humblot.

Schumpeter, J.A. (1912), *Theorie der wirtschaftlichen Entwicklung*, Leipzig: Duncker and Humblot.

Schumpeter, J.A. (1926), *Theorie der wirtschaftlichen Entwicklung: Eine Untersuchung über Unternehmergewinn, Kapital, Kredit, Zins und den Konjunkturzyklus*, 2nd rev. edn, Munich and Leipzig: Duncker & Humblot.

Schumpeter, J.A. (1927), 'The Explanation of the Business Cycle', in J.A. Schumpeter (1951), pp. 21–46.

Schumpeter, J.A. (1928), 'The Instability of Capitalism', in J.A. Schumpeter (1951), pp. 47–72.

Schumpeter, J.A. (1932), 'Das Woher und Wohin unserer Wissenschaft: Abschiedsrede gehalten vor der Bonner staatswissenschaftlichen Fachschaft am

20. Juni 1932', in J.A. Schumpeter (1952), *Aufsätze zur ökonomischen Theorie*, (eds) E. Schneider and A. Spiethoff, J.C.B. Mohr (Paul Siebeck), Tübingen, pp. 598–608.

Schumpeter, J.A. (1933), 'The Common Sense of Econometrics', in J.A. Schumpeter (1951), pp. 100–107.

Schumpeter, J.A. (1934), *The Theory of Economic Development: An Inquiry into Profits, Capital, Credit, Interest and the Business Cycle*, London: Oxford University Press.

Schumpeter, J.A. (1939), *Business Cycles: A Theoretical, Historical, and Statistical Analysis of the Capitalist Process*, 2 vols, New York and London: McGraw-Hill.

Schumpeter, J.A. (1949), 'The Historical Approach to the Analysis of Business Cycles', in J.A. Schumpeter (1951), pp. 308–15.

Schumpeter, J.A. (1950), *Capitalism, Socialism and Democracy*, 3rd enlarged edn, New York: Harper.

Schumpeter, J.A. (1951), *Essays on Economic Topics*, ed. R.V. Clemence, Kennikat, Port Washington, New York.

Schumpeter, J.A. (1954), *History of Economic Analysis*, ed. E.B. Schumpeter, London: Allen and Unwin.

Silverberg, G., G. Dosi and L. Orsenigo (1988), 'Innovation, Diversity and Diffusion: A Self-Organization Model', *Economic Journal*, **98**, 1032–54.

Silverberg, G. and B. Verspagen (1994), 'Collective Learning, Innovation and Growth in a Boundedly Rational, Evolutionary World', *Journal of Evolutionary Economics*, **4**, 207–26.

Smith, A. (1976), *An Inquiry into the Nature and Causes of the Wealth of Nations*, 2 vols, ed. R.H. Cambell and A.S. Skinner, Oxford: Clarendon.

Smithies, A. (1951), 'Memorial: Joseph Alois Schumpeter, 1883–1950', in S.E. Harris (ed.), *Schumpeter: Social Scientist*, Cambridge, Mass.: Harvard University Press, pp. 11–23.

Sraffa, P. (1926), 'The Laws of Returns Under Competitive Conditions', *Economic Journal*, **36**, 535–50.

Stigler, G.J. (1951), 'The Division of Labour is Limited by the Extent of the Market', *Journal of Political Economy*, **59**, 185–93.

Swedberg, R. (1991), *Schumpeter: A Biography*, Princeton, N.J.: Princeton University Press.

Vassilakis, S. (1987), 'Increasing Returns to Scale', in J. Eatwell, M. Milgate and P. Newman (eds), *The New Palgrave: A Dictionary of Economics*, **2**, London and Basingstoke: Macmillan, 761–5.

Veblen, T. (1898), 'Why is Economics Not an Evolutionary Science?', *Quarterly Journal of Economics*, **12**, 373–97.

Veblen, T. (1899–1900), 'The Preconceptions of Economic Science, I–III', *Quarterly Journal of Economics*, **13–14**.

Winter, S.G. (1984), 'Schumpeterian Competition in Alternative Technological Regimes', *Journal of Economic Behavior and Organization*, **5**, 287–320.

Winter, S.G. (1987), 'Natural Selection and Evolution', in J. Eatwell, M. Milgate and P. Newman (eds), *The New Palgrave: A Dictionary of Economics*, **3**, London and Basingstoke: Macmillan, 614–7.

Witt, U. (ed.) (1993), *Evolutionary Economics*, Aldershot: Edward Elgar.

Wood, J.C. (ed.) (1991), *J.A. Schumpeter: Critical Assessments*, 4 vols, London and New York: Routledge.

Young, A.A. (1928), 'Increasing Returns and Economic Progress', *Economic Journal*, **38**, 527–42.

6. Economic Growth: An Evolutionary Perspective

Gerald Silverberg and Bart Verspagen

---

1 INTRODUCTION

Evolutionary thinking and economic growth would seem to be two subjects with a natural affinity. Yet historically, nothing could be further from the case. Formal growth theory of the Harrod–Domar sort arose as an attempt to dynamize the Keynesian model, while the Solovian full-employment alternative succeeded in making factor substitution a saving grace. Until the recent advent of endogenous growth theory, these early approaches have dominated all later thinking on the matter. But none of them, including endogenous growth theory in its various forms, bears the least resemblance to an evolutionary process.

While an evolutionary perspective has been urged upon economists since at least Marshall (1890; see Hodgson, 1993, for a recent reiteration), what has been lacking until recently, at least for a large portion of the economics profession, has been a body of formal theory and quantitative analysis on an explicitly evolutionary basis. This has changed since the work of Nelson and Winter in the 1960s and 1970s (summarized in Nelson and Winter, 1982), which operationalized and extended many of the concepts going back to Schumpeter (1919), Schumpeter (1947), Alchian (1950), Downie (1955), Steindl (1952), and others. Since then a number of authors have been enlarging on this foundation and systematically extending the evolutionary economics paradigm in a number of directions. A survey of some of these can be found in Nelson (1995).

In this chapter we intend to deal with the basics of a formal evolutionary approach to technical change, economic dynamics and growth. In so doing we will leave out for the most part the burgeoning new areas of application of evolutionary ideas to game theory, learning dynamics and bounded rationality, organization theory, financial markets, industrial organization, and the interface of economics, law and culture. Instead we will concentrate on a general discussion of evolution, growth and technical change, and the outcomes of a specific model of growth and dynamics, to see whether a viable alternative paradigm to the mainstream, neoclassical approach, as well as a new class of insights, are emerging.

There are essentially two reasons for believing that an evolutionary approach is applicable to economics. One is based on analogy and an appeal to the type of explanation common in biology: that forms of competition, innovation, variation and selection have analogues in the two subjects and thus that similar reasoning can profitably be applied in the nonbiological domain. Here most authors stress that the analogy should not be taken too seriously, so that it is useless to search for whatever corresponds exactly to genes, sexual reproduction, crossover or mutation in the economic sphere. Moreover, discredited forms of evolution such as Lamarckianism, the inheritance of acquired characteristics, may be perfectly conceivable in the socioeconomic realm.

The second takes a more universalist perspective. It argues that, just as biological evolution has passed through distinct stages (prokaryotic and eukaryotic life, asexual and sexual reproduction, as well as a prebiotic stage), so modern industrial society is just a distinct stage of this single process, subject to the same underlying laws if constrained by specific features of its current realization. Thus economic evolution would be an intrinsic component of a larger evolutionary process, and not merely something accidentally amenable to certain forms of reasoning by analogy.

What reasons might we have to believe this? Lotka (1924) proposed the concept of 'energy transformers' to capture the common thermodynamic features of all life forms. This is quite similar to what later was termed dissipative systems (Nicolis and Prigogine, 1977), that is, thermodynamically open systems, far from equilibrium, which maintain a high state of internal organization by importing free energy from their environment, consuming it for purposes of self-repair and self-reproduction, and exporting the resulting waste as high entropy back to the environment. Thus the apparent paradox of life, already pointed out by Henry Adams (1919), of complex structure emergence in the face of the Second Law of Thermodynamics (that in thermodynamically closed systems entropy, that is, disorder, must increase) is transcended.[1] Life (or at least carbon-based life as we know it until the industrial revolution) can be seen as a sea of such 'converters'

---

[1].   The observation that open systems (in particular, organisms) can seemingly circumvent the second law of thermodynamics by exporting entropy to the environment (or equivalently, importing 'negentropy' or free energy, that is, energy of a higher 'quality' than the ambient heat, which can be converted to mechanical work) goes back at least to Bertalanffy (1932) and Schrödinger (1945).

living off the waterfall of free energy flowing between the sun and the low-value infrared radiation reflected by the earth into deep space.[2]

From this perspective human civilization is distinguished from earlier forms of biological evolution by the fact that the information carriers of the self-organizing structures, rather than being encoded in a form like DNA internal to the organism, now have attained an *exosomatic*[3] (Lotka, 1945) form. Information is encoded both in an intangible sphere existing between human minds known as culture, and a more tangible sphere consisting of writing and other forms of representation, and cultural and industrial artefacts. But the fact remains that, within the constraints imposed by the various physical substrates of information storage and transmission, evolution still must proceed along the basic Darwinian lines of (random) variation and selection. The complication associated with modern socioeconomic evolution is that we now have to deal with a mosaic of simultaneous biological (DNA), culturally tacit (existing in the human psychomotoric systems of individuals and groups) and culturally codifiable (existing in exosomatic artefacts) information transmission and variation mechanisms, the latter category being increasingly machine based.

The task of an evolutionary theory of economic growth, then, might be to formulate a population dynamics of this multilevel evolutionary process, taking account both of the human components and of the increasingly sophisticated forms of artefactual energy and information transformers collectively referred to by economists in a rather undifferentiated manner as

---

[2]. 'Summarizing we may say that selforganization is necessarily connected with the possibility to export entropy to the external world. In other words, selforganizing systems need an input of high-valued energy and at the same time an output of low-valued energy. In the interior of selforganizing systems a depot of high-valued energy of another form is observed. The evolution processes on our planet are mainly pumped by the "photon mill" with the three levels sun–earth–background radiation (let us mention however that the geological processes are pumped by the temperature gradients between the centre of the earth and the surface). On the cosmic scale the general strategy of evolution is the formations of islands of order on a sea of disorder represented by the background radiation'. (Feistel and Ebeling, 1989, p. 91)

[3]. There is of course another level of *endosomatic* information processing based on the neuronal system of animals, which Edelman (1987) hypothesizes to function according to neuronal group selection. This allows organisms to learn from experience during their lifetimes, that is, a type of acquired characteristic with clear survival value. However, until the advent of language and culture, which permit *intergenerational* transmission, the neuronal system in itself cannot serve as a basis for long-term evolution but must still rely on the DNA substrate to generate further development.

capital.[4] But even if we agree that this more fundamental perspective on economics as an integral part of the evolutionary process has a certain validity, the 'genetic code' of the various non-DNA-based levels still remains to be discovered. Even in biology, in fact, where a firm understanding of the molecular basis of genetics has emerged since the 1950s, many extreme simplifications of a phenomenological sort still have to be made in formal models of population genetics and evolution.[5] Thus from a practical point of view it may not make much difference whether we apply evolutionary thinking to economics as an exercise in restrained analogizing or regard the economics of human societies as a specific stage in a universal evolutionary process, until such time as canonical descriptions of the 'genetic deep structure' of socioindustrial processes can be agreed upon.[6] For the time being we will have to do with more or less plausible and heroic assumptions about the entities and variation and transmission mechanisms implicated in economic evolution, and judge them on the basis of a limited range of micro and macroeconomic 'stylized facts'.

2 BEHAVIOURAL FOUNDATIONS AND FORMAL EVOLUTIONARY MODELLING IN THE ECONOMICS OF GROWTH AND SCHUMPETERIAN COMPETITION: SELECTION

Formalization of evolutionary thinking in biology began with Fisher (1930), who introduced what are now called replicator equations[7] to capture Darwin's notion of the survival of the fittest. If we consider a population to be composed of n distinct competing 'species' with associated, possibly frequency-dependent fitnesses $f_i(x)$, where x is the vector of relative

---

[4]. This is the theme of Boulding (1978) and Boulding (1981), without the author proceeding very far down the road of formal modelling, however.

[5]. Thus one often assumes asexual rather than sexual reproduction to simplify the mathematics.

[6]. One difference, however, is the central importance placed upon energetic and environmental constraints associated with the latter perspective. These, for better or worse, will not play any explicit role in the following discussion.

[7]. See Sigmund (1986) and Hofbauer and Sigmund (1988, pp. 145–6) for a discussion of their basic form and various applications.

frequencies of the species $(x_1, x_2, ..., x_n)$, then their evolution might be described by the following equations:

$$\dot{x}_i = x_i(f_i(x) - \bar{f}(x)), \ i = 1, ..., n, \ \text{with} \ \bar{f}(x) = \sum_{i=1}^{n} x_i f_i(x).$$

The intuition is simple: species with above-average fitness will expand in relative importance, those with below-average fitness will contract, while the average fitness $\bar{f}(x)$ in turn changes with the relative population weights. If the fitness functions f_i are simple constants, then it can be shown that the species with the highest fitness will displace all the others and that average fitness will increase monotonically until uniformity is achieved according to

$$\frac{d\bar{f}}{dt} = var(f) \geq 0,$$

where *var(f)* is the frequency-weighted variance of population fitness. Thus average fitness is dynamically maximized by the evolutionary process (mathematically, it is referred to as a Lyapunov function). This is known as Fisher's Fundamental Theorem of Natural Selection, but it should be noted that it is only valid for constant fitness functions. In the event of frequency-dependent selection, where fitness depends on population shares, including a species' own share, and increasing and decreasing 'returns' may intermingle, multiple equilibria are possible and no quantity is *a priori* necessarily being maximized (see Ebeling and Feistel, 1982, for an extensive discussion of maximal principles). The replicator equation only describes the relative share dynamics and thus takes place on the unit simplex S^n (where $\sum_{i=1}^{n} x_i = 1$), an $n-1$ dimensional space. To derive the absolute populations it is necessary to introduce an additional equation for the total population level. An alternative description due to Lotka and Volterra, which will be used in the model that we apply below, is based on growth equations for the population levels y_i (with the frequently used log-linear version on the right-hand side):

$$\dot{y}_i = g_i(y) = r_i y_i + \sum_{j=1}^{n} a_{ij} y_i y_j.$$

A theorem due to Hofbauer asserts that Lotka–Volterra and replicator systems are equivalent (see Hofbauer and Sigmund, 1988, p. 135).

Most evolutionary economics models to a considerable extent consist of giving the functions f_i or g_i economic meaning in terms of market competition or differential profit rate driven selection mechanisms. The former usually defines a variable representing 'product competitiveness', which may be a combination of price, quality, delivery delay, advertising

Economics and Evolution

and other variables (for examples see Silverberg, Dosi and Orsenigo, 1988 or Kwasnicki and Kwasnicka, 1992). The latter assumes that product quality and price are homogeneous between producers (or subject to fast equilibrating dynamics compared to the evolutionary processes of interest) but unit costs of production differ, so that firms realize differential profit rates. If their growth rates are related to profits, as seems reasonable, then their market shares or production levels (corresponding to x_i and y_i in the biological models) can be described by replicator or Lotka–Volterra equations, respectively.

The model we apply below, as most other growth models in the evolutionary tradition, focuses primarily on technical change as the central driving element of the evolutionary processes with which they are concerned. A major distinguishing characteristic is whether technology is 'capital embodied' or 'capital disembodied', that is, whether changes in technological performance are primarily (though not necessarily exclusively) related to investment in new equipment or not. In the former case technical change is highly constrained by investment in physical capital (as well as possible complementary factors); in the latter case it is not and can be almost costless. Yet even on the assumption of embodied technical change, there can be important differences in formal treatments. The classical approach to embodied technical change uses the 'vintage' concept going back to Salter (1960), Solow (1960) and Kaldor and Mirrlees (1962), as in essence do national statistical offices with the perpetual inventory approach to the measurement of the capital stock. One assumes that at any given time there is a single best-practice technology in which investment is made. The capital stock consists then of the vintages of past investment going back in time until the scrapping margin, that is, the moment when the oldest vintage is on the verge of being discarded due to technological obsolescence and/or wear and tear. This defines a technological lifetime of capital equipment.[8] The aggregate capital stock is a sum or integral (in the discrete and continuous time cases, respectively) over the vintages during this lifetime, and average technical coefficients (labour productivity, capital/output ratios) are the corresponding vintage-weighted sums or integrals. Vintage capital stock may be easy to compute from data, but they have two disadvantages which detract from their realism and tractability. First is the assumption of a single best-practice technology, which rules out multiple competing technologies at the investment frontier, a topic dear to the hearts of most

---

[8]. Except in the case in which capital is assumed to decay exponentially according to some presumed depreciation rate, in which case its lifetime is infinite, although older vintages rapidly become insignificant.

evolutionary economists and students of innovation diffusion. This can be overcome to some extent by assuming multiple, parallel vintage structures of distinct technologies, as in Silverberg, Dosi and Orsenigo (1988). The second is that, although particularly discrete-time vintage capital stocks can be easily calculated from data, when they are embedded in a dynamic framework with endogenous scrapping they can lead to awkward mathematical complications. Delay difference or differential equations and even age-structured population dynamics become involved whose mathematical properties, except under extremely simple assumptions, are still poorly understood compared to systems of ordinary difference or differential equations.

An alternative implicitly exploited in the model below, as well as in models by Metcalfe (1988), Iwai (1984a,b), Henkin and Polterovich (1991), Silverberg and Lehnert (1993, 1994), might be termed a 'quasi-vintage' framework. Capital 'vintages' are labelled by their type instead of their date of acquisition, so that the service age no longer plays any role, only the technical characteristics (although decay by type independently of age is still possible). Thus several qualitatively distinct technologies can diffuse simultaneously into and out of the capital stock. Furthermore, only ordinary differential (or difference) equations are needed to handle the quasi-vintage structure, a considerable mathematical simplification. This gain in realism and tractability is compensated for by an inability to track the vintages by chronological age, however. But quasi-vintages lend themselves more naturally to the kind of multiple replacement dynamics investigated by Marchetti and Nakicenovic (1979), Nakicenovic (1987), and Grübler (1990). And one view on evolution holds that its essence resides exactly in the sequence of such replacements (Montroll, 1978), whether related to technologies, behavioural patterns, or social structures.

The disembodied side of technical change (disembodied at least in the sense that it is not representable by tangible equipment) is still even more of a black box than the embodied side. It can reside in (tacit) human skills or organizational and societal capabilities, but little is known of a very fundamental nature about how it is accumulated, stored, and refreshed. 'Learning by doing' (Arrow, 1962) is a standard phenomenological approach finding expression in power laws for the relationship between productivity and cumulative investment or production. Recently, it has also become central to much of the neoclassical endogenous growth literature. The effects of technological spillovers between competitors have also received considerable attention. One possible way of combining learning by doing and spillovers in a dynamic framework is Silverberg, Dosi and Orsenigo (1988), but nothing along these lines has been attempted in an evolutionary growth model, to our knowledge. The net effect of both of these phenomena is usually one form or another of increasing returns, such as increasing returns to adoption or agglomeration, network externalities, and so on (see Arthur, 1988, 1994). Within the replicator framework this means that the fitness functions $f_i(x)$ truly depend on the frequencies x, resulting in multiple equilibria, threshold phenomena, lock-in, and so on.[9]

3 BEHAVIOURAL FOUNDATIONS AND FORMAL EVOLUTIONARY MODELLING IN THE ECONOMICS OF GROWTH AND SCHUMPETERIAN COMPETITION: INNOVATION AND LEARNING

Evolution would soon come to an end were it not for the continual creation of new variety on which selection (as well as drift) can act. This is especially crucial for growth models, where the ongoing nature of the technical change process is at the fore, although other aspects may well converge to stable stationary patterns. Thus considerable attention has to be devoted to how innovation is realized by firms, individually and collectively. In principle most scholars agree that innovation should be modelled stochastically, to reflect the uncertainty in the link between effort and outcome. The details on how this is done may vary considerably, however. The classical formulation is due to Nelson and Winter, who lump technologies and behavioural rules/strategies together under the concept of 'routines'. Since technical change is disembodied in their model, this equivalence is perhaps admissible, since a change in technique for a firm's entire capital stock requires only the expenditure necessary to undertake innovative or imitative search, not investment or training per se. While there is technological learning at the economy-wide level, firms themselves are completely unintelligent, since they operate according to given search and investment rules that cannot be modified as a result of experience. Instead, the firm is subject to selection as a consequence of the technologies it has stumbled upon. A somewhat peculiar aspect is the very literal application

---

[9].   The increasing returns phenomenon was studied by Arthur, Ermoliev and Kaniovski using the Polya urn stochastic tool, which assumes an indefinitely increasing population to establish asymptotic results. The alternative case of a fixed population size with stochastic effects can be studied using Master equation methods (see Feistel and Ebeling, 1989; Bruckner, Ebeling, Jiménez Montaño and Scharnhorst, 1994; and especially Jiménez Montaño and Ebeling, 1980, for a stochastic formulation of the Nelson and Winter model). We will only make limited use of stochastic tools in the following, so that the deterministic replicator equation will serve our purposes.

of Simon's notion of satisficing to mean that firms only undertake innovative search if their performance is unsatisfactory.[10]

An interesting elaboration of search activity and entry in the original Nelson and Winter model is presented in Winter (1984),[11] where firms are broken down into two types: primarily innovative or imitative. Further, the notion of 'technological regime' is introduced (going back to the early or later Schumpeter) depending on whether the source of technical progress is external to the firm (for example from publicly available scientific knowledge bases) or from firms' own accumulated technological capabilities. These regimes are referred to as the 'entrepreneurial' and the 'routinized' and are exogenously imposed by means of specific parameter settings. Although firms can be of two types, neither type is capable of learning. Instead, the market is shown to select between the two depending on the technological regime. Entry of new firms also assumes a greater importance than the mere supporting role to which it is relegated in most evolutionary models, being stimulated in the entrepreneurial regime.

While learning based on selection/mutation dynamics has begun to play a major role in the evolutionary games literature (for example Kandori, Mailath and Rob, 1993; Young, 1993), very little has found entrance into evolutionary models of a general economic orientation. A first stab at changing this state of affairs for the theory of growth was undertaken by Silverberg and Verspagen (1994a,b; 1995a; 1996), drawing on the evolution strategy literature (Schwefel, 1995). Here mutations are local around the current strategy, and the probability of imitation is an increasing function of dissatisfaction with current performance and the size of the imitated firm. In contrast to the Nelson and Winter tradition, strategies and technologies are treated separately. The learning algorithm applies only to the firms' R&D expenditure strategies; their technological performance then follows in a somewhat complex manner from these decisions and market feedbacks. In this way it is possible to implement simple boundedly rational decision rules gleaned from actual business practice, such as targeted R&D/total investment or R&D/sales ratios, or a combination of the two.

Genetic algorithms and classifier systems have also been gaining favour in recent years as mechanisms for operationalizing learning with artificial

---

[10]. This should be contrasted with the Silverberg and Verspagen models, where firms undertake behavioural 'imitation' with increasing probability the more unsatisfactory their performance is.

[11]. The discussion of the model is couched in terms of industry dynamics, not economy-wide growth, although there is nothing in the basic assumptions to preclude analysis of the latter.

agents.[12] Although these appeal even more directly to a discrete genetic mechanism of inheritance *à la* biological DNA than social scientists may feel comfortable with, they may also be employed agnostically simply as algorithmic tools to allow learning to happen, if not as models of how learning actually happens. The goal of an 'artificial economics' modelling philosophy as espoused by Lane (1993) is to put together a basic web of economic interactions between artificial agents endowed with a *tabula rasa* knowledge of their environment, but fairly sophisticated abilities to learn, and see what sorts of markets, institutions and technologies develop, with the modeller prejudicing the developmental possibilities as little as possible. Something along these lines has already been implemented to a certain extent in the 'sugarscape' model of Axtell and Epstein (1995), paralleling the artificial worlds movement in the biology domain (cf. Langton, 1989; Langton, Taylor, Farmer and Rasmussen, 1992). While this direction of research has generated much excitement, it has not avoided the fate of many over-hyped scientific trends in the form of a sceptical backlash (see Horgan, 1995).

4 THE MODEL

In the following, we will present the basic structure of a model which takes into account the elements of an evolutionary perspective on economic growth. Thus, the central elements of our model will be the formalization of selection, technical change and behavioural learning. To deal with these different aspects of the problem, we have constructed the model around three basic blocks. The first block describes how the artificial economy evolves with a given set of technologies and firms, with selection taking place at both levels. This block consists of equations for the rate of capital accumulation, the diffusion of new technologies in the total capital stock of the firms, and the real wage rate. The second block describes a set of rules that is used to introduce new technologies and firms into the economy. This block takes the behaviour of firms as given, and then describes the probability that individual firms will make an innovation, as well as how innovations are introduced. The third block describes how innovative behaviour changes under the influence of the evolution of the economy and firm learning. This block, in other words, describes a feedback from

---

[12]. See Booker, Goldberg and Holland (1989), and Goldberg (1989) for basic theory and methodology and Holland and Miller (1991), Kwasnicki and Kwasnicka (1992) and Lane (1993) for some economic applications.

performance to innovative behaviour and thus a form of collective learning. The parameters of the model and the values used in the simulations are summarized in the Appendix on page 166.

a. Selection in the Artificial Economy

The basic framework for selection in the model is a set of Lotka–Volterra equations, as in Silverberg and Lehnert (1993), which in turn draws on Silverberg (1984) and Goodwin (1967). Let hats above variables denote proportional growth rates, w be the (real) wage rate, v the employment rate (persons employed as a fraction of the labour force), and m and n parameters (both positive). Then the wage rate is determined by the following differential equation:

$$\hat{w} = -m + nv. \tag{6.1}$$

It is assumed that there is a fixed number q of firms in the economy, while each of these firms has a variable number p_q of different types of capital goods that it utilizes to produce a homogeneous product. New capital arises from the accumulation of profits, a process described by the following equation:

$$\hat{k}_{ij} = (1-\gamma_{1i})r_{ij} - \frac{\gamma_{2i}}{c} + \alpha(r_{ij}-r_i) - \sigma. \tag{6.2}$$

The capital stock is denoted by k, r stands for the profit rate, and σ is the exogenous rate of 'physical' depreciation of capital (technological obsolescence is an endogenous component of the model itself). The subscript i $(1,...,q)$ denotes the firm, and j $(1,...,p_q)$ the type of capital (the absence of any of these indices indicates an aggregation over this particular dimension). Equation (6.2) assumes that the principal source for type ij-capital accumulation is profits generated by ij-capital. This is modelled by the first term on the rhs of (6.2), that is, $(1-\gamma_i)r_{ij}$. A firm-specific portion of profits (denoted by γ_{1i}) plus a firm-specific portion of total output (sales; denoted by γ_{2i}) is used for the development of knowledge (R&D) (when $r_i<0$, γ_{1i} is set to zero).

However, profits may also be redistributed in such a way that more profitable types of capital accumulate even faster, less profitable even slower, than would otherwise be the case. The mechanism used to model this was first proposed by Soete and Turner (1984), and is represented by the second term on the rhs of equation (6.2). By changing the value of α, redistribution of profits takes place faster (larger α) or slower (smaller α).

It is assumed that each type of capital is characterized by fixed technical coefficients, c and a (for capital coefficient and labour productivity, respectively). The capital coefficient is assumed to be fixed throughout the economy (and time), while labour productivity is assumed to change under the influence of technical progress. The profit rate of ij-capital is then given by $(1-w/a_{ij})/c$.

The principal variable used to describe firm dynamics is the share of the labour force employed on each capital stock. Production is assumed to be always equal to production capacity (the influence of effective demand is absent), so that the amount of labour employed by each capital stock is equal to $k_{ij}/(a_{ij}c)$. Dividing this by the labour force (assumed to grow at a fixed rate β) gives the share of labour employed, v_{ij} (called the employment share hereafter). The expression for the growth rate of this variable is

$$\hat{v}_{ij} = \hat{k}_{ij} - \beta = (1-\gamma_i)r_{ij} - \frac{\gamma_{2i}}{c} + \alpha(r_{ij}-r_i) - (\beta+\sigma). \tag{6.3}$$

R&D also has an employment effect. We assume that the ratio between R&D expenditures and R&D labour input is equal to a fraction δ of the economy-wide labour productivity. The employment rate v_q resulting from production is then found by summing v_{ij} over i and j. Under these assumptions, it can then be shown that the overall employment rate v is equal to $(1+\delta(\gamma_1 rc+\gamma_2))v_q$.

Equations (6.1) and (6.3) together form a Lotka–Volterra system, and thus create a selection mechanism in our artificial economy. Equation (6.3) describes how more profitable (that is, with above-average labour productivity) technologies tend to increase their employment share, whereas more backward (below-average) technologies tend to vanish. The real Phillips curve equation (6.1) ensures that real wages tend to track labour productivity in the long run. In a situation in which new technologies are continually being introduced, this implies that all technologies, after an initial phase of market penetration and diffusion, will eventually vanish from the production system.

However, for a given set of technologies, long-run per capita growth is no longer possible once all firms converge to exclusive employment of the highest productivity technology. The next section outlines how new technologies can enter the system and thereby open up the possibility of long-run growth.

b. Introducing Technological Change

It is assumed that in each time period, firms devote resources (R&D) to the systematic search for new production possibilities (that is, new types of capital). The outcome of this search process is assumed to be stochastic.

The structure of the 'technological space' is assumed to be a simple directed graph (Figure 6.1). More complicated graphs could well be imagined with branching and even merging nodes; this remains a subject for future research.

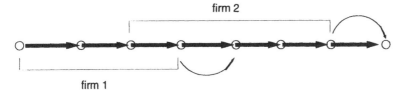

Figure 6.1   *The technology space. Firms' current capital stocks are bracketed, and their next innovations are shown by the circular arrows*

Each time an innovation occurs, the firm creates a new type of capital. The labour productivity of this type of capital is given by the following process:

$$a_{i,t}^{*} = (1+\tau)a_{i,t-1}^{*}, \tag{6.4}$$

where τ is the fixed proportional increase in labour productivity between innovations and $a_{i,t}^{*}$ is the firm-specific best practice labour productivity. The new type of capital is seeded with a small employment share (say 0.0001). In order to keep the total employment rate constant, this seed value is (proportionally) removed from the other types of capital of the innovating firm. The number of technologies employed by any given firm may vary in time.

As real wages rise over time, every technology will generate negative profits at some stage (because of its fixed labour productivity). It is assumed that these losses are financed by an equivalent decrease of the capital stock. In other words, losses imply that capital will be scrapped, and scrapped capital can be 'consumed' to cover the losses. Note that for individual capital stocks, the point at which scrapping occurs lies *prior* to the point where profits are negative, due to the α-related diffusion term in equation (6.2). When a technology's employment share falls below a specified (very small) value E, it is scrapped completely.

A firm's R&D activities as well as possibly those of its rivals enter an innovation potential function T_i. This in turn determines the firm's probability of making an innovation according to a Poisson process with arrival rate ρ_i. The simplest relation is simply linear:

$$\rho_i = AT_i + \rho_{min}, \tag{6.5}$$

where ρ_{min} is the (small) autonomous probability of making a fortuitous innovation without doing formal R&D, and A is the innovation function slope. One can also posit a nonlinear relationship with both increasing and decreasing returns to R&D, such as a logistic:

$$\rho_i = \frac{\rho_{min}\,\rho_{max}}{\rho_{min}+(\rho_{max}-\rho_{min})\,e^{-AT_i}}. \tag{6.6}$$

This logistic function has intercept ρ_{min} and (asymptotic) saturation level ρ_{max}. In this case, the parameter A determines the speed at which the saturation level is approached.

T_i, the innovation potential, is determined both by the firm's own R&D level (h_i, to be defined below) and its ability to profit from other firms' R&D (technological spillovers):

$$T_i = h_i + \phi_1 h + \phi_2 h h_i. \tag{6.7}$$

These spillovers can take two forms. First, there is a term related to the economy-wide value of h (written without subscript). The economy-wide R&D level h is defined to be the market share weighted average of firm-specific R&D levels. Second, there is a term related to the product of the economy-wide and the firm-specific value h_i. This latter term takes into account the argument that in order to assimilate spillovers, a firm has to have some technology-generating proficiency itself (see Cohen and Levinthal, 1989; Nelson, 1990). The parameters ϕ_1 and ϕ_2 determine the importance of each spillover mode.[13]

The firm-specific R&D level h_i is defined to be the ratio of a moving average of firm R&D investment to its total physical capital stock. A ratio is used to normalize for firm size, since otherwise such a strong positive feedback between R&D and firm growth exists that monopoly becomes inevitable. While *a priori* it is by no means clear why the size of individual R&D effort should not directly relate to innovative success, a pure scale effect must be ruled out by the continuing existence of competition and the ability of small countries to remain or even advance in the technology race. The exponential moving average RD_i on R&D for a lag of L (or a depreciation rate of $1/L$) is given by the following differential equation:

$$\frac{d}{dt}RD_i = ((\gamma_1 r_i + \gamma_2/c)k_i - RD_i)/L. \tag{6.8}$$

Hence the firm-specific R&D level is

---

13. Spillovers will not be dealt with in this paper. They are examined within the context of one-parameter strategies in Silverberg and Verspagen (1994a,b).

$$h_i = RD_i/k_i. \tag{6.9}$$

An innovation can be defined in a narrow or a wide sense. In the wide sense, the adoption of any technology not yet employed by a firm (or a country) is an innovation to that unit. In the narrow sense, only technologies that have never been employed before anywhere are considered innovations at their time of introduction. If firms innovate according to the above Poisson arrival rates in the narrow sense, however, a very considerable intertemporal externality is created, because firms' innovations always build on each other. Thus there can be no duplication of effort and, as long as firms maintain a minimal level of R&D, no cumulative falling behind. On the other hand, once an innovation has been introduced somewhere into the economy, it should be progressively easier for other firms to imitate or duplicate it; it should not be necessary to reinvent the wheel. We capture this by introducing a catching-up effect. Let the labour productivity of the economy-wide best practice technology be a^*, and the best practice technology of firm i a^*_i. Then firm i's innovation potential T_i will be augmented by a measure of its distance from the best practice frontier:

$$T_i' = T_i (1 + \kappa \ln(a^*/a_i^*)). \tag{6.10}$$

Thus, adopting an old innovation is facilitated for backward firms, but they are still required to invest in their technological capacity to reap these catchup benefits. Here, however, R&D efforts should be interpreted in the larger sense of technological training and licensing, reverse engineering, or even industrial espionage (all costly activities, if not as costly as doing state-of-the-art R&D).

We have also experimented with innovations in the narrow sense, but the results on strategic selection are rather ambiguous. This is not surprising, since the import of the intertemporal externality is indeed quite large. We consider the beginning in equation (6.10) therefore to be a justifiable first formulation, since technology adoption decisions are never passive, but rather require technological efforts of the adopting firm. However, it does place too much of the burden of catching up onto R&D.

In the artificial economy modelled here, entry of a new firm occurs only as a result of exit of an incumbent firm. Exit occurs whenever a firm's employment share (excluding its R&D employment) falls below a fixed level E. While exit of incumbent firms is completely endogenous, entry only occurs in case of exit, so that the total number of firms is constant. Naturally, this feature of the model is not very realistic, as in reality entry may be independent of exit and the total population of firms may vary. However, it is not the aim of this model to describe the phenomena of entry and exit as such. Instead, the main function of entry and exit is to maintain potential variety in the population of firms while providing for firm elimination.

Whenever entry occurs, the entrant is assigned a single technology with an amount of capital corresponding to an employment share of $2E$ (the remaining employment is proportionally removed from other firms so that total employment remains constant). The labour productivity of this technology is drawn uniformly from the range $[(1-b)A,(1+b)A]$, where A is the unweighted mean value of labour productivity of all the firms in the economy, and b is a parameter. The values for h and γ are (uniformly) drawn from the range existing in the economy at the time of entry.

c. Behaviour and Learning

In sections (a) and (b) we have outlined the system whereby innovating firms generate technical change and undergo selection in a closed economy model as a function of their R&D strategy parameters γ. Learning now enters the picture in the form of two 'genetic' operators, mutation and imitation. Thus 'behavioural evolution' takes place in a two-dimensional continuous space, where the economy at any given point in time is represented by a cloud of points (Figure 6.2).

With probability Π each decision period, which is set exogenously and is equal for all firms, a firm will draw from a normal distribution and alter one or both of its strategy parameters γ within the admissible range $[0,1]$ (mutation). Given that mutation occurs, each possibility (change either one or both parameters) occurs with equal probability:

$$\gamma_{1it}=Min(1,Max(\gamma_{1it-1}+\epsilon,0)), \quad \epsilon\sim N(0,s), \; or$$
$$\gamma_{2it}=Min(1,Max(\gamma_{2it-1}+\epsilon,0)), \quad \epsilon\sim N(0,s), \; or \qquad (6.11)$$
$$\gamma_{lit}=Min(1,Max(\gamma_{lit-1}+\epsilon_l,0)), \quad \epsilon_l\sim N(0,s), \quad l=1,2.$$

With variable probability Π^c_i the firm simply imitates the strategy of another firm. Again, given that imitation occurs, each possibility (imitate either one or both parameters) occurs with equal probability:

$$\gamma_{1it}=\gamma_{1jt-1}, \; j(\neq i)\in[1,...q]_i, \; or$$
$$\gamma_{2it}=\gamma_{2jt-1}, \; j(\neq i)\in[1,...q]_i, \; or \qquad (6.12)$$
$$\gamma_{lit}=\gamma_{ljt-1}, \; j(\neq i)\in[1,...q]_i, \; l=1,2.$$

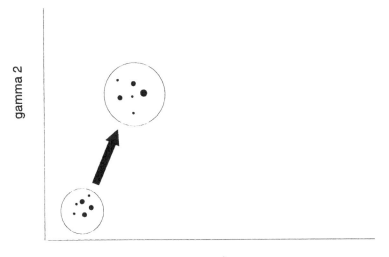

Figure 6.2   The space of behavioural evolution. A firm's strategy is represented as a point in a two-dimensional space whose diameter corresponds to the firm's market size. In the course of time the economy 'cloud' shifts through this space

The imitation probability is partly endogenous to reflect satisficing behaviour. Only firms with unsatisfactory rates of profit with respect to economy leaders will choose or be forced (for example by their stockholders or by hostile takeovers) to adopt the strategy of a competitor:

$$\Pi_i^c = \mu\left(1 - \frac{y_i - y_{\min}}{y_{\max} - y_{\min}}\right).$$ (6.13)

y_i is the firm's rate of expansion of physical capital (defined as $min(r_i - \gamma_{2i}/c,$ $(1-\gamma_i)r_i - \gamma_{2i}/c))$, $y_{\max}$ and $y_{\min}$ are the maximum and minimum values of y in the sample, and μ is the (exogenously determined) maximum imitation probability. Thus, the more profitable a firm is, the less likely it will change its strategy by imitating another firm. The most profitable firm has an imitation probability equal to zero; the least profitable the maximum probability μ. Once a firm has decided to imitate, it selects a firm to imitate randomly from the industry with weight equal to the target firm's market share in output. If neither imitation nor mutation occur, the firm simply retains its strategy from the previous period.

5 IDENTIFICATION OF STEADY STATES BY RANDOM AND SPONTANEOUS GENERATION

The model has been implemented to run on both MS-DOS and Unix computers. To make the solution as time-step invariant as possible, the selection mechanism, which is basically a system of differential equations, is solved using a fixed-step, fourth-order Runge–Kutta algorithm. The innovation decisions are executed during each computational step (using Poisson arrival rates scaled by the computation time step), and when an innovation is made, the corresponding changes in initial conditions, number of equations, and coefficients are made for the next step. Mutation and imitation are only performed at fixed intervals of one 'year', which may be many times the step employed in the Runge–Kutta algorithm.

In investigating the model, rather than simply presenting one or several simulation outcomes, we wish to focus on the question, which outcomes are robust features of the model? In other words, which outcomes are due to systematic underlying relationships in the model, and which are simply due to contingencies and random factors in the simulation?[14] To this end, we will perform multiple simulation experiments, with different randomizations for identical parameter sets, in order to explore the impact of stochastic factors, as well as 'step through' the key parameters to explore the impact of parameter variations. The results of these simulation experiments will be presented in the form of observed distributions of the relevant variables in the model.

The main feature of the model we will investigate in this way is the existence and nature of an 'evolutionary attractor' in the dynamics, that is, whether a 'stable' configuration of firm R&D strategies exists to which our artificial economy will converge from particular classes of initial conditions. We have initialized the system in two ways: first in a 'grapeshot' mode we term 'random generation' in which the initial γs are drawn from a uniform distribution over [0,1] and [0,0.2] (respectively for γ_1 and γ_2); and second, in a 'spontaneous generation' mode in which all initial γs are set to zero. We present the results of these experiments by means of density plots made on the basis of 3-dimensional histograms of the two γs. On the horizontal axis we plot the experimental parameter that is being varied through different simulation runs (A or μ). The (market share weighted) mean value of the strategy parameter over the firms in each run is shown on the vertical axis. The data are pooled from the last 1000 'years' of five

---

[14]. See Silverberg and Verspagen (1997, forthcoming) for a more detailed discussion of the dual role of 'chance' and 'necessity' in economic evolution.

simulation runs for each value of the experimental parameter, each generated with a different random seed. Darker shading indicates higher frequencies.

In Figure 6.3 (page 156) we plot the results for the runs initialized by random generation. The figure shows clearly that the converging behaviour of the two strategy parameters is quite different. Parameter 1 (the targeted R&D to profits ratio) does not converge very clearly, except for higher values of the innovation slope, when relatively high frequencies are found at values near zero. Parameter 2 targeting R&D to sales shows a more tight convergence, although there are still high frequencies near zero (the white band between the horizontal axis and the attractor is quite narrow). Thus, firms show a tendency to select a relatively tight range of values for parameter 2, while parameter 1 tends to drift or, if anything, go to zero. Summarizing, firms seem to display a tendency to select tightly defined strategies based upon parameter 2 and indifference to 1.

Figure 6.4 (page 157) shows corresponding results for the case of spontaneous generation, that is, a situation in which firms have to discover R&D as an activity. In this case, the economy starts out in a stagnant phase, with no intentional technical progress. As firms explore the strategy space by mutation and imitation, they may (or may not) find R&D a useful activity. The density plots show that in this case, the evolutionary attractor is much more clearly defined. The type 1 strategy parameter remains at values near zero (in our interpretation, the positive values found are largely attributable to random 'evolutionary' noise). The type 2 strategy parameter, however, shows a well-defined peak significantly distant from zero, as indicated by the white space bordering it from below.

This behaviour of the system can be interpreted as a particular form of lock-in or path dependency. When the system is started 'clean', without any form of 'commitment' to any type of R&D strategy, it will select a much more unambiguous evolutionary attractor than in the random generation case. This is not the case when only the type 1 strategy parameter is employed (compare Silverberg and Verspagen, 1994a,b). There the asymptotic steady states of the two initializations are identical.

For a logistic innovation function (equation [6.6]) we obtain similar patterns from the histograms over innovation opportunity (Figure 6.5, page 158). In contrast to the linear case, however, the steady-state value of parameter 2 does seem to decline somewhat with increasing technological opportunity. What is also remarkable is the sudden collapse of the technological regime below values of A of about 40. The steady-state values of parameter 2, in the range 20–30 per cent, are also higher than in the linear case.

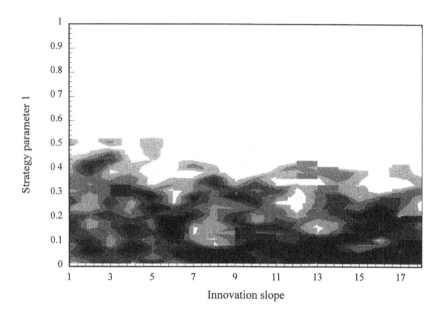

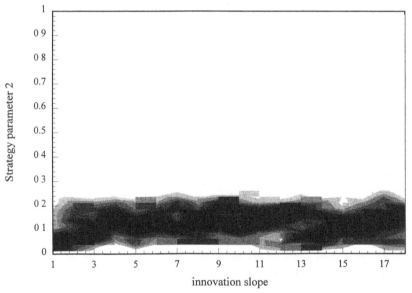

Figure 6.3   Density plots of strategy parameters from pooled data of five
runs per value, last 1000 years of 8000 year runs (random
generation), for a linear innovation function

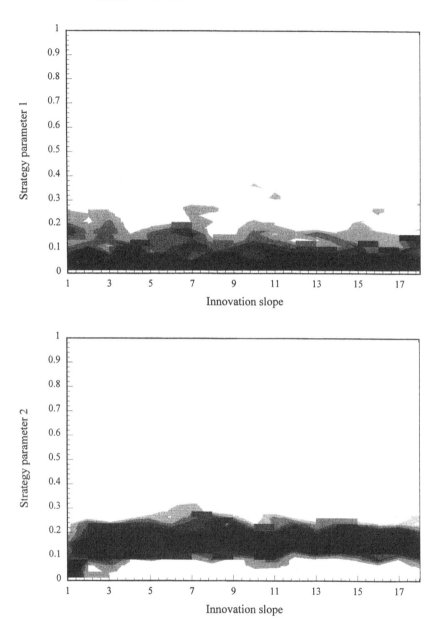

Figure 6.4   Density plots of strategy parameters from pooled data of five runs per value, last 1000 years of 8000 year runs (spontaneous generation), for a linear innovation function

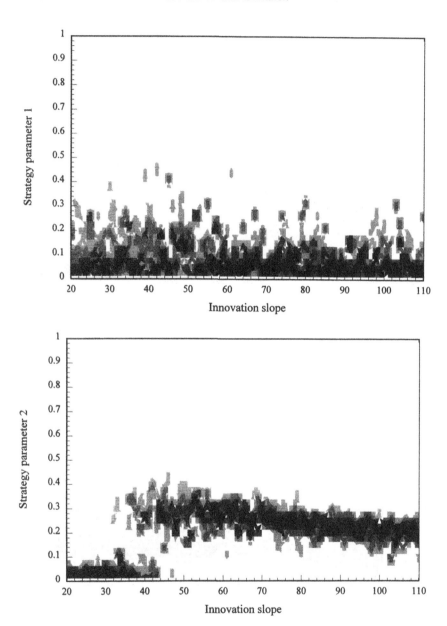

*Figure 6.5   Density plots of strategy parameters from pooled data of five
runs per value, last 1000 years of 8000 year runs (spontaneous
generation), for a logistic innovation function*

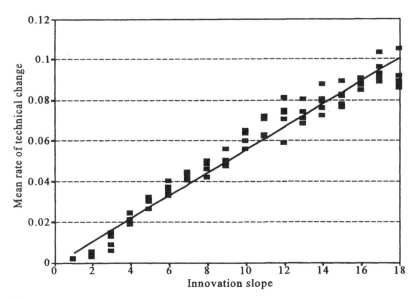

Figure 6.6   *The rate of technical change is an increasing function of the innovation slope (A = 10, 50 firms, spontaneous generation)*

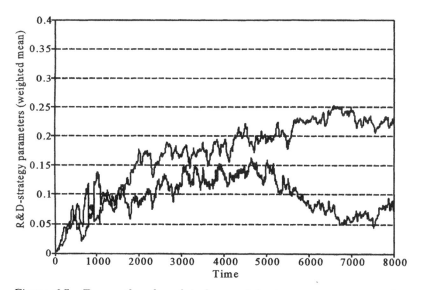

Figure 6.7   *Time paths of market share-weighted-strategy parameters in a spontaneous generation run (50 firms, $\tau = 0.04$). The light line is γ_1, the heavy line is γ_2*

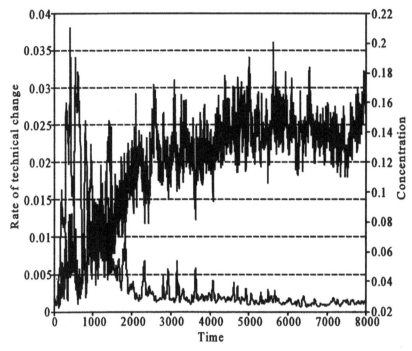

Figure 6.8   Time paths of rate of technical change (light line) and Herfindahl index of concentration (heavy line) for the same run as in Figure 6.5

Why is strategy parameter 2 subject to positive selection, while parameter 1 displays either drift or is constrained to zero? Our interpretation is that R&D comes to be regarded as a 'core' business activity in the model, for, due to the 'Goodwin' business cycles of the underlying economy, profits are more variable than sales. Thus, firms which base their R&D expenditures upon profits will have more fluctuating R&D stocks than firms which base their R&D on sales. The selection environment seems to favour the latter firms because, in the long run, their R&D behaviour provides a more reliable stream of innovations.

Whereas the steady-state values of the strategy parameters do not appear to depend on technological opportunity, as represented by the value of A,[15] the rate of technical change is a simple linearly increasing function of it

---

[15]. This is not true when only parameter 1 is used. In this case, the value gradually *falls* with increasing A.

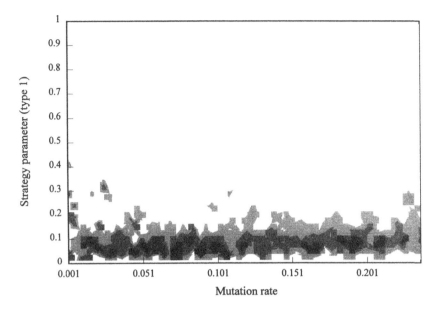

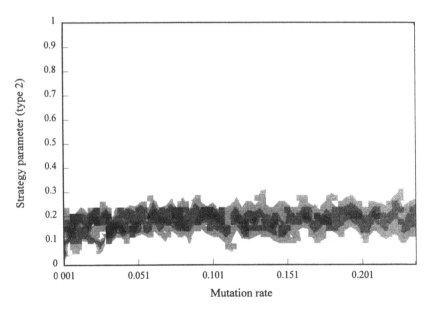

Figure 6.9 Density plots of strategy parameters for varying rates of the mutation probability (A = 10)

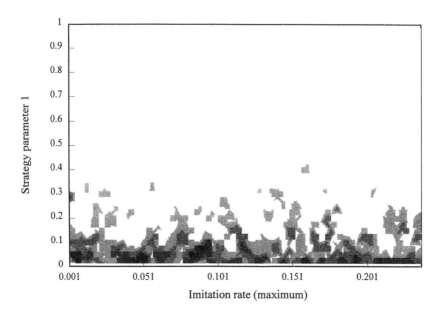

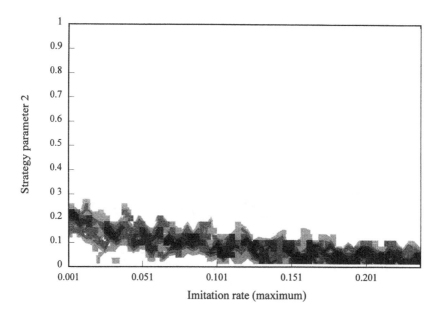

Figure 6.10 Density plots of strategy parameter for varying rates of the maximum imitation parameter (A = 10)

(Figure 6.6, page 159). The transient time paths in the spontaneous generation case on the way to a growth steady-state are also of interest in themselves. Figure 6.7 (page 159) displays the market-share-weighted values of the two strategy parameters for a single run over 8000 years. Convergence is relatively rapid in comparison with the single parameter case. Figure 6.8 (page 160) shows the time paths of the rate of technical change and the Herfindahl concentration index.[16] Viewed as a process in historical time and not just as out-of-equilibrium transient, this figure recapitulates a piece of virtual economic history. The economy starts off with no R&D and an essentially vanishing rate of technical change. Within this regime the rate of market concentration is quite high, although the identity of the near monopolist changes at almost regular intervals, as indicated by the breaks in the level of concentration. As the γs rise with time and with them the overall rate of technical change, this market regime breaks down. It is replaced by low levels of concentration and considerable market turnover.

We have also begun to investigate how the structure of the evolutionary learning process affects the outcomes of these experiments. Recall that the variables Π and μ, representing the probability of mutation and imitation, are exogenously imposed. We have compiled histograms for the two strategy parameters by varying each of these rates separately. Figure 6.9 (page 161) shows the results for mutation, Figure 6.10 (page 162) for imitation, for runs with $A = 10$ and random generation initial conditions. Varying the mutation probability does not change the picture in any essential way. In contrast, increasing the ceiling on the imitation probability leads to a progressive collapse of γ_2 selection. If firms imitate each other too strongly, they become involved in an evolutionary game of musical chairs, and no nontrivial strategy is able to establish itself.

6 DISCUSSION AND CONCLUSIONS

In this paper we have developed an evolutionary model describing the relation between endogenous technological change and economic growth along the lines of an evolutionary modelling philosophy. By this we mean that the economy is disaggregated into diverse individual behavioural subunits (instead of the representative agent so prevalent in most macroeconomic modelling) connected by nontrivial nonlinear dynamic

---

[16]. This is defined as $H = \Sigma f_i^2$, where f_i is the market share of the ith firm. It ranges from $1/n$, for n equally sized firms, to 1, for complete monopoly.

interactions based on plausible notions of disequilibrium competition and investment. Rather than search for a strategic equilibrium based on a concept of rationality, we have assumed that these agents use boundedly rational behavioural procedures. In the present case this is an extremely simple rule for the R&D/profits (or gross investment) and R&D/sales ratios, which is parameterized by two real numbers between 0 and 1. Learning is modelled by allowing for mutation and imitation rules operating on the agents's strategy parameters. An element of behavioural realism is injected into the model by insisting that mutations are local in the strategic 'genotype' space, and that imitation is only prompted by less than satisfactory performance.

Using both a linear and a logistic innovation function we were able to show that evolutionary steady states exist that are attractive in the behavioural space, but may differ depending on 'history'. Thus the model does establish a case for endogenous growth in the sense of demonstrating that economic competition, even with very relaxed   assumptions about individual goal-seeking behaviour and profit maximization, leads to an approximately steady-state growth path with a positive rate of technical change and R&D investment.

However, the spontaneous generation experiments underline the fact that the mere existence of such a steady state does not mean that history does not matter. Quite the contrary. A society starting with no or low rates of R&D will pass through a phase of very high market concentration, but with periodic upheavals or 'palace revolts' of market leadership on a time scale of centuries. Eventually such an economy will 'bootstrap' itself to higher rates of R&D and technical change.[17]

In many evolutionary growth models found in the literature (for example Dosi et al., 1994; Chiaromonte and Dosi, 1993; Nelson and Winter, 1982) one implication of modelling technological change stochastically is that a wide range of 'economic histories' is possible, some of which seem to be compatible with the 'stylized facts' of actual empirical observations. While these results are often used to justify a 'minimalist' position that an evolutionary theory can explain the phenomena explained by mainstream theory but with a more realistic (Nelson, 1995, p. 67) microeconomic foundation, we wish to argue that evolutionary theory would have to be more precise on the possible range of outcomes it predicts. For example, in the model outlined in this paper, we asked the question under what

---

[17]. This should be compared with the one-parameter strategy case, where the evolution is slower and passes through at least three distinct historical phases.

circumstances a fairly 'narrow' band of outcomes exists, in the sense of a small range of values for our 'strategy parameters'.

Such an approach admittedly does not help us much in understanding specific events in economic history. It does not give us an answer to the question why a 'takeoff' of the strategy parameters (or its possible counterpart in reality, the industrial revolution) takes place at a given point of time. However, given the argument of evolutionary theory that clearcut monocausal mechanisms explaining phenomena like these do not exist, the further development of methods like the one applied here could provide a powerful analytical tool, which would take the field a step further than the currently available results. In order to stimulate other contributors to the evolutionary debate to take a similar perspective in the future, further work on methodological issues, such as the status of simulation experiments relative to analytical results, or the statistical evaluation of results generated by computer simulations, is obviously required.

Although we do not wish to overburden our simple model with historical interpretations, it would be unfortunate to restrict the concept of endogenous growth to steady-state growth paths with no real structural development, social learning, and historical contingency. For this reason an evolutionary approach like the one proposed here, appears to offer an attractive alternative explanation of how an economy can 'bootstrap' itself in historical time through a succession of growth phases and market structures. The concepts of growth or development stages, takeoffs and changes of regime were prominent in a classical line of thought associated with Marx, Schumpeter and later Rostow. The criticism that these theories smacked of rigid mechanistic determinism is overcome by the artificial worlds methodology, which demonstrates that reversions, variable delays, and path dependence resulting from underlying stochasticity and nonlinearity cannot be excluded. Needless to say, such a broad and differentiated perspective on economic growth has mostly fallen by the wayside in the postwar literature on growth and development (cf. Rostow, 1990).

Our model also demonstrates that a bounded rationality approach to the theory of the firm, coupled with an evolutionary framework for analysing market selection and collective learning, does yield dividends both in terms of explaining how identifiable patterns of behaviour emerge from 'profit-seeking' rather than completely rational 'profit-maximizing' assumptions, and how market structures and growth regimes may be simultaneously endogenized. We believe that the apparent inconvenience of bounded rationality and an artificial worlds, computer-based modelling strategy, is more than outweighed by the ability to go far beyond the mere reproduction of conventional wisdom and open up a range of phenomena and relationships to theoretical and quantitative empirical study that historians have repeatedly emphasized but economists have for the most part ignored.

APPENDIX

A summary of the parameters and the values employed in the runs analysed in the paper is presented below.

$q = 10$	number of firms
$m = 0.9$	parameter of the Phillips curve eq. 6.1
$n = 1$	parameter of the Phillips curve eq. 6.1
$\alpha = 1$	Soete–Turner coefficient eq. 6.2
γ (endogenous)	R&D/investment ratio in eq. 6.2
$c = 3$	capital–output ratio
$\sigma = 0$	rate of physical depreciation in eqs. 6.2 and 6.3
$\beta = 0.01$	rate of growth of labour force eq. 6.3
$\delta = 1$	ratio of productivity in goods and R&D sectors
$\tau = 0.06$	proportional jump in labour productivity eq. 6.4
A (variable)	innovation slope in eq. 6.5
$\rho_{min} = 0.01$	autonomous rate of innovation eq. 6.5
ϕ_1 (variable)	type 1 spillover coefficient in eq. 6.7
ϕ_2 (variable)	type 2 spillover coefficient in eq. 6.7
$L = 5$	lag for R&D moving average eq. 6.8
$\kappa = 4$	catch-up parameter eq. 6.10
$\Pi = 0.02$	mutation probability eq. 6.11
$s = 0.02$	standard deviation of mutation step size eq. 6.11
$\mu = 0.02$	maximum imitation probability eq. 6.12
$E = 0.005$	exit level in employment share
$b = 0.1$	labour productivity bandwidth for entrants

REFERENCES

Adams, H. (1919/1969), *The Degradation of the Democratic Dogma*, New York: Harper & Row.

Alchian, A.A. (1950), 'Uncertainty, Evolution, and Economic Theory', *Journal of Political Economy*, **58**, 211–22.

Arrow, K. (1962), 'The Economic Implications of Learning by Doing', *Review of Economic Studies*, **29**, 155–73.

Arthur, W.B. (1988), 'Self-Reinforcing Mechanisms in Economics', in P.W. Anderson, K.J. Arrow and D. Pines (eds), *The Economy as an Evolving Complex System*, Reading, Mass.: Addison-Wesley.

Arthur, W.B. (1994), *Increasing Returns and Path Dependence in the Economy*, Ann Arbor, MI: University of Michigan Press.

Axtell, R. and J. Epstein (1995), 'Agent-Based Modeling: Understanding Our Creations', *Bulletin of the Santa Fe Institute*, Santa Fe, NM, Winter, 28–32.

Bertalanffy, L.v. (1932), *Theoretische Biologie*, 1, Berlin: Borntraeger.

Booker, L., D. Goldberg and J. Holland (1989), 'Classifier Systems and Genetic Algorithms', in J. Carbonell (ed.), *Machine Learning: Paradigms and Methods*, Cambridge, MA: MIT Press.

Boulding, K.E. (1978), *Ecodynamics: A New Theory of Societal Evolution*, Beverly Hills and London: Sage.

Boulding, K.E. (1981), *Evolutionary Economics*, Beverly Hills and London: Sage.

Bruckner, E., W. Ebeling, M.A. Jiménez Montaño and A. Scharnhorst (1994), 'Hyperselection and Innovation Described by a Stochastic Model of Technological Evolution', in L. Leydesdorff and P. van den Besselaar (eds), *Evolutionary Economics and Chaos Theory*, London: Pinter.

Chiaromonte, F. and G. Dosi (1993), 'Heterogeneity, competition, and macroeconomic dynamics', *Structural Change and Economic Dynamics*, 4, 39–63.

Cohen, W.M. and D.A. Levinthal (1989), 'Innovation and Learning: The Two Faces of R&D', *Economic Journal*, 99, 569–96.

Dosi, G., S. Fabiani, R. Aversi and M. Meacci (1994), 'The Dynamics of International Differentiation: A Multi-Country Evolutionary Model', *Industrial and Corporate Change*, 3, 225–41.

Downie, J. (1955), *The Competitive Process*, London: Duckworth.

Ebeling, W. and R. Feistel (1982), *Physik der Selbstorganisation und Evolution*, Berlin: Akademie Verlag.

Edelman, G.M. (1987), *Neural Darwinism: The Theory of Neuronal Group Selection*, New York: Basic Books.

Feistel, R. and W. Ebeling (1989), *Evolution of Complex Systems*, Berlin: VEB Deutscher Verlag der Wissenschaften.

Fisher, R.A. (1930), *The Genetical Theory of Natural Selection*, Oxford: Clarendon Press.

Goldberg, D. (1989), *Genetic Algorithms in Search, Optimization, and Machine Learning*, Reading MA: Addison-Wesley.

Goodwin, R.M. (1967), 'A Growth Cycle', in C.H. Feinstein (ed.), *Socialism, Capitalism and Economic Growth*, London: Macmillan.

Grübler, A. (1990), *The Rise and Decline of Infrastructures. Dynamics of Evolution and Technological Change in Transport*, Heidelberg: Physica-Verlag.

Henkin, G.M. and V.M. Polterovich (1991), 'Schumpeterian Dynamics as a Non-linear Wave Theory', *Journal of Mathematical Economics*, 20, 551–90.

Hodgson, G. (1993), *Economics and Evolution: Bringing Back Life into Economics*, Ann Arbor, MI: University of Michigan Press.

Hofbauer, J. and K. Sigmund (1988), *The Theory of Evolution and Dynamical Systems*, Cambridge: Cambridge University Press.

Holland, J.H. and J.H. Miller (1991), 'Artifical Adaptive Agents in Economic Theory', *American Economic Review Papers and Proceedings*, 81, 363–70.

Horgan, J. (1995), 'From Complexity to Perplexity', *Scientific American*, June 1995, 74–9.

Iwai, K. (1984a), 'Schumpeterian Dynamics. I: An Evolutionary Model of Innovation and Imitation ', *Journal of Economic Behavior and Organization*, **5**, 159–90.

Iwai, K. (1984b), 'Schumpeterian Dynamics. II: Technological Progress, Firm Growth and "Economic Selection"', *Journal of Economic Behavior and Organization*, **5**, 321–51.

Jiménez Montaño, M.A. and W. Ebeling (1980), 'A Stochastic Evolutionary Model of Technological Change', *Collective Phenomena*, **3**, 107–14.

Kaldor, N. and J.A. Mirrlees (1962), 'A New Model of Economic Growth', *Review of Economic Studies*, **29**, 174–92.

Kandori, M., G.J. Mailath and R. Rob (1993), 'Learning, Mutations, and Long Run Equilibrium in Games', *Econometrica*, **61**(1), 29–56.

Kwasnicki, W. and H. Kwasnicka (1992), 'Market, Innovation, Competition: An Evolutionary Model of Industrial Dynamics', *Journal of Economic Behavior and Organization*, **19**, 343–68.

Lane, D.A. (1993), 'Artificial Worlds and Economics. Parts 1 and 2', *Journal of Evolutionary Economics*, 3(2&3), 89–108, 177–97.

Langton, C.G. (ed.) (1989), *Artificial Life*, Redwood City, CA: Addison-Wesley.

Langton, C.G., C. Taylor, J.D. Farmer and S. Rasmussen (eds) (1992), *Artificial Life II*, Redwood City, CA: Addison-Wesley.

Lotka, A.J. (1924/1956), *Elements of Mathematical Biology*, New York: Dover.

Lotka, A.J. (1945), 'The Law of Evolution as a Maximal Principle', *Human Biology*, **17**, 167–94.

Marchetti, C. and N. Nakicenovic (1979), *The Dynamics of Energy Systems and the Logistic Substitution Model*, Research Report RR-79-13, Laxenburg, Austria: IIASA.

Marshall, A. (1890), *Principles of Economics*, London: Macmillan.

Metcalfe, J.S. (1988), 'Trade, Technology and Evolutionary Change', University of Manchester, mimeo.

Montroll, E.W. (1978), 'Social Dynamics and the Quantifying of Social Forces', *Proceedings of the National Academy of Sciences, USA*, **75**, 4633–7.

Nakicenovic, N. (1987), 'Technological Substitution and Long Waves in the USA', in T. Vasko (ed.), *The Long-Wave Debate*, Berlin: Springer-Verlag.

Nelson, R.R. (1990), 'What is Public and What is Private about Technology?', Berkeley: CCC Working Paper No. 90–9.

Nelson, R.R. (1995), 'Recent Evolutionary Theorizing About Economic Change', *Journal of Economic Literature*, **33**, 48–90.

Nelson, R.R. and S.G. Winter (1982), *An Evolutionary Theory of Economic Change*, Cambridge MA: The Belknap Press of Harvard University Press.

Nicolis, G. and I. Prigogine (1977), *Self-Organization in Non-Equilibrium Systems*, New York: Wiley-Interscience.

Rostow, W.W. (1990), *Theorists of Economic Growth*, Oxford: Oxford University Press.

Salter, W. (1960), *Productivity and Technical Change*, Cambridge: Cambridge University Press.

Schrödinger, E. (1945), *What is Life? The Physical Aspect of the Living Cell*, Cambridge: Cambridge University Press.

Schumpeter, J. (1919/1934), *Theorie der wirtschaftlichen Entwicklung*, English translation, *The Theory of Economic Development*, Cambridge, MA: Harvard University Press.

Schumpeter, J. (1947), *Capitalism, Socialism, and Democracy*, New York: Harper.

Schwefel, H.P. (1995), *Evolution and Optimum Seeking*, New York: Wiley

Sigmund, K. (1986), 'A Survey of Replicator Equations', in J.L. Casti and A. Karlqvist (eds), *Complexity, Language and Life: Mathematical Approaches*, Berlin, Heidelberg, New York and Tokyo: Springer-Verlag.

Silverberg, G. (1984), 'Embodied Technical Progress in a Dynamic Economic Model: the Self-Organization Paradigm', in R. Goodwin, M. Krüger and A. Vercelli (ed.), *Nonlinear Models of Fluctuating Growth*, Berlin, Heidelberg, New York: Springer Verlag.

Silverberg, G., G. Dosi and L. Orsenigo (1988), 'Innovation, Diversity and Diffusion: A Self-Organisation Model', *Economic Journal*, **98**, 1032–54.

Silverberg, G. and D. Lehnert (1993), 'Long Waves and "Evolutionary Chaos" in a Simple Schumpeterian Model of Embodied Technical Change', *Structural Change and Economic Dynamics*, **4**, 9–37.

Silverberg, G. and D. Lehnert (1994), 'Growth Fluctuations in an Evolutionary Model of Creative Destruction', in G. Silverberg and L. Soete (eds), *The Economics of Growth and Technical Change: Technologies, Nations, Agents*, Aldershot: Edward Elgar.

Silverberg, G. and B. Verspagen (1994a), 'Learning, Innovation and Economic Growth: A Long-Run Model of Industrial Dynamics', *Industrial and Corporate Change*, **3**, 199–223.

Silverberg, G. and B. Verspagen (1994b), 'Collective Learning, Innovation and Growth in a Boundedly Rational, Evolutionary World', *Journal of Evolutionary Economics*, **4**, 207–26.

Silverberg, G. and B. Verspagen (1995a), 'An Evolutionary Model of Long Term Cyclical Variations of Catching Up and Falling Behind', *Journal of Evolutionary Economics*, **5**, 209–27.

Silverberg, G. and B. Verspagen (1996), 'From the Artificial to the Endogenous: Modelling Evolutionary Adaptation and Economic Growth', in E. Helmstädter and M. Perlman (eds), *Behavioral Norms, Technological Progress and Economic Dynamics*, Ann Arbor, MI: University of Michigan Press, pp. 331-54.

Silverberg, G. and B. Verspagen (1997) (forthcoming), 'Evolutionary Theorizing on Economic Growth', in K. Dopfer (ed.), *The Evolutionary Principles of Economics*, Norwell, MA: Kluwer Academic Publishers.

Soete, L. and R. Turner (1984), 'Technology Diffusion and the Rate of Technical Change', *Economic Journal*, **94**, 612–23.

Solow, R. (1960), 'Investment and Technical Progress', in K.J. Arrow, S. Karlin and P. Suppes (eds), *Mathematical Methods in the Social Sciences 1959*, Stanford: Stanford University Press.

Steindl, J. (1952), *Maturity and Stagnation in American Capitalism*, New York: Monthly Review Press.

Winter, S.G. (1984), 'Schumpeterian Competition in Alternative Technological Regimes', *Journal of Economic Behavior and Organization*, **5**, 137–58.

Young, H.P. (1993), 'The Evolution of Conventions', *Econometrica*, **61**, 57–84.

7. New Technology and Windows of Locational Opportunity: Indeterminacy, Creativity and Chance

Ron Boschma and
Bert van der Knaap

1 INTRODUCTION

One of the main topics in economic evolutionary thinking is to provide explanations for the emergence of novelty (Hodgson, 1993; Andersen, 1994). There is much debate about the extent to which novelties may be determined by specific circumstances, or should be regarded as the outcomes of chance events (see, for example, Silverberg and Verspagen, Chapter 6). This chance–necessity controversy may also throw light on another debate concerning the nature of the dynamics of technological evolution in particular and economic development in general, which is a topic central to evolutionary theory (Nelson, 1995). This relates to the problem whether novelties reflect gradual, continuous or dramatic, discontinuous tendencies of change. The conflicting views about the nature of change in systems, known as the controversy between the gradualist approach and the punctuated equilibrium perspective (see, for instance, Hall, 1994) can also be found in other scientific fields, such as biology (Monod, 1972), philosophy of science (Kuhn, 1970), physics (Prigogine and Stengers, 1984) and economic history (Mokyr, 1991).

Economic geographers are dealing with similar questions. On the one hand, they are much interested in analysing the driving forces behind the spatial pattern of major technological innovations, that is, the extent to which chance and necessity may be involved in their spatial manifestation. On the other hand, they explore the way these novelties may affect the evolution of spatial economic systems, that is, whether these bring about the rise of new growth regions at the expense of old industrial regions (Scott, 1988). In this chapter an attempt is made to address both problems from a particular spatial angle. This is done by introducing the Windows of

Locational Opportunity (WLO) concept (Boschma, 1994). To this end, we will focus attention on the problem as to how to explain the location of major innovations that give birth to new industries (such as the transistor, the integrated circuit and the microprocessor that led to the emergence of a new computer industry). First, we will discuss whether indeterminacy, human agency and chance rather than deterministic mechanisms may be involved in the spatial emergence of new industries. We will conclude, for example, that newly emerging industries are likely to develop rather independently of established spatial structures and conditions. Second, the WLO concept addresses the fundamental problem whether the ability of regions to generate new industries is likely to be subject to fundamental change in the course of time. With respect to the latter, it emphasizes a potentially, but not necessarily unstable evolution of the spatial system.

When addressing these items, we will discuss or refer to key concepts in evolutionary thinking (indeterminacy, randomness, selection environment, the cumulative, localized nature of innovation) when these may be helpful to specify and define the main features of the WLO concept. We will point out, for example, that the selection environment is unlikely to determine where new industries will emerge and prosper in space, due to a mismatch between their new requirements and the existing production environment. As a result of this lack of fitness, new industries will shape and transform the local selection environment according to their needs as their development proceeds.

This contribution is divided into three sections. In Section 2, we will set out the main traits of two particular notions of innovation. The first is the cumulative, localized and primarily incremental concept of innovation, which refers to the evolutionary theory of technical change proposed by Nelson and Winter (1982). The second is the revolutionary, random, unpredictable and disruptive concept of innovation, which has been adopted by (among others) evolutionary reasoning in chaos theory (see, for instance, Leydesdorff and van den Besselaar, 1994). The two notions of innovation not only throw a different light on the role of chance and necessity when explaining their origins, but these also reflect different views regarding the nature of the dynamics involved (gradual versus dramatic change). This will enable us to define more clearly in Section 3 the main features of the WLO concept, which attempts to come to grips with the mechanisms behind the spatial manifestation of the latter notion of innovation, that is, new industries. As far as the chance–necessity debate is concerned, we will discuss successively in sections 3.1, 3.2 and 3.3 whether indeterminacy, human agency and randomness are involved. In other words, we will specify the extent to which the existing environment determines the place where new industries will emerge, that is, the extent to which chance and necessity are involved in their spatial manifestation. We will claim, for instance, that the spatial pattern of new industries is unlikely to reveal predictable tendencies of necessity and regularity, not in the least because spatial structures and conditions laid down in the past are unlikely to determine their spatial manifestation. As far as the nature of change is concerned, we will focus attention in Section 3.4 on the extent to which the evolution of the spatial system may be subject to fundamental change when new industries emerge, that is, to what extent these novelties require so-called new growth regions rather than old industrial regions to develop. We will relate this to the mechanisms behind the location of new industries described previously in terms of indeterminacy, creativity and randomness. In Section 3.5 we will claim that the rate of discontinuity of the new industry involved may determine what type of spatial change occurs. In Section 4 we will draw some conclusions.

2   TWO NOTIONS OF INNOVATION

To start with, a distinction will be made between two notions of innovation. We will first discuss the nature, origins and impacts of technical change as defined by Nelson and Winter (1982). It lays emphasis on a localized, cumulative and primarily incremental concept of innovation, which results from the localness of searches for new technologies, the importance of cumulative trajectories of innovative behaviour and the transmission and amplification of feedback between firms operating in clusters. Next, the features of the concept of the discontinuous innovation will be presented, which sharply contrasts with the previous notion of innovation in many respects. This outline will be partly based on insights of the neo-Schumpeterian long-wave theory (Freeman et al., 1982). However, we will also draw from those evolutionary strands that refer to chaos theory in order to underline the catastrophic nature of major innovations (see, for example, Hodgson, 1993) or acknowledge the importance of major innovations because these lay at the roots of new technological trajectories (Dosi, 1982; Silverberg, 1988; Mokyr, 1990). In short, this discontinuous concept takes notice of the indeterminate and unpredictable origins of major innovations or new techno-industrial trajectories, because large numbers of (small, arbitrary) potential triggers and (weak) selecting mechanisms are involved. Moreover, it accounts for the disruptive and destabilizing impacts of major innovations, such as changes in the economic and institutional structure.

This distinction will serve several purposes. The main features of the notion of the discontinuous innovation will be used to construct a theoretical concept in Section 3, which endeavours to come to grips with the mechanisms behind the spatial manifestation of new industries. The outline of the notion of the continuous innovation will be helpful to specify and sharply define the main features of this discontinuous concept, while it will also make clear that the evolutionary notion of technical change introduced by Nelson and Winter (1982) is rather unfit to address such a research question.

2.1 The Notion of the Continuity of Innovation

The evolutionary theory of technical change as defined by Nelson and Winter (1982) focuses attention on the importance of uncertainty in which the innovation process takes place. Complex and dynamic environments do not provide freely available and readily accessible information. As a consequence, economic actors face uncertainties resulting from a wide range of possible alternative paths of behaviour and the inability of firms to assess the merits and drawbacks of each of these options. In order to cope with this uncertainty, decisions of firms are guided by routines (Nelson and Winter, 1982) or behavioural rules (Heiner, 1983). Such attitudes of firms, embedded in skills and experience show regular, continuous and relatively predictable patterns, because uncertainty requires behaviour to be reduced to simplified patterns while firms have limited awareness of alternatives. As a consequence, firms tend to employ conservative, risk-averse behaviour: they will hesitate moving into unknown territory, because in this case, there is no prior experience to benefit from.

This does, however, not imply that change does not take place. On the contrary, economic actors exhibit innovative behaviour, defined as changes in routine (Nelson and Winter, 1982) despite high uncertainty and risks. Nevertheless, innovative behaviour is believed to be guided to a considerable degree by prevailing routines. Firms are considered to carry out so-called searches, that have been described by Nelson and Winter (1982) as routine-guided efforts to explore possibilities of routine-changing innovations. This search behaviour is undertaken locally because uncertainty is more likely to be kept under control when this search is directed to more familiar markets, technologies and existing routines. In fact, when innovative behaviour is regarded as a result of a problem-solving response initiated by perceived troubles with existing routines (stagnant or declining markets, technological anomalies in established routines, or threats of innovative rivals), the latter tend to push firms to look in directions not unrelated to their past achievements. When innovative behaviour is considered to be induced by the challenge of technological opportunity because the use of existing technology offers scope for considerable improvements in the near future, innovations are likely to be closely related to existing products and the organization of production processes. However, this does not imply that search outcomes may not still be subject to stochastic processes. For example, potential adaptations to a changing environment, although heavily constrained by existing routines may be quite numerous (Hall, 1994). This is why changes in an evolutionary perspective are often described in probabilistic terms.

This historical nature of the continuous notion of innovation may be further illustrated by the fact that innovative behaviour is seen to proceed along specific paths or technological trajectories (Dosi, 1982). These are described as regular guidelines of exploratory activities specific to a particular technology, or to a wider range of technologies, so-called technological paradigms. This importance of path-dependency implies that the historical accumulation of information, knowledge and experience tends to structure available options and probable outcomes of searches, while it constrains the ability of economic agents to react to changing market signals. Innovative behaviour may show a certain internal logic, that acquires momentum as it proceeds along trajectories. This continuous, cumulative pattern of innovative behaviour along trajectories has often been related to learning processes: the use of a new technology may result in further improvements because new opportunities are identified based on practical knowledge and previously acquired experience (Rosenberg, 1976). On the one hand, this may take place within firms, bringing about the accumulation of firm-specific advantages or competencies (Dosi, 1984), especially when 'technology is not a free good, but involves specific, often idiosyncratic, partly appropriable knowledge which is accumulated over time through equally specific learning processes' (Dosi and Orsenigo, 1988, p. 16). This asymmetry between firms, the varying techno-industrial positions of firms with regard to a particular technological frontier is likely to be consolidated due to firm-specific learning processes, skills, R&D abilities and economies of scale (Nelson and Winter, 1982; Dosi, 1984). On the other hand, these cumulative, self-reinforcing processes may occur within clusters of closely linked firms. In fact, the transmission, exchange and feedback of technological knowledge, resulting from 'reciprocal stimuli, bottlenecks, information flows, spillovers of technological knowledge, etc.' (Dosi and Orsenigo, 1988, p. 28) may spark off a dynamic innovative process in those firms that are either linked into such a network or have (local) access to these externalities.

This implies that evolutionary change is, to a large extent, cumulative and gradual (De Bresson, 1987). This notion of cumulative innovative behaviour has, in fact, often been associated with series of continuous, small-scale, incremental changes, such as quality improvements of products and minor cost reductions of production processes. Rosenberg (1982) states that the economic significance of the cumulative effect of many minor, incremental innovations is actually very large, although each of them has a very limited economic impact.

Institutions (industrial associations, universities, government bodies) may be considered part of the selection environment: these regulate and coordinate the behaviour of actors in general and influence innovative behaviour in particular (see Nelson, 1995). The so-called 'regulation approach' (Lipietz, 1986; Boyer, 1988) regards the role of the socio-institutional structure as an 'essential underpinning of efficient capitalist production systems' (Scott and Storper, 1992, p. 5). What is essential here is that this regulatory influence of the institutional environment is believed to support the continuous development of innovative behaviour along trajectories for a long period of time as soon as a wide range of durable institutions has matched their requirements (Freeman and Perez, 1988).

Although the notion of continuous innovation may be regarded as a disequilibrating force, it takes place in a relatively ordered manner (Dosi and Orsenigo, 1988). This may be associated with its main features mentioned above, that is, the continuous and cumulative patterns of technological change along trajectories; the local character of search and imitation in terms of routine-guided adjustments; the relatively stable and self-reinforcing diffusion patterns among clusters of interrelated firms; and the regulatory influence of durable, supporting institutional structures. Further, the selection environment imposes heavy constraints on new technologies that strongly deviate from the established trajectories, even if these novelties possess superior qualities;[1] these will therefore not survive. This brings about stable patterns of dynamic economic development for at least some time.

2.2 The Notion of the Discontinuity of Innovation

Following Schumpeter (1939), major innovative breakthroughs represent dramatic breaks or 'quantum leaps' in the direction of techno-industrial development. It is therefore unlikely that the information, knowledge and experience accumulated along trajectories, as stressed by the evolutionary theory of Nelson and Winter may determine or stimulate the appearance of this notion of innovation. In fact, the emergence of major innovations is accompanied by new and not standardized knowledge and fundamentally different kinds of information, while qualifications of the labour force, the R&D commitments and the established institutional environment (knowledge

---

[1]. If such is the case, path dependency has resulted in lock-in.

infrastructure, capital suppliers, government) are not compatible with the new requirements of major innovations. It is even very likely that prevailing routines and institutions act as impediments for the adoption of major innovations (Perez, 1983). As a consequence, discontinuity is regarded as of such a dramatic nature that any specific, predictable influence from past structures and practices may be ruled out. It is, however, important to note that this dramatic nature has not so much to do with the pace of change; it is rather a rule than an exception that the adoption and diffusion of breakthroughs takes place rather slowly (Rosenberg, 1976). This may be related to their discontinuity mentioned above.

This lack of positive influence from past events, combined with the numerous hindrances attributed to prevailing routines and the presence of high uncertainties attached to the introduction of major innovations explain why concepts like heroic Schumpeterian entrepreneurship and Keynesian animal spirits have been used to explain why major innovations occur (Freeman and Perez, 1988). The prospect of superprofits, resulting from patent protection, imperfect competition and other first-mover advantages is regarded as the only incentive that makes firms introduce breakthroughs in the economic system. Their discontinuity may also explain why the rise of new industries is often associated with newly emerging firms (Dosi, 1982). The emphasis on firm-specific advantages by the evolutionary theory of Nelson and Winter (1982) provides a powerful explanation for the reluctance of established firms to adopt major innovations. In fact, this inability may be explained by the large gap that exists between the techno-economic competence of existing firms on the one hand and the new requirements of major innovations that deviate strongly from prevailing routines on the other hand (Heiner, 1983).[2]

According to modern evolutionary thinking, the emergence of novelty is subject to a random variation, that stands in sharp contrast to the notion of continuous innovation. Breakthroughs are either regarded as unforeseen, unexpected outcomes of searches (Nelson and Winter, 1982; Mokyr, 1990)

---

[2]. However, there may be differences between major innovations concerning their discontinuity. For example, Rosenberg (1976) states that the ability of firms to adapt depends on 'the complexity of the new techniques, the extent to which they are novel or rely on skills already available or transferable from other industries, etc.' (p. 197). In the case of major process innovations (new production methods), it is not impossible that the (established) firms can make use of existing know-how about the product, market demand and existing sale and distribution facilities, which make them fitter to implement these breakthroughs (Teece, 1988). We will discuss this more in detail in Section 3. We will conclude there that only inquiry may determine in each particular case the extent to which firms, regions or countries have fallen back on existing routines and conditions to generate, imitate or apply major innovations.

or conceived to be induced by small, arbitrary factors analogous to the so-called 'butterfly effects' in chaos theory (Dosi, 1982; Silverberg, 1988; Arthur, 1989). We will only briefly analyse here the extent to which major innovations, in spite of their discontinuity, may be subject to influences of existing practices and environmental conditions. This topic is likely to throw light on the chance–necessity debate mentioned in the introduction, and will be analysed more thoroughly in Section 3.3. In short, we will argue that it is impossible to predict which major innovations will emerge, by which specific triggers they are induced, and by which elements of the environment they are selected. The fundamental uncertainty about their sources and impacts is likely to preclude an *ex ante* logic behind the emergence of major innovations in time and space (Silverberg, 1988). Dosi was right when he claimed that it is impossible 'to draw any conclusions on the directions of change of the system without first seeing it moving in each single part' (1984, p. 108).

As far as the uncertainty about the specific impact of triggers providing opportunities and/or challenges is concerned, this is not only because a multitude of small, arbitrary events, that are hard to generalize about, are likely to be involved (Arthur, 1989). This can also be related to the fact that only a few out of an infinite number of potential triggers or focusing mechanisms will actually result in breakthroughs (Rosenberg, 1976). As far as the uncertain and unpredictable impact of the selection environment is concerned, this may not only be explained by the fact that this environment contains so many potentially influential elements (a wide range of technological, economic, political and institutional factors) that it is impossible to predict which one(s) will exercise a (decisive) influence. This is also because the favourable impacts of the environment are likely to be rather weak, due to its poor match with the new requirements of major innovations as explained by their discontinuity above.[3] It not only means that major innovations survive despite the fact that they reflect, almost by definition, unfit changes, but it also implies that a technological breakthrough that became dominant after a process of competition between rivals is not necessarily the superior or the most efficient one (see David, 1985; Arthur, 1989). In Section 3 we will argue that the lack of specific stimuli from the environment necessitates firms to create or attract their own supporting conditions, such as input requirements (Storper and Walker, 1989). This favours the view of a dynamic growth process, wherein

---

[3].   It should be noted that major innovations are regarded here as historical accidents because indeterminacy is involved, and not because specific environmental conditions happened by chance to match perfectly the needs of these new technologies.

supporting conditions (skilled labour, useful knowledge and information, dynamic user-supplier linkages, responsive capital suppliers) come into being as the development of new industries proceeds. This view differs from the continuous perspective because such a development process in their initial stage of growth is not based on the presence of favourable conditions. On the contrary, the environment is shaped according to their needs because such a supportive production environment is lacking.

Major innovations are likely to have disruptive and pervasive effects on the economic system. On the micro-level, we already explained why prevailing routines and high adjustment costs may hamper the ability of established firms to divert into totally different fields of technology. On the meso-economic level, major innovations may bring about structural changes, altering and displacing the previously existing economic structure, because breakthroughs have different impacts on the various industries in an economy. Further, institutional structures have to be adjusted because the prevailing institutional environment is probably incompatible with the requirements of new breakthroughs because they are discontinuous (Perez, 1983). On the macro-economic level, it has been stressed by many authors that major innovations may only have a small economic effect unless they occur in clusters (Frischtak and Rosenberg, 1983). In a long-wave perspective, these are believed to pave the way for the resurgence of long-term economic growth, because they offer new opportunities for investments (new markets) and productivity gains, whereas their diffusion is likely to sustain a prosperity phase for some time (Freeman, Clark and Soete, 1982; Kleinknecht, 1990). It is not surprising then that major innovations are often considered a prerequisite for securing the long-term survival of the economic system: they not only overcome limitations of existing structures such as the exhaustion of technological and economic possibilities, but they also break down institutional rigidities enabling new activities to occur (Dockès and Rosier, 1992).

The differences between the two notions of innovation are summarized in Table 7.1. The features of the notion of discontinuous innovation will be used to construct a theoretical concept in Section 3, which will deal with the mechanisms behind the spatial manifestation of new industries. The notion of continuous innovation may be regarded as unfit to address such a problem, because it neglects the issue of discontinuity. However, we will argue in Section 3.5 that such a framework is more appropriate to describe the spatial formation of new industries when they build on conditions inherited from the past in order to adjust the local environment in accordance with their own needs.

Table 7.1 The main differences between the two notions of innovation

	The notion of continuous innovation	The notion of discontinuous innovation
Nature of innovation	Small, incremental	Radical
Role of history	Continuous, cumulative, routine-guided changes	Discontinuous, breaks with the past
Triggers	Local problems and opportunities within existing routines	Accidents, small and arbitrary events, many potential triggers
Selection environment	Strong selection due to role of supporting environment	Weak selection due to lack of stimuli: creative behaviour
Predictable pattern of change	High	Low
Economic impact	Small, cumulative impact may be large	Large, especially in the case of clusters
Economic dynamics	Dynamic stability	Instability and transformation
Firms	Mostly established firms due to firm-specific advantages	Mostly newly created firms due to flexible nature
Institutional structure	Relatively good match: in general supporting	Mismatch: structural crisis of adjustment, transformation

3   WINDOWS OF LOCATIONAL OPPORTUNITY

The principles behind the notion of discontinuous innovation will now be applied to develop a theoretical concept, called the 'Windows of Locational Opportunity' (WLO), that endeavours to understand the mechanisms of the spatial manifestation of major innovations that give birth to new industries. The WLO concept partly builds on the work of Scott and Storper (1987), Scott (1988), Perez and Soete (1988) and Storper and Walker (1989).

   In the following sections, we will first successively discuss whether indeterminacy, human action and accidental events are involved in the spatial emergence of new industries. By doing so, we will specify the extent to which the existing spatial environment may exercise influence on, or even determine the location where new industries will emerge. In other words, we will define the extent to which chance and necessity are involved in their spatial manifestation. Next, the WLO concept is applied to the problem whether newly emerging industries will disrupt the long-term evolution of the spatial system, that is, whether the ability of regions to generate novelty is subject to fundamental change in the course of time. It basically regards the problem to what extent these novelties require new growth regions rather than old industrial regions to develop. This will strongly depend upon the mechanisms behind the location of new industries, which has been described in terms of spatial indeterminacy, creativity and randomness. With respect to both matters, the WLO concept states that new industries are likely to emerge and develop in space rather independently of established spatial structures and conditions, while it lays emphasis on a potentially unstable evolution of the spatial system. This will be illustrated by a few examples taken from a long-term spatial analysis of Great Britain and Belgium (Boschma, 1994).

   By doing so, the WLO concept uses some topics and notions dealt with by modern evolutionary thinking, such as randomness and selection environment. This concept claims, for example, that the rise of new industries in space, though highly unpredictable is not an entirely accidental outcome because it is often triggered by existing practices and structures that provide challenges or opportunities. Moreover, it states that the selection environment is unlikely to determine where new industries will emerge and prosper in space, due to a mismatch with their new requirements. Because of this lack of fitness, it is wrong to treat the local selection environment as given; newly emerging industries shape and transform their production space according to their needs as their development proceeds.

3.1 Spatial Indeterminacy

To begin with, the discontinuous nature of major innovations set out in Section 2.2 implies that the spatial formation of new industries involves spontaneity or indeterminacy because it is unlikely to be determined by or bound to particular places. Storper and Walker (1989) assert that because new industries differ from existing ones, they require unique 'locational specifications' that need to be met in space in order to support their further development. This discontinuity involves a fundamental problem of adaptation for regions: their own particular histories (trajectories), which have resulted in a particular technological, economic and institutional specialization make them unfit to seize these new opportunities. This can be explained with the assistance of the particular evolutionary framework presented in Section 2.1: there probably is a large gap between the new (locational) needs of new industries and the prevailing techno-industrial structure (the techno-economic competence of firms and industries) and the institutional environment in regions. The larger the gap, the higher the adjustment costs related to, for instance, the acquisition of new knowledge, information and skills, and the more difficult it is for regions to draw on available local conditions to restructure their local economies. This negative element of path dependency may explain why old industrial regions are sometimes incapable of generating new technologies that deviate considerably from their established trajectories. In fact, industrial regions may become 'locked' into a production environment which is strongly geared to their established techno-industrial structure that they become incapable of responding to any fundamental changes.

Whereas the idea behind discontinuity explains the severe adjustment problems confronting regions, the notion of spatial indeterminacy suggests that it is impossible that their ability to adapt is determined by past experiences. Due to a mismatch with the new requirements, spatial practices and conditions that have been accumulated in the past, will not provide any stimuli to the development of new industries and, therefore, will not predetermine where they will emerge. This view stands in contrast with a widely-held belief in location theory that claims that new industries will develop most rapidly in those regions where their static, quasi-fixed, pregiven locational needs (for instance, a highly skilled population) can be most effectively matched with local conditions accumulated in the past (Hall, 1985). Their spatial manifestation should be regarded then as 'essentially random and indifferent to the specificities of place' (Gordon, 1991, p. 178) rather than as an automatic and predictable outcome of spatial structures and practices laid down in the past. Accordingly, many spatial outcomes are possible. We will not take the view, however, that potential impacts of space should be neglected, a topic to which we shall return in Section 3.3. There we will argue that this set of possible spatial outcomes may be more limited than is suggested here.

3.2 Creation of Production Space

The importance of spatial indeterminacy leaves room for human agency or creativity to be involved in the spatial formation of newly emerging industries. For reasons set out above, new industries can hardly draw on available conditions to support their development in space, which is why they must rely on their creative capacity to generate or attract their own supportive conditions in space (Storper and Walker, 1989). This creative ability compensates for the lack of stimuli from the spatial environment. In fact, new industries steadily create their favourable conditions (such as required labour, capital, suppliers, markets, institutions) *in situ* or attract them from outside, rather than being tied to pre-existing, independent locational factors (Scott and Storper, 1987).

For this reason, it would be wrong to treat the local environment as a static selection mechanism. By contrast, newly emerging industries will shape and transform it according to their needs as their development proceeds. Hence, the local environment is likely to be adjusted to their requirements only in those places where new industries have actively manifested themselves. This implies that a supportive and efficient local environment is more likely to be an outgrowth of, rather than a pre-condition for, the rise of new industries.

There is no reason to believe that the location where a new industry emerges is necessarily the most efficient of all possible places. The lack of a favourable impact of the environment discussed previously implies that locations of new industries are unlikely to be selected, let alone be the most suitable ones. In fact, it is difficult to think of optimal locations when the specific needs of new industries at their earliest stages of development are not pre-given but come gradually into being as these develop. We will turn to this issue in the next section. Even so, the presence of high returns in the early stages of growth, which results from patent protection, technological inappropriability and (temporary) price inelastic demand allows new industries to locate and survive in arbitrary places where, for example, 'labor supplies are apt to be poor or inappropriate, linkages to relevant suppliers and buyers spotty, local markets weak, infrastructure poorly developed, and so forth' (Storper and Walker, 1989, p. 73). Moreover, the local presence of high costs is likely to be offset by the creative ability of new industries, because it brings efficiency in their local production environment.

Another implication is that the development of newly emerging industries at their initial stage of growth should be viewed as a creative process associated with the lack of a supportive environment, rather than as a process of positive feedback founded on the presence of favourable local conditions. However, this process of positive feedback, which is related to Veblen's notion of cumulative causation, may take place at a later stage of their development (see Dicken and Lloyd, 1990; Storper, 1992). Then, entry barriers will be imposed on lagging regions. We will focus attention on this latter topic in Section 3.4.

The relevance of creative ability may be illustrated by a historical example relating to Great Britain and Belgium (Boschma, 1994). The example is interesting because it challenges the common belief of economic historians that in the late eighteenth to early nineteenth century, given the poor transport facilities, a ready local access to coal and iron deposits could explain why regions endowed with such natural resources witnessed the rise of coke-based iron making and steam engineering (Hudson, 1992). We will argue that, though a prerequisite, local supply of coal and iron ore was certainly not sufficient for regions to develop such dynamic industries (Pollard, 1981). In fact, the development and growth of these new industries only became possible through the creative ability of firms to generate or attract a supportive local environment, because such a favourable environment was, to a high degree, lacking. This was achieved through, among other things, the import and creation of a (skilled) labour force (based on apprenticeship, on-the-job training, learning by doing), the development of a strong local network of techno-industrial linkages between ancillary or complementary activities, the construction of a canal and railway infrastructure, and the supply of capital based on the practice of reinvested profits and, at a later stage, the establishment of new (local) joint-stock banks.

3.3 Spatial Accidents

In the foregoing, we have suggested that newly emerging industries may have a complete freedom to locate anywhere, due to their discontinuity (Section 3.1) and creative ability (Section 3.2). However, the WLO concept rejects the view that their emergence takes place in a spaceless vacuum. In fact, technological change should not be understood as exogenous to space, but as interacting with its spatial context (Gertler, 1992). When spatial conditions vary markedly from place to place because of different histories, the capacity of regions to generate or attract new industries, and their ability to adapt their local environment, may also differ.

For this purpose, we will analyse here under what circumstances the foundation of new industries may actually depend upon, or be conditioned by, the spatial environment, and how to relate this to their discontinuity and creative ability in space. In other words, we will focus attention on whether the notions of spatial indeterminacy and creativity may still be valid when situating newly emerging industries in their local context. Taking into account what has been said in Section 2.2, we will successively examine those situations in which regions (a) provide initial triggers or incentives in terms of location-specific problems and opportunities, or (b) offer a local environment favourable to meet the new requirements of new industries. By doing so, we will examine the extent to which random events are still involved in the spatial emergence of new industries (see Chapman, 1992).

a Triggers
As has been set out in Section 2, major innovations may be triggered by existing (spatial) structures and practices, that reveal specific problems (factor scarcity, conflictual industrial relations, environmental threats, technological bottlenecks) or demands (market pressures, government regulations). We will claim that, contrary to the local character of searches along trajectories (Section 2.1), it is uncertain and unpredictable where triggers will actually induce the emergence of new industries. This may, firstly, be related to the evolutionary view that regards technological breakthroughs as unpredictable, unexpected outcomes of searches (Nelson and Winter, 1982; Mokyr, 1990). Moreover, small, arbitrary events, or even accidents are likely to be involved, which are hard to generalize about (Arthur, 1989). Further, we can think of general triggers, which are anything but confined to particular places, like high input costs (oil prices, labour costs) or government regulations (restrictive environmental policy). Another reason for the uncertainty about the location of new industries is the fact that there is an infinite number of location-specific potential triggers, that are present in every possible type of region. In fact, it remains an open question why certain potential triggers set in motion the development of new industries in particular regions, and why others (in the same or other regions) do not. We are dealing here with a fundamental problem of uncertainty and unpredictability *ex ante* concerning the actual spatial manifestation of new industries. This is illustrated in Figure 7.1, which shows the presence of many potential location-specific triggers in all of ten distinct regions in a country, but induce major innovations in only three of them. Although each of these major innovations can be related to a location-specific trigger, they may still be regarded as accidental events, because we cannot explain why similar innovations did not occur in the

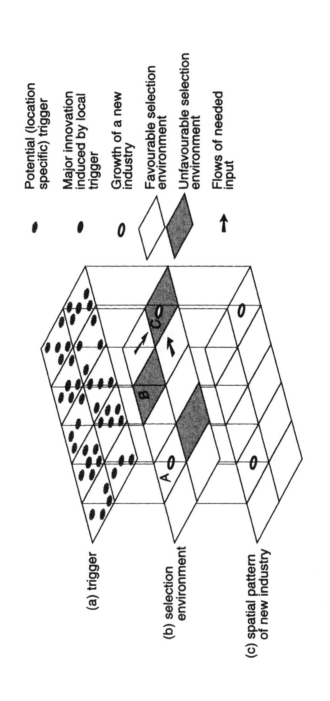

Potential (location specific) trigger

Major innovation induced by local trigger

Growth of a new industry

Favourable selection environment

Unfavourable selection environment

Flows of needed input

(a) trigger

(b) selection environment

(c) spatial pattern of new industry

Figure 7.1   An illustration of the accidental way in which new industries emerge in space

other regions. This reasoning is similar to the selection processes determining choices of technology set out by Arthur (1989): the actual outcome largely depends on small, arbitrary events, magnified by a positive feedback mechanism, which, in our approach, is achieved by the creative ability of firms that build up a favourable local production milieu around them.

b Selection environment
Once triggered, it is not unlikely that a particular spatial environment, that provides a mixture of constraints, advantages and capabilities carried over from the past may be more beneficial for, or more responsive to, the development of new industries than others. This is exactly what the notions of heredity and selection in evolutionary thinking are about (Metcalfe, 1989; Witt, 1991). We want to point out again, however, that it is still not possible to predict where new industries will emerge.

We already explained in Section 2 that the selection environment consists of many potentially influential elements of a technological, economic, political, social and institutional nature. Moreover, these will only determine their location in case these are spatially differentiated. Even so, it has already been pointed out before that the discontinuity of new industries implies that potentially favourable impacts of the local environment are likely to be rather weak, because they hardly meet their requirements. Even more so because the specific needs of new industries are often not given but come into being as a result of their development in the regions concerned. In this respect, it is essential to make a distinction between so-called 'generic' and 'specific' conditions: in their initial stage of growth, new industries can only make use of generic, non-specific resources (basic knowledge and skills). As their growth proceeds, their creative ability turns out to be an essential mechanism, because it transforms the generic resources into specific ones (highly skilled labour, specialized knowledge). It may seem rather paradoxal that such discontinuity leads to the conclusion that the creation of a suitable production milieu, based on such generic resources, may be regarded as a gradual process, that steadily emerges out of its environment. In fact, it is this discontinuity that explains why the growth of the new industry smoothly transforms the local milieu to serve its development.

It may imply that regions endowed with particular generic conditions may, to a certain extent, be fitter to adjust than other regions. The WLO concept claims, however, that potentially favourable generic conditions are likely to be widely available in space, while these will only influence rather than determine the ability of regions to adjust. Though the local presence of generic conditions may be regarded as potentially beneficial, it is far from sufficient to sustain the rise of new industries. In sum, the emergence of a new industry in a particular region may be described as a rather adventitious process; the beneficial, generic conditions are unlikely to be confined to only this successful region. Its creative ability may not prevent the development of the new industry in regions where those generic, potentially favourable resources are absent.

This is illustrated in Figure 7.1. The rise of a new industry in region A may be explained by its potentially favourable environment. However, it may also be viewed as a rather accidental event, because we cannot provide an explanation for the fact that other regions endowed with similar beneficial conditions did not succeed to develop the new industry. The only thing we can explain is that regions lacking such basic requirements are more likely to fail to generate new industries (see Crafts, 1977). This is shown in Figure 7.1 by region B, where a major innovation induced by a local trigger did not give rise to a new, fully-developed industry. This touches upon the way of reasoning common to evolutionary theory, that is to explain '*what is not* likely to occur' (De Bresson, 1987, p. 754) (emphasis in the original). One should, however, not forget that superprofits, for instance, do not stop new industries from developing in unfavourable, high cost regions as well. In fact, Figure 7.1 illustrates a case, where region C shows an ability to generate a new industry, despite its unfavourable production milieu. Here, we can argue that its creative ability, which includes drawing resources (skilled labour) from surrounding regions endowed with favourable environments (illustrated by the arrows drawn in Figure 7.1) has been able to offset the lack of local stimuli. The fundamental problem here is that we cannot explain why region C was able to do so, and why region B was not.

We will briefly illustrate this adventitiousness of the spatial pattern of new industries on the basis of two examples derived from a long-term spatial study of Great Britain and Belgium (Boschma, 1994). In both cases we will relate the rise of a particular new industry to a favourable local environment, determine whether such an environment was confined to the host regions involved, and assess the importance of the ability of the new industry to create its own supportive local environment.

The first example relates to the rise of the mechanized cotton industry in some textile regions (Lancashire and Ghent) in both countries in the late eighteenth and early nineteenth century. There, the new textile mills could profit from favourable conditions associated with local linen and wool trades, such as pools of skilled entrepreneurs, readily available reservoirs of experienced labour, and established networks of suppliers and markets. In fact, a tradition of a domestic 'putting-out' system had led to a local accumulation of skills and experience in this semi-capitalist type of production. This facilitated the inflow of required labour in the new textile mills in those regions (Marshall, 1987). Further, local networks of suppliers and buyers, linked into a chain of successive stages of textile production (spinning, weaving, bleaching, printing) favoured the absorption of the strongly growing cotton output. These favourable conditions should, however, not be regarded sufficient; many textile areas in Britain and Belgium endowed with similar conditions were unable to participate in this new sector. Furthermore, the innovative firms showed a well-developed capacity to create or attract their own beneficial conditions *in situ*. In fact, the rise of specialized (textile) machine-building firms and the rapid expansion of heavy chemicals (Leblanc soda and bleaching powder) in these dynamic textile regions were largely a response to the rapid mechanization of the cotton industry, supporting its subsequent development. Moreover, required skills had to be created locally through practical experience and on-the-job-training within the firms themselves, in order to compensate for the lack of skills and the absence of a technical education system. Firms also depended heavily on a massive inflow of labour (from Ireland in the case of Britain, from England in the case of Belgium) to secure the mobilization of necessary workers for the new textile mills. They managed to avoid the traditional labour force by making use of untapped, more disciplined segments of labour supply such as women and children, which were widely available.

The second example refers to newly emerging industries such as electrical engineering and automobiles, that developed in a range of British and Belgian areas during the late nineteenth and early twentieth century. These localities were characterized by a multiplicity of metalworking, engineering and instrument trades, from which were drawn pools of readily available experienced labour and skilled entrepreneurs. However, the randomness of their spatial appearance may be related to the fact that these trades were widely available in space at that time in both Britain and Belgium: many regions involved in these trades in the past were incapable of reaping the benefits from these new industries. Further, the importance of their creative ability may be briefly illustrated by the fact that these initial developments were at a later stage followed by the establishment of supportive technical schools (for instance, King's College in London) in the regions concerned. These were created and financed by the local firms themselves to overcome the lack of skilled personnel and the absence of government involvement (see Boschma, 1994).

3.4 Spatial Dynamics: Windows of Locational Opportunity

In the previous section we presented a theoretical concept, that adopted a particular view with respect to the extent to which chance and necessity are involved in the spatial manifestation of newly emerging industries. The WLO concept is used to describe the mechanisms behind the location of new industries in terms of spatial indeterminacy, creativity and randomness. By doing so, one can account for the fact that newly emerging industries are likely to develop rather independently of established spatial structures and conditions.

From the WLO perspective, we will now focus attention on the problem whether these novelties may bring about elements of flux or stability in the long-term evolution of the spatial system, a topic which is regarded central to evolutionary thinking (see Nelson, 1995). This pertains to the question to what extent the evolution of the spatial system is subject to fundamental change when new industries emerge, that is to what extent these novelties require so-called new growth regions rather than old industrial regions to develop. We will relate this to the notions of indeterminacy, creativity and randomness discussed above. According to the WLO concept, the long-term evolution of the spatial system is in principle unstable. The discontinuity of major innovations, combined with their disruptive impacts described in Section 2.2 is likely to change the ability of regions to generate or attract new industries in the course of time. Major innovations often create opportunities for lagging and backward regions, whereas leading regions are not necessarily winners in many cases. However, there still is much uncertainty about whether regional dynamics take place because there is much uncertainty about the location where the new industry will sprout: the location of new industries is probably not determined by any specific, beneficial factors.

Empirical evidence lends support to the view that long-term structural shifts in techno-industrial leadership between regions have actually taken place in the major industrial countries. Former leading regions are often unable to maintain their dominant positions. We have illustrated this in Figure 7.2 for Great Britain and Belgium. In this figure the long-term evolution of regions is presented on the basis of their relative shares in employment in (clusters of) innovative industries, so-called location quotients. A quotient higher than one indicates that a region's number of employed in the innovative sectors exceeds the national average (Boschma, 1994). It is evident from the data that both Wallonia and the north of Britain were already losing their dominant position by 1910. It has completely vanished by 1950. At the same time new industrial regions emerge in Flanders and the south of England to become prominent in 1950.

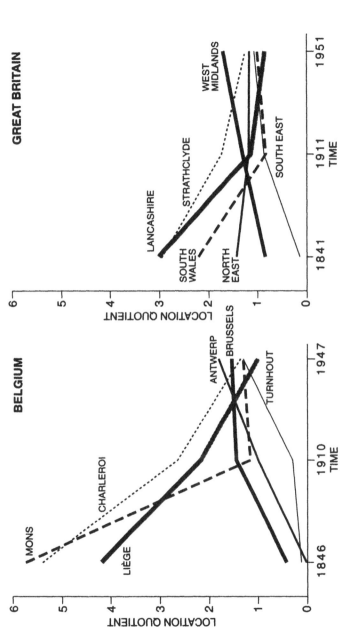

Figure 7.2 *The long-term ability of selected regions to participate in new techno-industrial fields in Belgium and Britain, expressed as location quotients*

Source: Boschma, 1994

The difference between the regions in terms of their ability to generate or attract new (clusters of) innovative industries has disappeared. Moreover, it has been demonstrated in many studies that these newly emerging industrial regions in both countries have consolidated and often improved their performance in the post-war period (see, for instance, Hall and Preston, 1988; Boschma, 1994).

The outcomes seem to support the widely-held view that new industries will emerge in regions different from those where traditional industries are declining, due to so-called 'inhibiting inheritances' in specialized industrial regions (Norton, 1979; Hall, 1985). The ability of this latter type of region to generate new industries is often considered to be weakened or eroded in the course of time, because they become too strongly orientated towards their techno-industrial legacy of the past, a topic which has also been addressed in Section 3.1 (see, for instance, Rees, 1979; Markusen, 1985; Booth, 1986).

Our claim here is that it is uncertain whether major innovations cause instability in the long-term evolution of the spatial system in terms of substantial shifts between techno-industrial positions of regions. There are several reasons for this. Recent processes of structural adjustment in some traditional industrial regions (Boston area, Jura region, Ruhr area) have demonstrated that the loss of techno-industrial leadership and a structural process of decay are anything but inevitable destinies of this type of regions. Moreover, we argued earlier that the spatial pattern of existing advantages and constraints accumulated in the past may be hardly of relevance because of the discontinuity of major innovations. In fact, the creative ability of new industries should be able to offset any hindrances, including the earlier mentioned negative lock-in effects, whereas the rather accidental nature of their spatial formation (their sensitivity to small, arbitrary factors) leaves open many possibilities.

We will, therefore, make use of the notion of window of locational opportunity, because it incorporates the uncertainty with respect to regional dynamics. The WLO concept has also been used elsewhere, though in a slightly different way (see Scott and Storper, 1987; Perez and Soete, 1988; Storper and Walker, 1989). In our view windows of locational opportunity open up in the event of newly emerging industries. New industries develop independently of established spatial structures because of their discontinuity, creativity and randomness. It is uncertain whether major techno-industrial changes cause regional dynamics, because it is uncertain where new industries will emerge. For this reason, it is probable but not inevitable that major innovations bring about regional dynamics. In fact, we may, for example, not rule out the possibility that a new industry emerges in traditional industrial regions, consolidating their dominant position in the spatial system, although hardly any conditions present in those regions could be held responsible for this. Hence, it is uncertain whether the long-term evolution of the spatial system is subject to major instability as a result of major innovations. In sum, the concept of window of locational opportunity claims that the long-term evolution of the spatial system is potentially, but not necessarily, unstable.

The concept of window of locational opportunity may be related to the two notions of innovation described in Section 2 and summarized in Table 7.1. The notion of discontinuous innovation and the notion of continuous innovative behaviour along trajectories may be successively associated with disruptive and cumulative tendencies in the long-term evolution of the spatial system, wherein windows of locational opportunity may successively open and close in the course of time (see also Storper and Walker, 1989). In fact, the rather indeterminate spatial manifestation of new industries may be followed by a logic of cumulative, self-reinforcing tendencies of spatial development.

This may be explained by an ideal type stage-model of a new industry in space, which is summarized in Table 7.2. In the first stage of their growth cycle, new industries may emerge spontaneously in arbitrary places, which may upset the foundations of the spatial system. The discontinuity and randomness of major innovations implies that the spatial emergence of new industries is unlikely to reveal predictable tendencies of necessity and regularity, because specific structures and conditions laid down in the past are unlikely to determine their location. For example, their extreme sensitivity to a multitude of small, arbitrary triggers in space and the importance of generic resources during their initial phase of development imply that new industries may well develop in a variety of alternative locations. In other words, the windows of locational opportunity are widely open at this stage of development. The next stage of development is characterized by a cumulative, self-reinforcing development in a few selected places, which exercises long-lasting exclusion effects on lagging regions. This is achieved by a self-reinforcing feedback between the continuous nature of innovative behaviour along trajectories, the build-up of localization economies, the creation and development of specific knowledge resources, the build-up of a socio-cultural climate of consensus and commitment often materialized in particular institutions (inter-firm associations, government regulations, industrial relation systems, educational and research facilities, financial organizations) and strong local economic growth within these dynamic regions (see, for instance, Camagni, 1991). In fact, successive rounds of innovative behaviour and local growth bring about higher volumes of output, which allow the dynamical regions to benefit from economies of scale, higher rates of specialization and more agglomeration advantages like a larger, more diversified labour market, an accumulated pool of skills, knowledge and experience, a larger supply of capital, a better provision of infrastructural facilities, and so forth. Once the spatial system has entered this phase, change will become merely marginal: the unfolding of cumulative, self-reinforcing development tends to reinforce the persistence of regional disparities, because the leading regions continue to stay ahead at the expense of lagging regions. Hence, the windows of locational opportunity have closed around the most dynamic areas, while entry barriers or exclusion effects have been imposed on lagging regions.

Table 7.2   The two sequential stages of discontinuous and cumulative development of a new industry in space

	The first stage of discontinuous evolution	The second stage of cumulative evolution
Nature of spatial pattern	Arbitrary places: optimization irrelevant	Spatial clustering: localized external economies
Origins of spatial pattern	Spatial indeterminacy	Cumulative mechanisms in space: localization economies
Footlooseness	High	Low
Predictability	Low	High
Windows of locational opportunity	Open	Closed
Dynamics in spatial system	Potentially unstable but uncertain	Relatively stable and fixed

3.5   Two Types of Spatial Change

By and large, the notion of discontinuous innovations plays an essential part in the foregoing, because it is strongly related to the notions of spatial indeterminacy, creativity and randomness discussed above. Nevertheless, it remains an open question to what extent each major innovation actually give evidence of a sharp discontinuity in space, that is, how big is the discrepancy between the new needs of the major innovation and the local environment inherited from the past. We think it is a big challenge for future research to define and measure this discrepancy empirically, because it would increase our understanding of evolutionary notions like fitness and selection. Moreover, this sort of analysis may be regarded as essential to determine whether novelties reflect gradual, evolutionary rather than dramatic, discontinuous changes in spatial economies.

For this purpose, we present in Table 7.3 an analytical framework, which attempts to shed some light on the problem of how to define spatial discontinuity. We suggest that the rate of discontinuity of each major innovation may be assessed in terms of the extent to which it can build on a local environment when the new industry has to organize its required inputs (labour, capital, technological knowledge and other inputs) and to serve its markets. We take also into account whether it can benefit from existing facilities provided by the (local) government (Metcalfe, 1994).

If a major innovation can hardly draw on available local conditions to support its development in space, it will be associated with a revolutionary tendency of spatial change: it would reveal deep techno-industrial cleavages in the evolution of spatial economies. Because of such a fundamental shortage of necessary resources, new industries have to rely on their creative ability in order to mobilize or attract these themselves. As shown in Table 7.3, for example, new skills and flexible labour at their initial stage of development will be acquired, in this case by on-the-job training, the start-up of new learning trajectories, the creation of new (or the adaptation of old) educational institutes, the inflow of external labour, and the use of new flexible labour segments. We already presented at an earlier stage in this contribution examples of the spatial emergence of new industries in Great Britain and Belgium that could be associated with this revolutionary type of change.

By contrast, an evolutionary tendency of spatial change will then be associated with situations in which new industries can build to some extent on existing local (though often generic) conditions when adjusting the local environment in accordance with their needs. In this latter case, a continuous framework would be more appropriate to explain their spatial emergence. As shown in Table 7.3, for example, new skills required at their initial stage of growth may be acquired, in this case by building on and applying existing skills, knowledge and experience accumulated in established local firms, educational facilities and the local environment. There are examples of new techno-industrial sectors that emerged in the last two centuries in Great Britain and Belgium, that could be associated with this evolutionary type of spatial change. These sectors could largely build on structures

Table 7.3   Two ideal types of spatial change

	Evolutionary tendency of spatial change	Revolutionary tendency of spatial change
New labour	Builds on existing skills and experience in local firms, educational system and local environment	Old skills obsolete: on-the-job training/new learning trajectory/new educational facilities/inflow of external labour/flexible labour
New capital	Addition to old capital: provision by established firms and existing local capital suppliers	Replacement old capital: provision by new firms (family capital, reinvested profit)/new suppliers (venture) of capital/external capital
New techno-knowledge	Builds on and reinforces applicability of existing knowledge (R&D, experience)	Old knowledge irrelevant: new technological trajectory/new R&D facilities/inflow of external knowledge
New input supplies	Builds on existing capability of current suppliers	New inputs: inhouse production of firms/creation of new suppliers/inflow of external supplies
New markets	New product sold on new or established market: use of existing market knowledge	New markets: substitution of old markets/creation of new markets/supply of external markets
New government institutions	Minor adjustments of established knowledge, capital, law and infrastructural institutions: builds on existing ones	Disfunctioning of established institutions: new knowledge and capital institutions/new regulations/new infrastructure

carried over from the past, strongly related to, and often actually incorporated in traditional activities in the regions concerned. This is, for example, true for highly innovative industries such as iron making, mechanical engineering and steel making in the nineteenth century, that were erected upon the foundations of heavy industrial complexes laid down in the preceding era of the first Industrial Revolution. It was this supportive environment that largely determined the locations of these industries. The ability of established (iron) firms to divert into these related techno-industrial fields could be attributed to the local accumulation of large sums of fixed capital (creating entry barriers for new regions), localization economies (skills, experience, infrastructure) and strong local linkages between major up- and downstream activities. This led to a consolidation of the leading positions of established iron regions in both countries. Indeed, it seems that the windows of locational opportunity never really opened up in these situations.

The WLO concept may be related to the two types of spatial change that are distinguished here. To begin with, the windows of locational opportunity are likely to be widely open if a revolutionary process of spatial change is involved, because it reflects a high rate of spatial discontinuity. Because the new industry can hardly draw on local conditions to support its growth in this case, each type of region starts from a more or less equal position and, thus, has more or less the same probability to host the new industry despite the fact that their histories may differ considerably. Hence, the new industry provides an opportunity for lagging regions to escape the vicious circle of former constraints and exclusion effects, while leading industrial regions can no longer build on local advantages related to their techno-industrial leadership. There is thus much uncertainty not only about the place where the new industry will germinate, but also about whether regional dynamics may take place.

This last mentioned point also applies to the evolutionary type of spatial change. The windows of locational opportunity will, however, be opened up to a lesser extent in this case because a relatively lower rate of spatial discontinuity is involved. As set out in Section 3.3, the creative ability of the new industry in this case can build to some degree on particular (though often generic) conditions inherited from the past. That is why regions endowed with these potentially favourable conditions have a higher probability to generate and develop the new industry. The probability still depends, however, on the extent to which these (locally available) conditions may be regarded as essential to develop the new industry, and on the extent to which these may also be created *in-situ* in order to compensate for their absence. We mentioned in Section 3.3, for example, that their often generic nature may imply that they are likely to be widely available in space, whereas the creative ability may not prevent the development of the new industry in regions which lack generic, potentially favourable resources. In other words, it is still very likely that the windows of locational opportunity are widely open when an evolutionary type of spatial change is involved, although the rate of openness is expected to correlate positively with the degree of spatial discontinuity.

4 CONCLUSION

In this chapter we employed the 'window of locational opportunity' concept to answer the question whether the spatial emergence of novelty, such as major innovations that give birth to new industries, should be attributed to chance events rather than deterministic mechanisms, and how this relates to the particular nature of change in the long-term evolution of the spatial system. By doing so, we accounted for a complex interplay between spontaneity, creativity, randomness and windows of locational opportunity.

We have specified whether elements like indeterminacy, human agency and chance are involved in the spatial formation of newly emerging industries. We came to the conclusion that their discontinuity and randomness imply that their spatial pattern does probably not reveal predictable tendencies of necessity and regularity, because spatial structures, conditions and capabilities laid down in the past are unlikely to determine their spatial manifestation. This happens in spite of the fact that new industries may be induced or triggered by existing practices and structures which provide opportunities and/or challenges. This is also despite the fact that the formation of new industries may be influenced by the production environment, that is facilitated in regions endowed with beneficial (though generic) conditions. Nevertheless, such potential impacts of space were considered to be highly unpredictable: latent triggers or incentives are manifold, whereas the selection environment may operate very weakly. In fact, we claimed that their discontinuity actually necessitated the incorporation of notions of human agency and accidents to 'explain' the spatial pattern of new industries, because the selection environment will not provide a full explanation for the location of novelty.

Because there is much uncertainty about the site where new industries will emerge, windows of locational opportunity tend to open up in the event of newly emerging industries: because of their discontinuity, creativity and randomness they are likely to bring about regional dynamics, without requiring so-called new regions instead of old industrial regions to develop. In other words, the WLO model leads to the conclusion that the long-term evolution of the spatial system is potentially unstable.

In our view future research should focus more on the problem of how to define and specify the rate of discontinuity of novelties, because this would increase our understanding of evolutionary notions like fitness and (the potential impact of) the selection environment. According to Hodgson (1993), 'such a standpoint avoids the extremes of either determinism or complete indeterminacy' (p. 224). In fact, we share the idea expressed by De Bresson (1987), Hodgson (1993) and Silverberg and Verspagen (this volume) that evolutionary theory should explicitly focus attention on the reduction of the possible range of outcomes and, at the same time, clarify why it is impossible to predict and determine exactly when and where novelty will emerge.

REFERENCES

Andersen, E.S. (1994), *Evolutionary Economics. Post-Schumpeterian Contributions*, London: Pinter Publishers.

Arthur, W.B. (1989), 'Competing technologies, increasing returns, and lock in by historical events', *The Economic Journal*, **99**, 116–31.

Booth, D.E. (1986), 'Long waves and uneven regional growth', *Southern Economic Journal*, **53**(1), July, 448–60.

Boschma, R.A. (1994), *Looking through a window of locational opportunity. A long term spatial analysis of techno-industrial upheavals in Great Britain and Belgium*, Tinbergen Institute Research Series no. 75, Amsterdam: Thesis Publishers.

Boyer, R. (1988), 'Technical change and the theory of regulation', in G. Dosi, C. Freeman, R. Nelson, G. Silverberg and L. Soete (eds), *Technical Change and Economic Theory*, London: Pinter Publishers, pp. 67–94.

Camagni, R. (ed.) (1991), *Innovation Networks: Spatial Perspectives*, London/New York: Belhaven Press.

Chapman, K. (1992), 'Continuity and contingency in the spatial evolution of industries: the case of petro-chemicals', *Transactions of the Institute of British Geographers*, **17**, 47–64.

Crafts, N.F.R. (1977), 'Industrial Revolution in England and France. Some thoughts on the question: why was England first', *The Economic History Review*, **30**, 429–41.

David, P.A. (1985), 'Clio and the economics of QWERTY', *American Economic Review*, **75**(2), 332–7.

De Bresson, C. (1987), 'The evolutionary paradigm and the economics of technological change', *Journal of Economic Issues*, **21**(2), 751–62.

Dicken, P. and P.E. Lloyd (1990), *Location in Space; Theoretical Perspectives in Economic Geography*, 3rd edition, New York: Harper and Row.

Dockès, P. and B. Rosier (1992), 'Long waves and the dialectic of innovations and conflicts', in A. Kleinknecht, E. Mandel and I. Wallerstein (eds), *New Findings in Long-wave Research*, London: Macmillan, pp. 301–15.

Dosi, G. (1982), 'Technological paradigms and technological trajectories; a suggested interpretation of the determinants and directions of technical change', *Research Policy*, **11**, 147–62.

Dosi, G. (1984), *Technical Change and Industrial Transformation; the Theory and an Application to the Semiconductor Industry*, London: Macmillan.

Dosi, G. and L. Orsenigo (1988), 'Coordination and transformation: an overview of structures, behaviours and change in evolutionary environments', in G. Dosi, C. Freeman, R. Nelson, G. Silverberg and L. Soete, (eds), *Technical Change and Economic Theory*, London: Pinter Publishers, pp. 13–38.

Freeman, C., J. Clark and L. Soete (1982), *Unemployment and Technical Innovation; a Study of Long Waves and Economic Development*, London: Frances Pinter.

Freeman, C. and C. Perez (1988), 'Structural crisis of adjustment: business cycles and investment behaviour', in G. Dosi C. Freeman, R. Nelson, G. Silverberg and L. Soete (eds), *Technical Change and Economic Theory*, London: Pinter Publishers, pp. 38–66.

Frischtak, C.R. and N. Rosenberg (1983), 'Long waves and economic growth; a critical appraisal', *American Economic Review, Papers and Proceedings*, **73**, 146–51.

Gertler, M.S. (1992), 'Flexibility revisited: districts, nation-states, and the forces of production', *Transactions of the Institute of British Geographers*, **17**, 259–78.

Gordon, R. (1991), 'Innovation, industrial networks and high-technology regions', in Camagni R. (ed.), *Innovation Networks: Spatial Perspectives*, London/New York: Belhaven Press, pp. 174–95.

Hall, P.G. (1985), 'The geography of the fifth Kondratieff', in P.G. Hall and A.R. Markusen (eds), *Silicon Landscapes*, Boston: Allen and Unwin, pp. 1–19.

Hall, P. (1994), *Innovation, Economics and Evolution. Theoretical Perspectives on Changing Technology in Economic Systems*, London: Harvester Wheatsheaf.

Hall, P.G. and P. Preston (1988), *The carrier wave; new information technology and the geography of innovation 1846–2003*, London: Unwin Hyman.

Heiner, R.A. (1983), 'The origin of predictable behaviour', *The American Economic Review*, **73**, 560–95.

Hodgson, G.M. (1993), *Economics and evolution. Bringing life back into economics*, Cambridge: Polity Press.

Hudson, P. (1992), *The Industrial Revolution*, London: Edward Arnold.

Kleinknecht, A. (1990), 'Are there Schumpeterian waves of innovation?', *Cambridge Journal of Economics*, **14**, 81–92.

Kuhn, T. (1970), *The Structure of Scientific Revolutions*, Chicago: University of Chicago Press.

Leydesdorff, L. and P. van den Besselaar (eds) (1994), *Evolutionary Economics and Chaos Theory. New Directions in Technology Studies*, London: Pinter Publishers.

Lipietz, A. (1986), 'New tendencies in the international division of labor: Regimes of accumulation and modes of regulation', in A.J. Scott and M. Storper (eds), *Production, Work, Territory: the Geographical Anatomy of Industrial Capitalism*, London: Allen and Unwin, pp. 16–40.

Markusen, A. (1985), *Profit Cycles, Oligopoly and Regional Development*, Cambridge: MIT Press.

Marshall, M. (1987), *Long Waves of Regional Development*, London: Macmillan.

Metcalfe, J.S. (1989), 'Evolution and economic change', in A. Silberstone (ed.), *Technology and Economic Progress*, London: Macmillan, pp. 54–85.

Metcalfe, J.S. (1994), 'Evolutionary economics and technology policy', *The Economic Journal*, **104**, 931–44.

Mokyr, J. (1990), *The Lever of Riches. Technological Creativity and Economic Progress*, New York: Oxford University Press.

Mokyr, J. (1991), 'Evolutionary biology, technological change and economic history', *Bulletin of Economic Research*, **43**(2), 127–49.

Monod, J. (1972), *Chance and Necessity: an Essay on the National Philosophy of Modern Biology*, London: Collins.

Nelson, R.R. (1995), 'Recent evolutionary theorizing about economic change', *Journal of Economic Literature*, **33**, 48–90.

Nelson, R.R. and S.G. Winter (1982), *An Evolutionary Theory of Economic Change*, Cambridge: Cambridge University Press.

Norton, R.D. (1979), 'Agglomeration and competitiveness from Marshall to Chinitz', *Urban Studies*, **29**(2), 155–70.

Perez, C. (1983), 'Structural change and the assimilation of new technologies in the economic and social systems', *Futures*, **15**(5), 357–75.

Perez, C. and L. Soete (1988), 'Catching up in technology: entry barriers and windows of opportunity', in G. Dosi, C. Freeman, R. Nelson, G. Silverberg and L. Soete (eds), *Technical Change and Economic Theory*, London: Pinter Publishers, pp. 458–79.

Pollard, S. (1981), *Peaceful Conquest; the Industrialization of Europe 1760–1970*, Oxford: Oxford University Press.

Prigogine, I. and I. Stengers (1984), *Order Out of Chaos*, London: Fontana.

Rees J. (1979), 'Technological change and regional shifts in American manufacturing', *Professional Geographer*, **31**, 45–54.

Rosenberg, N. (1976), *Perspectives on Technology*, Cambridge: Cambridge University Press.

Rosenberg, N. (1982), *Inside the Black Box: Technology and Economics*, Cambridge: Cambridge University Press.

Schumpeter, J.A. (1939), *Business Cycles: a Theoretical, Historical, and Statistical Analysis of the Capitalist Process*, 1st edition, 2 volumes, New York: McGraw-Hill.

Scott, A.J. (1988), *New Industrial Spaces: Flexible Production Organisation and Regional Development in North America and Western Europe*, London: Pion.

Scott, A.J. and M. Storper (1987), 'High technology industry and regional development: a theoretical critique and reconstruction', *International Social Science Journal*, **112**, 215–32.

Scott, A.J. and M. Storper (1992), 'Industrialization and regional development', in M. Storper and A.J. Scott (eds), *Pathways to Industrialization and Regional Development*, London/Boston: Routledge, pp. 3–17.

Silverberg, G. (1988), 'Modelling economic dynamics and technical change: mathematical approaches to self-organisation and evolution' in G. Dosi, C. Freeman, R. Nelson, G. Silverberg and L. Soete (eds), *Technical Change and Economic Theory*, London: Pinter Publishers, pp. 531–59.

Storper, M. (1992), 'The limits to globalization; technology districts and international trade', *Economic Geography*, **68**(1), 60–93.

Storper, M. and R. Walker (1989), *The Capitalist Imperative; Territory, Technology and Industrial Growth*, New York: Basil Blackwell.

Teece, D. (1988), 'Technological change and the nature of the firm' in G. Dosi, C. Freeman, R. Nelson, G. Silverberg and L. Soete (eds), *Technical Change and Economic Theory*, London: Pinter Publishers, pp. 256–81.

Witt, U. (1991), 'Reflections on the present state of evolutionary economic theory', in G.M. Hodgson and E. Screpanti (eds), *Rethinking Economics. Markets, Technology and Economic Evolution*, Aldershot: Edward Elgar, pp. 83–102.

Name Index

Subject Index

Adaptation 84–5
Adaptive learning 44, 52, 63
Agent 74–5, 80
American Economic Association 69
Analytical tool 114–16, 124, 165
Animal spirits 30, 177
Anti-reductionism 27, 29–30, 110
Asset specificity 90–2.
Association for Evolutionary
  Economics 9
Asymmetrical information 89, 96
Austrian economics 3, 9–14, 20,
  44–8, 71, 100, 102

Behavioural evolution 152–3
Behavioural rule 73, 88, 119,
  122–3, 126, 144, 146, 164, 174
Behaviouralist theories 69, 78, 83,
  86
Belgium 184, 188–91, 195
Biological evolution 45, 51, 63, 72,
  138–9
Biological metaphor 3, 16, 18,
  71–2, 113–29
Biology 10, 13, 15–17, 19, 26, 28,
  44, 47, 100, 113, 138, 140,
  171
Bounded rationality 5, 52, 89–90,
  98, 102, 137, 164–5
Business Cycles 114, 160
Butterfly effect 20, 178

Capital stock 119–20, 122, 142–4,
  146–50,
Change 85, 97, 109, 125
Chaos theory 10, 14, 20–1, 102,
  172–3, 178

Chicago economists 3, 47–8
Choice 19, 20, 87
Coasian approach 70, 78, 88–9
Comparative statics 77, 117
Competence 75, 87, 91–5, 99–100,
  175, 177, 182
Competition 84, 93, 138, 141, 177–8
Complexity 10, 87, 96, 125, 130
Computer simulation 10, 54, 62, 86,
  110, 119, 165
Contractual economics 70, 80, 87–93,
  100
Contractual theory of the firm 4, 70,
  78–9, 88, 90, 93, 97–101
Coordination problem 75, 93, 127,
  130
Creativity 14, 19, 75, 171, 173, 181,
  183, 185, 190, 192, 194, 198
Cultural evolution 50, 63–4
Culture 14, 75, 85, 100, 138
Cumulative causation 43, 184

Darwinian theory 51–2, 139
Determinism 20, 27–8, 60, 74, 102,
  172, 199
Discontinuity 129, 177–8, 185, 187,
  194
Division of labour 114, 127–8

Economic agent 53, 56–7, 61–2, 64,
  74–5, 113
Economic change 1, 2, 43, 48–9, 51,
  54–5, 119
Economic evolution 47, 49, 51, 54,
  63, 65, 72, 74, 82, 111, 113–15,
  117, 119, 124, 138, 140